VOICES LONG SILENT

AN ORAL INQUIRY INTO THE JAPANESE AMERICAN EVACUATION

Edited by

Arthur A. Hansen

and

Betty E. Mitson

JAPANESE AMERICAN PROJECT

CALIFORNIA STATE UNIVERSITY, FULLERTON, ORAL HISTORY PROGRAM

1974

"SOUL CONSOLING TOWER"

Manzanar Cemetery

TO THOSE WHO DARED TO DREAM: THE ISSEI

"Women, if they've ever been raped, don't go around talking about it, you know, 'I was a victim of rape,' or anything like that. This is exactly the kind of feeling that we as evacuees, victims of circumstances, had at the time of evacuation. A lot of Nisei and Issei are actually ashamed of the fact that they have to own up to the fact that they were in a concentration camp. You just don't talk about having been a victim of rape, and I think this is where our mental block is; therefore, it is very hard for the young people to go to their parents and ask them 'Have you had this experience?'"

Amy Uno Ishii (Nisei), April 17, 1973

"A group of college students became involved in setting up Asian American Studies programs on different campuses, and one of the things they wanted to talk about was the evacuation and internment period. Most of them complained, to me and to others, that their parents didn't want to talk about it, that the information was not coming from their parents, and they wanted personal interviews, personal experiences.

. . . . .

"An NBC reporter asked [Jim Matsuoka], 'How many people are buried here in the [Manzanar] cemetery?' and he said, 'A whole generation. A whole generation of Japanese who are now so frightened that they will not talk. They're quiet Americans. They're all buried here.'"

Sue Kunitomi Embrey (Nisei), November 15, 1973

"The Sansei and the Yonsei, the third and fourth generation, question us and they bombard us with these things, you know, 'Why? Why didn't you resist? If we went through the same process now, would you accept it?' Sure, hypothetically we can say this, and we can say that. If you get in a position where a person points a gun at you, or you point a gun at them, you can certainly rationalize and say things now, but you don't know what your reaction would be at the time when something happens for real. So this is the only rebuttal that I have for our children."

Mas Uyesugi (Nisei), April 16, 1971

CONTENTS

PREFACE

The pathos of a people so completely meriting acceptance as fellow Americans yet so consistently confronted with misunderstanding and prejudice was a significant theme in United States social history even before World War II. But the nation's reaction during those tense days following Pearl Harbor, culminating in the evacuation and incarceration of those on the West Coast of Japanese ancestry, escalated Japanese-American experience to a theme of major importance.

Despite its significance, until recently it appeared that the basic documentation necessary for an in-depth understanding of the Japanese-American past would never be extant. For, while the special meaning of being Japanese American was stamped indelibly in the memory of many persons, most seemed willing to leave those recollections undisturbed until death obliterated them. This situation has now been altered, however, due largely to those scholars who have begun to tape record the individual experiences of these people. In greatly augmenting our fund of information on the subject, these oral historians have familiarized themselves with the available sources, then listened carefully and questioned extensively in assisting the narrators to convey their recollections.

Since its inception in 1967, the California State University, Fullerton, Oral History Program has begun to play a role in collecting this crucial oral history. It was almost inevitable that such a program dedicated to documenting the common man's role in history would be attracted to this topic, for the university is located in an area, a large portion of which was developed by Japanese Americans in agricultural and business endeavors, and where many still reside.

However, the contribution of CSUF's Oral History Program would not be nearly so significant were it not for the capable and dedicated efforts of the Japanese American Project's director, Arthur A. Hansen, and associate director, Betty E. Mitson. These two scholars recognized the value of the work already done in this field and the vast potential for further documentation. During the past three years, they have spent a major portion of their time and attention in developing CSUF's now quite substantial collection. Furthermore, in the finest tradition of scholarship, they have determined to go beyond mere oral documentation by analyzing, synthesizing and making the material available to others.

The California State University, Fullerton, Oral History Program is proud to be involved in the publication of Voices Long Silent, for it exemplifies some of the finest research being carried on within the overall program.

Gary L. Shumway, Director
Oral History Program
California State University, Fullerton

ACKNOWLEDGMENTS

The ways in which people have assisted in the production of this publication are so varied and numerous as to make the detailing of them an impossible task. Without the contributions of those interviewees and interviewers listed in the Bibliography, this book would not have been possible. We further wish to acknowledge the invaluable contributions of the following people:

Annette Baca, Patrick Fukunaga, George Giacumakis, Jr., Janis Gennawey, Gerald Halbert, Roberta Hansen, Ken Hochfeld, Nancy J. Hunsaker, Ronald C. Larson, Susan McNamara, Jan Mikus, Kristen Mitchell, David Payne, Mary Ann Ranahan, Helen Riendeau, Bonnie Sharpe, Gary L. Shumway, Shirley E. Stephenson, Ernest W. Toy, Jr., and Kinji Ken Yada.

Particular thanks are extended to the CSUF Departmental Association Council and the Associated Students Senate for providing grants to Betty Mitson to further research and participation in endeavors connected with the Japanese American Project. Furthermore, a special appreciation goes to Dr. Samuel B. Hand who published the original version of the article "Looking Back in Anguish" in the ORAL HISTORY REVIEW 1974, journal of the Oral History Association.

INTRODUCTION

The World War II removal into concentration camps of more than 110,000 West Coast Japanese, the majority of them American citizens, is a topic which too long escaped the scrutiny of the scholar and layman. Until recently, most Americans, including most Japanese Americans themselves, seemingly were content either to forget or to rationalize the anomaly of a nation committed to democratic ideals while pursuing a policy characterized by the assignment of collective guilt and the infringement of civil liberties. But in the last decade or so, as more people have become sensitized to the necessity of confronting and explaining anomalies of this sort, social critics have exhumed the wartime experience of the Japanese Americans. Voices Long Silent is designed to carry this exhumation a step further.

Oral history is a tool of inquiry uniquely suited to deepening an understanding of the phenomenon of Japanese-American wartime evacuation. The most obvious reason is a temporal one. At a remove of only thirty years, countless prospective interviewees--policy makers, administrators, internees, and the general public--are available to recount experiences and impressions. At the same time, the intervening period offers these interviewees sufficient distance from events to insure a measure of perspective and to assure them immunity from reprisals.

A second reason is cultural. Prior to the contemporary movement of ethnic consciousness, non-Anglo Americans customarily were reluctant to identify themselves in terms of their ethnicity. Intimidated into silence about their cultural inheritance by the dominant society's insistence upon assimilation; i.e., Americanization, minority groups resorted to unobtrusive strategies for ethnic maintenance. This "conspiracy of silence" was abetted, even consecrated, by American historians. Acting either consciously or unconsciously as cultural custodians, their writings--aside from those of exceptions like Marcus Lee Hansen and Oscar Handlin--celebrated the triumph of America's "melting pot" and were mute or cavalier toward ethnic heritage and its persistence in American life. By contrast, the current upsurge of concern for cultural pluralism and ethnic revitalization has legitimated ethnicity and effected a corresponding transformation in historiographical treatment of ethnic subjects. In a general way then, this new cultural climate explains why oral historians are equipped to enrich our knowledge of modern ethnic topics like the Japanese-American experience.

There are, however, special reasons why this particular topic is preeminently amenable to examination through oral history. On the one hand, the wartime incarceration episode so severely traumatized the Japanese Americans, especially the second generation Nisei, that many were unwilling--perhaps unable--to recount their experiences, even to their children. Whereas the historian relying exclusively on written documents can do little more than bemoan this loss of crucial commentary, the oral historian, by adroitly employing interviews, can stimulate long silent Japanese-American voices into contemplative and analytical retrospection. On the other hand, most scholars who have addressed themselves to the topic of evacuation have been so bedeviled by guilt over America's departure from democratic practice that they have invariably assuaged their consciences by imaging the Japanese Americans within the comforting stereotype of patient, unprotesting, patriotic victims of American racism. While the interview technique affords no fail-safe protection against such compensatory stereotyping, its demand for person-to-person interchange of thoughts and emotions fosters a more holistic and complex appreciation of human behavior. The racist notion that "A Jap is a Jap" provided the theoretical impetus for the decision to incarcerate the Japanese Americans. Perhaps oral historians, by illuminating the variety of beliefs and actions within the interned population, can help move us beyond further stylized versions of this emasculative maxim into a more humane and authentic understanding of this critical chapter of Japanese-American history.

The present volume showcases the oral inquiry into the Japanese-American wartime evacuation being undertaken by the Oral History Program at California State University, Fullerton. Although several institutional and private oral history projects on the West Coast focus on this topic, the CSUF project is distinctive in several respects. Most importantly, it is student-centered; while the director is a History Department faculty member, the overwhelming majority of the interviewing and processing is carried out by students. Secondly, the program is designed not only to use the collection as an instructional tool, but also to promote original scholarship in the area of Japanese-American history and culture. Though in an early stage of development, the project has already spawned an assortment of theses, professional papers, and published articles. Thirdly, the project is geared toward utilization by anyone doing serious research in the subject, as all interviews are transcribed, bound, and deposited as volumes in the permanent library of the CSUF Oral History Program, along with a comprehensive annotated bibliography of the entire collection.

Voices Long Silent is arranged to illustrate the project's distinctive features. The opening section includes two articles which rely heavily on oral documentation in the collection. The first essay, Betty E. Mitson's "Looking Back in Anguish: Oral History and Japanese American Evacuation," surveys extant oral history collections relevant to wartime evacuation, discusses the contribution oral history has made to the scholarship of this subject, and employs a combination of oral and written sources to enlarge our understanding of the evacuation. The second essay, "The Manzanar 'Riot': An Ethnic Perspective," by Arthur A. Hansen and David A. Hacker, employs oral history as a conceptual tool and oral materials as corroborative or invalidative documentation in reevaluating one dramatic episode of the evacuation experience.

The middle section of the book is indicative of the array of oral history materials in the collection. The items here are intended to enlighten readers about aspects of the evacuation heretofore largely slighted by scholars. The first selection, "How to Survive Racism in America's Free Society." is a lecture delivered by Togo W. Tanaka, a prewar editor of the Rafu Shimpo (Los Angeles Daily Japanese News). Tanaka recounts the endemic anti-Japanese racism in California during the twenties and thirties--culminating in the events surrounding Pearl Harbor and the evacuation--experienced by himself and other Japanese Americans and the strategies they adopted to salvage their belief in the American credo of freedom and justice. The remaining three selections are drawn from interviews. "A Friend of the American Way: An Interview with Herbert V. Nicholson" describes the experiences of a Quaker missionary who served as an interpreter and witness in Department of Justice hearings for "potentially dangerous enemy aliens" in the months following Pearl Harbor and who ultimately launched a letter-writing campaign to close the internment camps and to open up the West Coast for occupancy again by people of Japanese ancestry. "They Don't Learn from History: An Interview with Anna T. Kelley" analyzes the impact of the Manzanar War Relocation Center on the surrounding communities in Owens Valley, California. The final selection, "Manzanar--The Continuing Struggle: An Interview with Sue Kunitomi Embrey" relates a Nisei woman's current activities with the Manzanar Committee and its successful fight to place a controversial commemorative plaque at the site of the former Manzanar Center.

An annotated bibliography of the CSUF Japanese American Oral History Project comprises the concluding section of the book. Of the 101 total items listed therein, 88 are interviews, 10 are lectures, and 3 are miscellaneous oral documents. Approximately half of these items derive from former internees among the Japanese-American population, while most of the remaining ones deal with former camp administrators and employees, residents in communities proximate to the two California camps of Manzanar and Tule Lake, and others who were involved in or affected by the evacuation experience. Until the past two years, the collection's chief concentration was on the Poston Center in Arizona, because the majority of Orange County (in which CSUF is situated) Japanese Americans were interned there. Since that time, however, as a perusal of the book's contents will reveal, the focus has shifted chiefly to Manzanar Center. There is a dual rationale for the emphasis on Manzanar: It is the nearest camp in California to the CSUF campus, and its population stemmed largely from Los Angeles County, which was the heart of the prewar Japanese-American community (and remains so even today).

It is hoped that this volume will stimulate further inquiry into the subject of the Japanese-American evacuation by serving as a repository for creative research, as an instructional aid for secondary and post-secondary classrooms, as a reference tool for libraries and historical societies, and as a suggestive model for oral history programs. More importantly, Voices Long Silent should remind us that to ensure freedom Americans must cultivate tolerance and safeguard justice.

A.A.H.
B.E.M.

PART ONE: ESSAYS

LOOKING BACK IN ANGUISH

ORAL HISTORY AND JAPANESE AMERICAN EVACUATION[1]

BETTY E. MITSON

The devastation of Pearl Harbor precipitated the evacuation and incarceration of more than 110,000 people of Japanese ancestry from the West Coast of the United States. Why? How? To where? With what effect? Answers lie not only in written documents but also within the minds of living people. Thus, scholars are attempting to resolve the enigmas of the period both by searching archives and conducting oral history interviews among those affected by the evacuation experience.

Individuals and institutions, particularly on the West Coast, are collecting taped reminiscences on the subject. Those that Audrie Girdner and Anne Loftis recorded for their book, The Great Betrayal,[2] are deposited in the Bancroft Library at the University of California, Berkeley. In addition to his personal oral history collection numbering fifty interviews, Donald Teruo Hata, Jr.[3] has begun an Asian American Research Project with his history students at California State College, Dominguez Hills, which currently contains about two hundred interviews dealing mainly with Japanese-American evacuation.[4] Under the aegis of the Japanese American Research Project, the late Joe Grant Masaoka[5] directed the collection of over five hundred oral history items (interviews, speeches, panel discussions, etc.) which are now housed in the Research Library Special Collections at the University of California, Los Angeles. The Bancroft Library's Earl Warren Project[6] includes materials from upper-echelon decision-makers and administrators with

---

[1]This article originally appeared, slightly modified, in the ORAL HISTORY REVIEW 1974, Samuel B. Hand, editor.

[2]See f. 16.

[3]As a small child Dr. Hata, a Yonsei, was evacuated with his family to Gila River War Relocation Center, Arizona. Those of Japanese ancestry living in the United States are customarily designated as Issei (first generation immigrants), Nisei (second generation), Kibei (Nisei who were raised and educated in Japan), Sansei (third generation), and Yonsei (fourth generation). In each instance the term is either singular or plural. The terms are Japanese in origin, sei meaning generation; however, since they are accepted terms in English, they are not italicized in the body of this work. Unless otherwise specified, the term Japanese used herein refers to all those of Japanese ancestry on the West Coast regardless of citizenship status.

[4]Though these interviews are not transcribed, accompanying each is a summary and an outline.

[5]Masaoka, a Nisei, was a "camp historian" at Manzanar War Relocation Center, California (along with Togo Tanaka who also figures in this essay).

[6]Earl Warren Oral History Project of the Regional Oral History

the relocation program. The 101 oral items now in the California State University, Fullerton collection[7] primarily focus on former evacuees; however, they also include administrators, and those who lived in communities neighboring the two camps located in California.[8]

This essay draws heavily on the oral documentation at Berkeley and Fullerton to illuminate some of the heretofore unknown, or only partially known, factors of the displacement period. The first section deals with the dilemma faced by the Japanese in America between Pearl Harbor and evacuation; the last concentrates on the prototype for all the centers-- Manzanar War Relocation Center--and on one family who figured largely in the volatile situation there.

America made its "worst wartime mistake"[9] when, on the basis of national and racial origins, it sent a resident group to concentration camps.[10] Asians had long been subject to exclusionary treatment, but the Japanese were singled out with particular suspicion because of Japan's ostensibly aggressor role in world affairs. During the weeks after Pearl Harbor when the prospects of a West Coast invasion created an atmosphere of fear and panic, opportunists seized upon the situation as a chance to move out all people of Japanese origins.[11] Sixty percent of those evacuated were American born. Circumstances were hardly conducive to resistance: the difficulty was that the citizens, averaging under twenty years of age, were too young and inexperienced, and their parents were aliens ineligible for citizenship.[12]

Office, The Bancroft Library, University of California, Berkeley, Japanese-American Relocation Reviewed, 2 volumes, 1974. Interviews with Tom Clark, Robert B. Cozzens, Edward J. Ennis, Ruth Kingman, Dillon S. Myer, James H. Rowe, Jr., and Herbert Wenig. The Kingman interview deals with the Fair Play Committee. See f. 59 regarding the committee. The Bancroft Library also houses an oral biography of the late Ralph P. Merritt, a director of Manzanar. Quotations are by permission of the Director of the Bancroft Library and hereafter cited as Earl Warren Project. (Acknowledgements also to Wendy Won and Willa Baum for assistance with those materials.)

[7]The Japanese American Oral History Project at California State University, Fullerton is used not only as a research tool but as a teaching tool as well in the subject of Japanese-American history. For a bibliography of the collection, see pages 193-209. Hereafter cited as CSUF.

[8]Sherry Turner has interviewed in the vicinity of Tule Lake camp; David J. Bertagnoli and Arthur A. Hansen in the area of Manzanar.

[9]The judgment of Eugene V. Rostow, then professor of law at Yale, in "Our Worst Wartime Mistake," Harper's, vol. 191, no. 1144, Sept. 1945, pp. 193-201.

[10]Former resident of Manzanar Relocation Center, Elaine Black Yoneda declares, "The minute I saw those barbed wires and those watchtowers, I knew it would be like a prison." Arthur A. Hansen, interviewer; O.H. 1377b, CSUF, March 2, 1974. The camps were by definition concentration camps; however, no interviewee has asserted that they were death

Over thirty years have elapsed since the West Coast sent its "potentially dangerous" people inland. Many, if not most, Americans have long forgotten that it ever happened. Except for a few, those who went to camps have kept the details to themselves and sublimated the memory of that experience.[13]

---

camps in the sense that the camps of Germany were. On April 14, 1973, California Registered Historical Landmark No. 850 was placed at Manzanar which carries the designation "concentration camps."

[11]Morton Grodzins, political and behavioral scientist, theorizes that group pressure, from such as the American Legion, Native Sons and Daughters of the Golden West, Western Growers Protective Association, chambers of commerce, labor, business and merchant associations, and countless others including the press, was the basic moving force for evacuation. He maintains that action was a "New manifestation of an old disregard for civil rights by certain California groups [particularly] economic groups [that] had histories which showed a willingness to violate rights of free speech and assemblage . . . ." (emphasis added) Morton Grodzins, "A Theory of Group Pressure," Leonard Pitt, ed., California Controversies (Glenview, Ill.: Scott, Foresman and Company, 1968), p. 183. Most of the "decision-makers" on the Earl Warren Project tapes express an agreement with this theory.

[12]The Naturalization Act of 1790 limited citizenship to "free white persons." The California Constitution of 1879 prevented the naturalization of "Mongolians," and a federal act in 1882 forbad United States citizenship to Chinese. In 1911 the Bureau of Immigration and Naturalization extended the citizenship ban to all but whites and blacks. Exclusion from naturalization was confirmed by the Supreme Court in the 1922 decision in Ozawa v. United States, 260 U.S. 178. Some seven hundred Issei veterans of World War I had been able to obtain citizenship in the 1930s through lobbying on the part of the Japanese American Citizens League (a Nisei organization) in Congress. In 1952 all racial barriers to naturalization were eliminated, again due to JACL lobbying.

[13]While interviewees show a willingness to relate their experiences, many indicate a hesitancy to discuss the evacuation and resettlement with their children. Following are quotations from the discussion period following a tape recorded lecture by Amy Uno Ishii, "The Japanese American Experience;" in series, Arthur A. Hansen, coordinator, Japanese American Internment During World War II (University of California Extension, Irvine; April 17, 1973; on deposit at CSUF). A Sansei: "My mother and father have never said one word to me about being relocated. The first time that I knew such a thing occurred was in high school from a history book." Another Sansei: "I was talking to my mom a couple of weeks ago, and there is a sort of hesitation on my part to ask her [about evacuation] because I feel embarrassed about it, to even just ask her. When I ask her, 'What about the camps? Were we there?' she acts very detached, very impersonal, like it didn't happen to her. This whole bit about the inability of the Nisei to express their feelings, I feel there is a lot of connection to the camps." A Nisei: "I think we can explain that women, if they've ever been raped, don't go around talking about it,

Several contemporary works appeared,[14] but after a lapse of many years, scholars have reawakened to the timeliness of the internment issue, some speculating on the implication for all of the precedent set in 1942.[15] The awareness that detainment for "variant" groups is not necessarily a thing of the past, coupled with rising ethnic consciousness among all groups, has proliferated books, articles, and visual media dealing with the camps of World War II.[16] Few, however, emphasize the oral history approach. Nor do former internees or those who had direct contact with camp life through visits or work experience publish their stories.[17] To date, most publications about evacuation and detainment have been based on written documentary evidence, largely because prospective informants have been reluctant, perhaps afraid, to speak of their experiences. Additionally, historians and archivists may be faulted for failing to seek out interviewees.[18]

---

you know, 'I was a victim of rape,' or anything like that. This is exactly the kind of feeling that we as evacuees, victims of circumstances, had at the time of evacuation. A lot of Nisei and Issei are actually ashamed of the fact that they have to own up to the fact that they were in a concentration camp. You just don't talk about having been a victim of rape, and I think this is where our mental block is; therefore, it is very hard for the young people to go to their parents and ask them, 'Have you had this experience?'"

[14]For example: Leonard Broom and Ruth Riemer, Removal and Return: The Socio-economic effects of the War on Japanese Americans (Berkeley: Univ. of Calif. Press, 1949); Morton M. Grodzins, Americans Betrayed: Politics and the Japanese Evacuation (Chicago: Univ. of Chicago Press, 1949); Alexander H. Leighton, The Governing of Men (Princeton: Princeton Univ. Press, 1945); Carey McWilliams, Prejudice, Japanese Americans, Symbol of Racial Intolerance (Boston: Little, Brown and Company, 1944); Dorothy Swaine Thomas and Richard S. Nishimoto, The Spoilage: Japanese-American Evacuation and Resettlement (Los Angeles: Univ. of Calif. Press, 1946).

[15]Justice Robert H. Jackson of the U.S. Supreme Court said that the precedent of the Japanese-American evacuation "lies about like a loaded weapon ready for the hand of any authority that can bring forward a plausible claim of an urgent need." As quoted in: Rostow, op. cit., p. 194.

[16]Among recent studies are the following: Paul Bailey, City in the Sun: The Japanese Concentration Camp at Poston, Arizona (Los Angeles: Westernlore Press, 1971); Allan R. Bosworth, America's Concentration Camps (New York: W. W. Norton and Company, 1967); Maisie and Richard Conrat, Executive Order 9066 (Cambridge: Massachusetts Institute of Technology Press for the Calif. Historical Society, 1972); Roger Daniels, Concentration Camps, USA: Japanese Americans and World War II (New York: Holt, Rinehart and Winston, Inc., 1972); Sue Kunitomi Embrey, ed., The Lost Years, 1942-1946 (Los Angeles: Moonlight Publications, 1972); Anne R. Fisher, Exile of a Race (Sidney, British Columbia: Peninsula Printing Co., 1965); Audrie Girdner and Anne Loftis, The Great

As approaches to history evolve, so also do attitudes toward the relating and the collecting of experiences for posterity. The recent increase in popularity of oral history has coincided with the desire of people to release information long bottled-up within them. There is a rising realization, not only among academicians but also among former internees and their offspring,[19] that America has much to learn from the internment story.

Interviewers usually ready themselves by studying the pertinent documents, particularly those published by the War Relocation Authority, the governmental agency that had administrative control of the "relocation centers."[20] Newspapers, both from the Japanese and the larger community, are rich sources of opinion in respect to evacuation. Other documents, such as letters, governmental reports, organizational minutes, etc., provide the scholar with a feel for what was going on in the dominant society at the time.

Betrayal: The Evacuation of the Japanese-Americans During World War II (New York: Macmillan Co., 1969); Dillon S. Myer, Uprooted Americans: The Japanese Americans and the War Relocation Authority During World War II (Tucson: Univ. of Arizona Press, 1971); Estelle Ishigo, Lone Heart Mountain (Los Angeles: Anderson, Ritchie & Simon, 1972).

[17]Of the authors listed in f. 16, Sue Kunitomi Embrey was interned at Manzanar, Estelle Ishigo (one of the few Caucasians who elected to accompany their spouse) was interned at Heart Mountain, and Dillon S. Myer was Director of the War Relocation Authority; still, their works are not primarily personal accounts.

[18]According to Alan T. Moriyama, of the UCLA Asian American Studies Center, "Some of the recent scholarship in the field have begun to use oral interviewing as a source of information, but thus far these attempts have been few and far between." "America's Concentration Camps: The Literature of the Field," a paper presented to the 1973 Western Conference of the Association for Asian Studies, Albuquerque, New Mexico.

[19]For instance, the aforementioned UCLA Japanese American Research Project (JARP) was initiated by the Japanese American Citizens League in 1962 with an initial grant of $100,000. This is mainly a sociological survey, but it includes the largest collection of Japanese-American oral history--about half in English, half in Japanese.

[20]War Relocation Authority permanent centers and listed capacities:
Central Utah, Topaz, Utah--10,000
Colorado River, Poston, Arizona (Army reception center initially)--20,000
Gila River, Rivers, Arizona--15,000
Granada, Amache, Colorado--8,000
Heart Mountain, Heart Mountain, Wyoming--10,000
Jerome, Denson, Arkansas--10,000
Manzanar, Manzanar, California (Army reception center initially)--10,000
Minidoka, Hunt, Idaho--10,000
Rohwer, McGehee, Arkansas--10,000
Tule Lake, Newell, California (A segregation center later)--16,000

Still, much of what decision-makers were saying and doing cannot be found in written documents, particularly since, operating in great haste, they relied heavily on the telephone.[21] What was happening among the Japanese must be garnered almost exclusively through oral means. An in-depth account cannot be readily obtained through contemporary documentary sources.[22] Even their camp newspapers are of little value to one looking for insights into the internees' perspectives, since those publications largely reflect administrative policies.[23]

Oral history that concentrates on the victim in any situation rather than on the milieu in which the victim is located is certainly open to challenge. Such questions as "How do you feel about the camps?" do not come to grips with the major issue of why there were camps. Danger lies in that the victim approach can divert attention from the real issues of causation. But if the victim has considerable awareness of the reasons for the problems the group faced or the victim's perspective provides a clue to those reasons, the interview technique proves a valuable tool. Former evacuees do exhibit exceptional knowledge and understanding which seem enhanced by retrospection. However, while most are articulate about the constitutional issue involved in their evacuation; i.e., the violation of the rights of citizens,[24] a good many

---

[21]Robert B. Cozzens states, "They had never had the privilege to move that fast in government. . . . We had the authority with us to do it. . . . If it cost a number of million dollars nobody had to ask anybody if they could do it or not. If I signed the papers, they could do it and they didn't wait till tomorrow to do it! . . . The speed with which this thing moved was unbelievable." "Assistant National Director of the War Relocation Authority," Earl Warren Project, 1971, p. 13, Rosemary Levenson, interviewer.

[22]This is not to discount those valuable contemporary documents that do exist. For instance, Togo W. Tanaka wrote voluminous contemporary documents, much of which now rest in the archives of the UCLA Research Library and the UC Berkeley Bancroft Library. Elaine and Karl Yoneda have a large personal collection of contemporary documents, some selections of which have been deposited in the UCLA Research Library. The JARP collection (ca. 1890-1974) at UCLA includes family papers; social, cultural, and organizational papers; consular papers; war relocation records; and rare ethnic newspapers, books and pamphlets. See also f. 89.

[23]Sue Kunitomi Embrey, former managing editor of the Manzanar Free Press, was asked, What control was there over what appeared in the paper with respect to administrative censorship? She replied, "Well, they didn't want us to write about things like . . . a strike going on at Lockheed or somewhere . . . somebody wrote a column . . . making some crack about 'Why are they on strike? Our government is having a war.' And we were asked not to include that, or after it was printed, we got feedback on it, 'We don't want things like that in the paper.' I don't recall that there was actual censorship of the articles. The editorials, I think, were checked before they were run pretty much." Arthur A. Hansen, interviewer; O.H. 1366a, CSUF, August 24, 1973, p. 34.

soft-pedal the aspect of racism.[25] That former evacuees tend to base whatever critical comments they may make on the issue of constitutional rights rather than on that of racism may indicate how, to a large extent, they absorbed, like most everyone else, the rationale of the day. They did not then and still do not see the issue as primarily one of racial discrimination.[26] The group's propensity to obey authority was frequently suggested as reason for compliance with the evacuation order:[27]

> I think this is one part that may have been a detriment to us, the fact that most Japanese people, through their parents and through their ancestry, are told to really respect authority. And when they tell you to move, you move. You really don't question it too much. You may question it, but you don't openly ask. At that time, at least, I don't think that most of the Japanese people were mentally in the position to even question it it. They weren't brought up that way.[28]

On the other hand, others are convinced that whether or not the group

---

[24]Martial law was not officially declared on the West Coast as it had been in Hawaii. Part of the constitutional issue, then, is the control the military exercised over civilians, not only in evacuation, but in curfews and restriction of movement in the Pacific Coast Military Area. For a discussion of the constitutional issue, see Rostow, op. cit.

[25]Among the rationale offered to justify evacuation were: (1) Japanese can't be trusted; (2) Japanese in Hawaii helped bombers find their way to Pearl Harbor; (3) Japanese are stockpiling weapons and short-wave radios; (4) Japanese tend to live near military installations; (5) it is impossible to distinguish trustworthy Japanese from subversive types; (6) Japanese are in danger and can't be protected; (7) wartime powers make the move constitutionally valid.

[26]There were more alien Italians than alien Japanese on the West Coast at the time. Race was the only basis upon which treatment of Germans, Italians, and Japanese differed. Nevertheless, most interviewees see the issue as mixed with other extenuating factors.

[27] On February 19, 1942, President Franklin D. Roosevelt signed Executive Order 9066 authorizing the exclusion of "any or all persons" from designated military areas and the erection of relocation camps to house them. However, mass evacuation was not a fait accompli until March 2, 1942, when Lt. Gen. John De Witt, Commander of the Western Defense Area, issued the order to evacuate all those of Japanese ancestry. On March 21, the first group of volunteers went to Manzanar. Initially, a voluntary movement inland had been encouraged, but that was terminated on March 29. Because of the periodic expansion of the "designated military areas," some found it necessary to move repeatedly before complete evacuation was mandated. For further information, see Dillon S. Myer, Uprooted Americans, op. cit., p. 26.

[28]Roy Uno, interviewee; John McFarlane, interviewer; O.H. 1070, CSUF, April 25, 1971, p. 16.

was willing to go is irrelevant:

> Oh, I feel that even if the Japanese Americans had been older
> and were able to put up a good fight or argument, I think the
> times were different then. I feel that the military and the
> emergency factor that was in existence at the time would have
> precluded any strong arguments on racial grounds or unconstitu-
> tionality. We may have been vociferous at the time, but I feel
> that because of the atmosphere of that time we wouldn't have
> been able to achieve our goals. I think the evacuation would
> have taken place no matter if we had put up a strong fight.[29]

The dichotomy between these opinions remains unresolved. No one knows
what eventualities confronted the people had they refused to go.[30]

What had happened to the leadership of the Japanese-American
community to interdict whatever political effectiveness it may have
exerted when evacuation eventually seemed imminent? According to
Herbert V. Nicholson,[31] the FBI and Naval Intelligence, assisted by
local law enforcement people, had

> picked up anybody that was the head of anything. The same
> thing they did when Lenin and the Communists took over in
> Russia. . . . Anybody that was a cho--that means head--he
> was picked up. Heads of prefectural organizations[32] were
> picked up. Just because we come from the same country, we
> get together occasionally, see, and just have a social time
> and talk about our friends back in Japan.[33] But everybody
> that was head of anything was picked up, which was a crazy
> thing.[34]

How about Buddhist ministers?

> They didn't touch them at first. They did later. . . .
> There were six hundred [people] picked up the first night,
> Sunday night, who were on the black list. . . . Because of
> public opinion and pressure, others were picked up later for
> all sorts of things. Buddhist priests and Japanese language
> schoolteachers were all picked up later . . . because of
> public opinion, they picked up more and more.[35]

---

[29]James Kanno, interviewee; John McFarlane, interviewer; O.H.
1070, CSUF, April 25, 1971, p. 16.

[30]Both evacuees and decision-makers agree in their opinion that
the evacuation could not have been stopped. Elaine Yoneda, op. cit.,
says, "It became apparent that we couldn't possibly fight it, knowing
the forces that the U.S. had at its command, knowing that the powers
that be would think nothing of dispatching a batallion or two with their
guns to evacuate the Japanese should there be resistance." The Assistant to Attorney General Biddle, James H. Rowe, Jr., declares, "We were
in a war, and as I look back now I don't really see that there was any
stopping this [evacuation]." "The Evacuation Decision," Earl Warren
Project, 1971, p. 36, Amelia Fry, interviewer.

Interviews have disclosed that, while the initial roundup included virtually all of the male and female leadership, many were powerless old men.[36] Some names were on the black list for what appear, in hindsight, absurd reasons.[37] Nicholson, who served as an interpreter[38] and, occasionally, a character witness at hearings for them, both in the Federal Building in Los Angeles and later in the Department of Justice detention camps,[39] is uniquely qualified to address himself to that aspect:

---

[31]Quaker missionary who has worked fifty-nine years among people of Japanese origins both in Japan and in the United States.

[32]A prefecture in Japan is comparable to a state in the United States. For a further explanation of prefectural organizations, see Harry H. L. Kitano, Japanese Americans: The Evolution of a Subculture (Englewood Cliffs, N.J.: Prentice-Hall, Inc., 1969), p. 94.

[33]Nicholson is a member of Ibaraki Kenjinkai prefectural organization.

[34]Rowe, op. cit., p. 20, agrees, "Some of this stuff they were charged on was as silly as hell."

[35]Herbert V. Nicholson, interviewee; Betty E. Mitson, interviewer; O.H. 1235, CSUF, April 19, 1973, pp. 27-29. James Rowe, op. cit., pp. 32-33, was asked, I understand that telegraphic approval from Biddle was required before making any arrest. There were so many arrested: 736 on just December 7th alone. . . . He responded, "I think those telegrams must have been prepared way ahead of time. That sort of thing was a very well-run job. Except that we picked up too many."

[36]According to the U.S. Dept. of Justice, Annual Report of the Attorney General [1941-1942] (processed, Washington, 1943), p. 8, "Each arrest was made on the basis of information concerning the specific alien taken into custody."

[37]Contrariwise, in correspondence to Fred Nitta on Feb. 24, 1970, Karl G. Yoneda stated, "In [respect to] my letter which appeared in the Jan. 16th issue of the Pacific Citizen, in regards to the Heimusha-kai (Overseas Ex-servicemen's Assn.) which was organized in 1937 to raise 'war chest' for the Japanese government and to which you take issue. I should have written that 'it was to raise war relief, at first, but soon also went into raising a war chest for the Japanese government.'" Yoneda detailed the prewar existence of numerous organizations which he termed "pro-Japan, super-militaristic and nationalistic" in a letter to Betty E. Mitson on March 19, 1974. "This organization [Heimusha-kai] grew to 8,000 members with 82 branches in the United States by 1940." Yoneda concedes that many people did not realize the significance of their contributions to such organizations, especially the "some 30,000 children attending Japanese Language Schools" who were giving their pennies. "These are some of the true facts of our past history that have been ignored although available, unfortunately it seems, only to those who read Japanese, but should be publicized for the benefit of those of Japanese ancestry and others. . . . [They] cannot and must not be buried, whether it did us good or not, if we want to relate our history

There was an old man here that was way past eighty, that had
been in the China War way back in 1896, and he was picked up
that night [December 7]--this old Mr. Hiraiwa. So I phoned
back over there [to the church people], and they said that Mr.
Sakamoto who had been in the Russo-Japanese War was picked up
about eight o'clock at night. The police came and got him.

When was your first opportunity to go and see any that had been
picked up?

I was right down there the next day, Monday afternoon. Then I
came back and told their wives about it, and then I was busy
every day there, from morning till night.

Was that at the jail that you went to see them?

Not the jail, it was the Immigration Service down at Terminal
Island. The Department of Justice had them confined there. I
don't know how many were there, but all up and down the Coast
there were six hundred. I think there must have been a couple
of hundred down there--at least two hundred of these old veterans were picked up, of the six hundred.[40]

Those arrested were alien Issei, with the exception of a handful who
who were Nisei and Kibei, native born citizens. One of the few citizens
hauled in was Togo W. Tanaka, young English language editor of the _Rafu
Shimpo_,[41] leading newspaper in Little Tokyo. To the interviewer's imputation of "leadership" to him Tanaka responded,

But I was not in a leadership position, as subsequent events
turned out [to show]. I don't think any of the Nisei were, in
a true sense, either accepted or qualified to lead this population. One, because the Issei were really men in their prime.
By and large the Nisei was a teen-aged group. The fact that
the Nisei were called upon to perform certain functions, and
largely they were a liaison between the community, as it was
constituted, and the authorities in the outside larger public.
To attempt to really lead so that you had a following proved
disastrous. . . . It was an impossible situation, because if
you're going to lead something, you've got to have a constitu-
ency. We had neither earned it--we had inherited it in a

---

as it really was and is." Except for the information in the two pieces
of correspondence to Nitta and Mitson, the foregoing quotations are from
"Letters from Readers," _Pacific Citizen_, Jan. 16, 1970.

[38]Nicholson served entirely without monetary compensation from the
government. In _op. cit._, p. 40, he recalls, "All I got out of it is a
pencil the secretary gave me."

[39]"Detention camps" were distinguished from "relocation centers"
in that the former held arrested "enemy aliens" suspected of being enemy
agents and eventually some of their wives and children and the latter
held all others.

[40]Nicholson, _op. cit._, pp. 25, 29.

situation where there was a great deal of fear and uneasiness
and mistrust and suspicion. This is, I think, what happened,
so that when the FBI and the Naval Intelligence . . . came in
and took the leadership of this community and put them into
camps, we really didn't have a base from which you could organize any resistance or anything. You just had people who
were fearful, uncertain, and didn't know their legal rights.

So the power base was taken away.

Completely.

The ones the people would normally look up to for advice were
gone.

That's right.[42]

Here, then, is a case for the viewpoint that resistance was neither prob-
able nor possible once the leadership was gone.

Tanaka was incarcerated without explanation and released eleven
days later, again without explanation (even though most detainees went
through a hearing).[43] According to Amy Uno Ishii, her father was detained
for seven years, being moved from one detention camp to another, and
never joining his family in the relocation center. She remains uninformed
as to why he was held so long.[44] Herbert Nicholson avers that release
and retainment were arbitrarily determined, often without "rhyme or
reason."[45]

---

[41]The Los Angeles Japanese Daily News.

[42]Togo W. Tanaka, interviewee; David Hacker and Betty E. Mitson,
interviewers; O.H. 1271a, CSUF, May 19, 1973, pp. 20-22. War Relocation
Authority Director Dillon Myer agrees: "Many of the best leaders in the
old Japanese community group were in Justice camps . . . and the Japanese
American Citizens League advised cooperation with the government once
evacuation was decided on. After all, the Army was a big army; . . .
there wasn't anything else for them to do." "War Relocation Authority:
The Director's Account," Earl Warren Project, 1969, p. 48, Amelia Fry,
interviewer. An Issei who was interned in the Santa Fe detention camp
says that so many talented and intellectual Issei were there that the
place was like a "cultural center." Iwami Kuratomi, interviewee; Betty
E. Mitson, interviewer; O.H. 1236b, CSUF, March 16, 1974.

[43]American born Karl G. Yoneda was also arrested, held 48 hours,
and had no hearing.

[44]Amy Uno Ishii, interviewee; Kristen Mitchell, interviewer; O.H.
1342b, CSUF, July 18, 1973, p. 34. Indications are that her father was
held because he had a son in the Japanese Army. (He had another serving
in the U.S. Army.) It appears that some were held accountable for the
activities of members of their families. For instance, Iwami Kuratomi,
op. cit., was kept on parole, required to report monthly to the FBI, and
not allowed to return to the West Coast for a period of three years
following cessation of hostilities. He belonged to no organizations
associated with Japan; however, his brother was a rear-admiral in the

The loss of such large numbers of older people set the rest of the community adrift in a sea of bewilderment. Not only were many families left without the traditional decision-makers and breadwinners, but they were also terrorized by fear for "Who will be next?" Complicating the situation was the knowledge that some Issei in the community had entered the country illegally. That had been the only means open to them after passage of the Exclusion Act of 1924.[46] One interviewee indicated that, since her father had come up through South America and crossed the Mexican border,

> he worried that he would be deported. Therefore, he was very, very cautious when it involved anything that had to do with law or regulations. It was really very sad for him to feel so insecure all through his life. He was so fearful of being deported that he led a very cautious and a very honest life. . . . He was very agreeable to whatever the Caucasians asked him to do-- very, very humble. He would never try to anger them in any way, and he was always trying to please them.[47]

In collecting material for his book, Americans Betrayed: Politics and the Japanese Evacuation, Morton M. Grodzins discussed with Togo Tanaka the impact that illegal entry may have had on compliance with the order to evacuate en masse. They both felt that it was a factor.[48] As Tanaka puts it, there existed "in-group solidarity"[49] which meant that further arrests and deportations (which surely faced Issei resisters) would have affected all, not just immediate families. "We cared about our parents who were legally defenseless and totally exposed," says Tanaka.[50] Furthermore, there was invariably no one of the grandparent generation to lend advice or a helping hand. Those still living were all in Japan. To resist, then, meant jeopardizing the entire community.

Japanese Navy. When Kuratomi was paroled to the Jerome Relocation Center, he was placed in charge of the agricultural program there.

[45]Director of the Alien Enemy Control Unit, Edward J. Ennis, says, "The Alien enemy control program was a system under which aliens of any nationality with something in their record showing an allegiance to the enemy, would be apprehended and put through a hearing procedure. We appointed hearing officers, civilians, throughout the entire country. Every alien who was arrested got a hearing to determine whether he would be released unconditionally, paroled subject to reporting, or interned for the duration." "A Justice Department Attorney Comments on the Japanese-American Relocation," Earl Warren Project, 1973, p. 3, Miriam Feingold, interviewer. For a description of hearings, see Nicholson, op. cit., pp. 33-56.

[46]In 1908 Theodore Roosevelt negotiated a "Gentlemen's Agreement" by which the Japanese government would limit emigration of Japanese laborers. From 1924 to 1952, exclusion was complete.

[47]Elaine S. Okimoto, interviewee; Betty E. Mitson, interviewer; O.H. 1080, CSUF, April 4, 1972, p. 3.

[48]Tanaka says that Grodzins estimated that five percent of the Issei were illegal immigrants. Karl Yoneda thinks they probably

The morning of December 8 Nicholson rushed to the Los Angeles office of the FBI. Having served in the mission field in Japan since 1915 and in a West Los Angeles Japanese Methodist Church[51] for a year before Pearl Harbor, he thought he knew those of Japanese background better than most anyone. Since two of his parishioners, in their eighties, had been picked up the night before, he felt impelled to act.

> The papers were full of terrible things the Japanese had
> done in Honolulu. They blocked the roads and, oh, they did
> all sorts of things. . . . The Monday morning papers were
> full of this; the radio was full of it--the terrible things
> the Japanese had done, see. And I said, "Now, that's not
> true." I said, "These are a lot of lies they have got in
> those papers. The Japanese wouldn't do that."[52] And the FBI
> man said, "I know it's not. They're lies." I said, "Then
> you do something to stop it. You get news in the paper right
> away that these reports aren't true. These things are all
> made up. Emotionally people are upset, and these things
> are being told, but they are lies, and tell them that you
> have already picked up all the dangerous Japanese. There
> is nobody left. I wish you would publicize that in the
> papers or over the radio." They said, "We're not in the
> publicity busines. We can't do it."
> And so I went then to Commander Ringle who I had known in
> Japan when he was a language officer at the embassy. He was
> head of Naval Intelligence in this area. I went to his office
> and found Ringle.[53] I had quite a talk with him. He didn't
> say that all of the reports were wrong. He said, "At least
> ninety-eight percent of these stories in the papers are lies.
> They're just not true." And I said one hundred percent of
> them were, but he said ninety-eight percent, so we let it
> go at that. And he said the same thing [as the FBI had said].
> He said, "I can't do anything about it. It's not my job to
> give publicity."
> And, you know, later on I found out that the G-2 and the
> Naval Intelligence, and the FBI all got together in Honolulu
> and filled the papers there with the facts. They did the

---

numbered over one thousand.

[49]Tanaka, op. cit., p. 19. For more on the "tightly knit" concept, see Jacobus ten Broek, et al., Prejudice, War and the Constitution (Berkeley: Univ. of Calif. Press, 1954), p. 275.

[50]Tape recorded lecture by Togo W. Tanaka, "How to Survive Racism in America's Free Society;" in series, Arthur A. Hansen, coordinator, Japanese American Internment During World War II (Univ. of Calif. Extension, Irvine; April 3, 1973; on deposit at CSUF). Hereafter cited as "How to Survive." See p. 83 in this volume.

[51]Owing to harassment by the police in Japan, Nicholson returned to Pasadena in 1940 after twenty-five years there. Since he had been a missionary and knew the Japanese language, he was prevailed upon to

thing they said they couldn't do here.

They <u>is</u> G-2?

That's the military intelligence.

<u>They did that right away?</u>

They started right away; they put these things in [the papers] because they realized things would get out of hand, because half the population was Japanese, you see. Down in Hawaii they had a situation on their hands, so they did something. But here they didn't do anything.[54]

Several aspects of the foregoing quotation need to be noted: (1) No documentary evidence has been uncovered by this writer to indicate that anyone, other than Nicholson, immediately appealed to the authorities directing the initial roundup. (2) The written documents are mute on the private conversations in the offices of the FBI and Naval Intelligence, yet those conversations are crucial to the total story of the Japanese evacuation, as they illustrate the inadequacy, the inertia, the refusal of bureaucracy to deal with the mounting hysteria in the outside community, particularly when the situation did not force it to take the initiative to allay the fears of the public. (3) There is an indication that matters were different in Hawaii where the "minority" Japanese represented the largest single national group--a sense of self-preservation and expedience[55] moved individuals to oil the wheels of government there. (4) There is indication that officials knew the facts as Nicholson relates they confessed them to him.[56] As he and other interviewees--both former internees and administrators alike--repeatedly state, rumor and confusion were the order of the day.

---

serve a Japanese Methodist congregation in West Los Angeles when their minister became ill. It meant compromising his Quaker principles which do not abide "hired preaching."

[52]There has never been a case of subversion by people of Japanese ancestry resident in the United States or the Territory of Hawaii.

[53]The Commander Ringle that Nicholson went to see reputedly authored an anonymous article declaring mass evacuation a mistake and presenting an alternative plan based on individual treatment. See, An Intelligence Officer, "The Japanese in America: The Problem and the Solution," <u>Harper's Magazine</u>, vol. CLXXXV, Oct. 1942, pp. 489-497.

[54]Nicholson, <u>op. cit.</u>, pp. 26-27.

[55]Ennis, <u>op. cit.</u>, p. 16, reflects, "It is curious that with a relatively much larger population of Japanese and Japanese-Americans in Hawaii, there was never any serious thought of evacuating Hawaii, for the practical reason that they didn't have the transport." A woman who grew up in Hawaii was asked, <u>So if they had sent all those of Japanese ancestry to camps</u> . . . ? She responded, "The laborers would have been gone, because the majority of the plantation workers were Oriental. All the labor was done by Orientals." Irene M. Kobayashi, interviewee; Betty E. Mitson, interviewer; O.H. 1077, CSUF, April 11, 1972, p. 11.

Even those who theoretically possessed citizenship rights, the Nisei, had been conditioned for what happened by a long history of prejudicial treatment. Several interviewees recall having been excluded, as children, from public bathing facilities and relegated to "Nigger Heaven" in the local movie houses.[57] Tanaka, a Phi Beta Kappa graduate of the University of California at Los Angeles, suffered the humiliation of being told "You can't live here" in 114 of the 119 attempts he made to look at prospective homes in the prewar Los Angeles community. Restrictive covenants kept his family out. His effort, in conjunction with the Pacific Development Company, to develop integrated housing outside the immediate Japanese community was quickly squelched by concerted hostility from Caucasians in the area.[58]

Tanaka was among the group of Japanese-American editors to whom California's Governor Culbert Olson[59] said,

> You know, when I look out at a group of Americans of German or Italian descent, I can tell whether they are loyal or not. I can tell how they think . . . but it is impossible for me to do this with the inscrutable Orientals, and particularly the Japanese. Therefore, I want all of you present here to pledge yourselves to make a sacrifice for your country, the United States of America. Promise to give up your freedom, if necessary, in order to prove your loyalty.[60]

In November 1941, Tanaka went to see Attorney General Francis Biddle in Washington to appeal, on behalf of his publisher, for permission to continue to print the Rafu Shimpo after war hit. He was grilled for a day at the War Department about how he knew that war was coming. His answer "Everyone knows it's coming" did not convince the authorities. He was unable to account for certain editorials in the Japanese language section of the Rafu stating that Nisei would be useful to Japan--editorials he (like most Nisei) couldn't even read! Tanaka told himself, "You're as

---

[56]Nicholson regularly visited almost all of the relocation centers and the detention camps. He relates that often administrators confided in him that they were aware of the innocence of their charges.

[57]"Such a thing like 'No Japs wanted,' or something like that, we took as a matter of course," states former evacuee, Clarence I. Nishizu. Richard Curtiss, interviewer; O.H. 5, CSUF, Jan. 1, 1966, p. 25.

[58]Tanaka, "How to Survive," op. cit.

[59]Olson was "acting chairman" of the Pacific Coast Committee on American Principles and Fair Play which was formed in August 1941. Ruth Kingman, an organizer of the group, states, "The first thing they did was to write a letter to fellow citizens just asking them to be alert to the actions of the Japanese government as differentiated from those of our perfectly loyal persons of Japanese ancestry here on the West Coast . . . ." Despite that stand, she says that the group "never opposed the evacuation as such." "The Fair Play Committee and Citizen Participation," Earl Warren Project, 1971, pp. 24-26, Rosemary Levenson, interviewer.

[60]As quoted by Tanaka from his diary in "How to Survive," op. cit.

good as dead--from here on it's all downhill." Years later Biddle sent
a copy of his book on Justice Holmes to Tanaka in which he inscribed
"With greetings and best wishes to Togo Tanaka who cherishes the secret
of happiness --freedom."[61]

Freedom is not what Tanaka had in 1942. Five months after his release from a cell atop the Hall of Justice he was incarcerated again--
this time at Manzanar--along with some ten thousand others. Manzanar,
the first camp to hold evacuees, was situated in what had been, around
the turn of the century, a prosperous fruit growing area at the foot of
Mount Whitney in California's Owens Valley. In 1908 Theodore Roosevelt
signed a bill permitting water to be brought by aqueduct over federal
lands from the Owens River to the Los Angeles basin. However, it was
not until the drought of the early twenties, when water north of the
headgates was also needed in the south, that Owens Valley was left high
and dry. The resulting decade of bitterness, dramatized by ruined
farmers repeatedly dynamiting the aqueduct, ended in a financial settle-
ment in which Los Angeles virtually "bought out the valley."[62] Thus it
was that Manzanar, a thriving community nestled in the heart of Owens
Valley, complete with general store, packing house and slaughter house,
became wasteland controlled by the Los Angeles Department of Water and
Power. Gaunt apple trees,[63] scarcely alive, gave mute testimony to what
once had been.

According to Robert L. Brown,[64] then Executive Secretary of the
Inyo-Mono Association, a valley-wide chamber of commerce, the Owens
Valley area was suggested to Biddle by Manchester Boddy, publisher of
the Los Angeles Daily News,[65] for the establishment of a receiving
center for resettlement inland. At that time, the plan was to bring
all evacuees there, at least temporarily, and then to disperse them to
"as many as fifty centers or work camps" by utilizing old CCC camps and
other abandoned facilities.[66]

When the Army Corps of Engineers began work at Manzanar, word got
around the neighboring towns of Independence and Lone Pine that there
were "100,000 Japs coming." Brown appealed to Tom Clark,[67] then Coordinator of the Alien Enemy Control Program for the Western Defense Command,
who agreed that the valley was not big enough for that many evacuees.
Almost immediately, Robert B. Cozzens[68] was drafted into the job of
Assistant National Director of the War Relocation Authority under
Milton Eisenhower who, in turn, had just been pressed into service by

[61]Tanaka, "How to Survive, op. cit.

[62]Erwin Cooper, Aqueduct Empire (The Arthur H. Clark Company,
Glendale, California, 1968), p. 66.

[63]"Manzanar" means "apple orchard" in Spanish.

[64]Brown, op. cit., Dec. 13, 1973. Brown later served both as
Reports Officer and Assistant Director of Manzanar Relocation Center.

[65]Rowe, op. cit., p. 37, remembers that "Boddy came in to see
Biddle and me in Washington. He'd run a great liberal paper in Los
Angeles, and here he was screaming bloody murder for evacuation against
Biddle."

[66]Dillon S. Myer, Uprooted Americans, op. cit., p. 127.

President Roosevelt.[69] Eisenhower charged Cozzens, "You have to select sites for 110,000 people and you have six weeks to do it." Cozzens outlined the criteria by which he selected the sites:

> I couldn't be close to a proposed military site in case we had to move back . . . . I could only use so many pounds of copper wire for hooking up the power, so I had to be close to that. I couldn't be close to an airport, I couldn't be close to any Navy installation that might be set up at any later date.
> I had to be able to produce . . . practically all the food that they were to use. . . . We finally wound up with not purchasing any sites. We either located on federal land, or Indian reservations, or things of that kind.[70]

Manzanar fit the bill, being isolated, publicly owned, and close to a large water supply. However, the people who were forced to live there saw it for the desolate place that it was; and Angelenos saw all kinds of possibilities of pollution, deliberate or otherwise, from the close proximity of a "Jap camp" to their water supply.[71]

The Inyo-Mono Association, recognizing the economic potential of a community destined to be the largest in the county, sent Brown on a speaking tour to extoll the camp's advantages to the area residents. Rumor and fear prevailed,[72] nevertheless, until money began pouring into the coffers of nearby merchants from the dozens of builders who came for tools and from the few residents of the camp who were allowed, in the early days, to come for supplies. Grumblings in the towns put a stop to internees coming in to shop, and the later attempt by an Independence merchant to reverse that situation came to no avail. Owens Valley people, however, continued to benefit economically through extensive employment in the center.

---

[67]Later, a U.S. Supreme Court Justice.

[68]Cozzens, op. cit., p. 2.

[69]In his Berkeley interview, op. cit., p. 2, Dillon Myer says, "He [Milton Eisenhower] was pushed into it. He didn't want the job. . . . The President poured the heat on. It was wartime. It was the only reason he took it because it was not his kind of job. He was capable, of course, and he had demonstrated that throughout the years. He didn't want it. He didn't like it, from the beginning." No mention is made by Myer in his book Uprooted Americans of the pressure placed by FDR on Eisenhower.

[70]Cozzens, op. cit., pp. 7, 8, and 16. In respect to military installations, Cozzens states, p. 6, "In locating the centers, I was given a map, both by the Navy and the Army, which showed how we would perform on later echelons if we were attacked and had to move back from the Coast. But I never divulged this to anyone. My assistants used to think I was crazy . . . because I would turn down sites that they had selected." Cozzens further indicates that land speculators attempted to bribe him: "You talk about pressures! I had offers of everything in the world—that I wouldn't have to work the rest of my natural life, had I

The buildings at Manzanar were far from ready for occupancy when, on March 21, the first volunteer group of eighty-six doctors, nurses, and others, headed by Dr. James Goto, moved in to staff the hospital. There were no windows, no lights, and no stoves--the wind blew unremittingly and ice formed on water overnight. Such were the conditions when Karl G. Yoneda arrived two nights later as part of the second volunteer contingent of eight hundred from the Los Angeles area, three hundred of whom had motored up.[73] The following day he noted in his diary:

> The dusty wind [blew] all day. White carpenters are hammering away. We went to the front office to inquire about working as carpenters' helpers and one of the officials said, "The Army is running the camp and we can't do anything about it." This was a promise the Maryknoll fathers in L.A. had given us--that we would be hired to build the camp and get union wages.[74] The volunteers are bitterly disappointed about the camp set-up.[75]

Yoneda's disappointment ran deeper than most for he had come with a dedication and purpose rooted in lifelong involvement in anti-militarist, anti-fascist, and pro-labor activities.[76] Indeed, he had volunteered precisely because this seemed an opportunity to further those causes. Being thirty-five, he was one of the few older second-generation Japanese Americans in the camp and, as such, felt a particular responsibility to the others as well as to the nation. Yoneda and his wife had resided in

---

done the things that certain people wanted me to do . . . if I would locate a site in a certain area, and buy that land, that I'd never have to work the rest of my natural life. . . . If we'd wanted to be crooked, we could have been. Thank God we weren't. We didn't have any of it. That's one thing. Mr. Myer told the President that WRA would be out of business six months after the war was over. We were out of business six months after it was over. We were the only war agency in government that _ever_ has gotten out of business."

[71]Myer, Earl Warren Project, op. cit., p. 16.

[72]According to Brown, op. cit., Dec. 13, 1973, a small group formed a militia to "save women and children."

[73]Elaine Yoneda, op. cit., relates, "Those who drove their cars, when they got to Manzanar, were told to park their cars in a certain area inside of the barbed wire encampment in the desert. They were not allowed to take their things out, and those who went by car, of course, took whatever they could in their cars. You know, they had more than the others who were going who could take only whatever they could carry. So that when we approached Manzanar, the first thing I was aware of . . . was this group of cars standing out there that were just laden with dust." The automobiles were never used again by evacuees. Later they were auctioned by the government and "blue book" price given their owners.

[74]The wage scale in the camps for full-time work ranged from $9 to $19--later $21--per month. Only those holding positions of comparative prestige, such as doctors, received $19.

[75]Karl G. Yoneda, Manzanar Diary, a forthcoming publication.

[76]Karl G. Yoneda, "A Brief History of Japanese Labor in the USA,"

San Francisco since 1933. However, they left there right after the funeral of prominent labor figure Tom Mooney; Mrs. Yoneda and son to stay with her parents in Los Angeles and Karl to go to Manzanar.

Yoneda was already well known because of frequent arrests for participating in strikes and hunger marches, and for distributing anti-imperialist leaflets during visits by Japanese Imperial Navy warships to U.S. ports. He was, moreover, the only longshoreman of Japanese descent on the mainland and the first Asian to run for state office in California, having been the Communist Party candidate for the 22nd Assembly District seat in 1934.[77] Furthermore, he wrote a regular column for Doho,[78] the only West Coast Japanese-American newspaper which consistently attacked Japan's militarism.

Karl had been vocal against the invasion of China in the prewar period, had promoted the boycott of Japanese goods, and had picketed ships loading scrap iron for Japan. He was among those "progressives of Japanese ancestry--native and foreign born"--who had telegraphed Roosevelt immediately after Pearl Harbor to offer their services in any capacity to defeat "our enemies."[79] He recognized the unconstitutionality of evacuating citizens, and now that his purposes appeared to be frustrated, he debated with himself over the rightness of his actions. "Had I, as a progressive labor leader, been right in evacuating voluntarily, along with some of the pro-Japan group who had come to Manzanar because they had no place else to go?" he asked himself. (He suspected later that a few of the pro-Japan group volunteered for other reasons.) His determination wavered only slightly, for uppermost in his mind was the thought that "the only way to speed victory over fascism and militarism" was to make every effort to expedite the evacuation "so that our country can turn her sights--unhampered--against the enemy."[80]

Meanwhile, Karl's wife, Elaine Black Yoneda, staying with their son Thomas Culbert[81] in the home of her parents, fully expected to contribute to the effort by finding war work and visiting Karl when she could. Elaine was of a like mind with Karl in respect to purposes. She, too, had been a labor activist, having been secretary in the district office of the International Labor Defense as well as that organization's Pacific

---

delivered to the Asian American Studies Class, UCLA, Nov. 12, 1969.

[77]He ran under the name of Karl Hama, the name by which he was known from 1926 until 1936, though his family name is Yoneda. As a Kibei, Karl fled to his native land in 1926 when he was drafted for service in the Japanese army. Largely in consideration of members of his family both in Japan and in the United States, he adopted the name Hama--a practice that was common in the Japanese community, particularly with those whose only way into the country was through illegal means. Fortunately, Karl's mother in Hiroshima had saved his American birth certificate.

[78]For a beginning study, see Ronald C. Larson, "Doho: The Communist Japanese-American Press, 1938-1942," a paper for a Historical Methodology class, Dec. 17, 1973, CSUF, Arthur A. Hansen, instructor.

[79]Manzanar Diary, op. cit., March 23, 1942.

[80]Ibid.

[81]Named for Thomas Mooney and Governor Culbert Olson.

Coast vice-president. It was she who had been instrumental in striking down the "$1,000 Vag" bail provision in California's Vagrancy Law which had been used mainly to harrass activists in San Francisco.[82] Photographs of the attractive Elaine Black pleading her own case made good news copy in the early thirties.

Karl's beating at the hands of the Los Angeles police in the Hunger March of 1931 was an incident that rated a series of three snapshots in the Los Angeles _Times_--the first, the clubbing; the second, the dragging; and the last, the carrying of a man unable to stand to the police wagon. Elaine met Karl when, as secretary for the ILD, it was her job to bail him out.

Their common interests drew them together, but marriage was postponed by California's anti-miscegenation law. It took a trip to Seattle to make their union legal. The Yonedas had endured much by evacuation time. The morning after Pearl Harbor he had been picked up at the docks as a "potentially dangerous enemy." She, in the meantime, was confronted in their home by FBI agents looking for him and refusing to be convinced that he could be employed at the time on the docks. Neighbors later told her that machine guns had been trained on their home while she was inside being interrogated.

Nothing, however, quite prepared Elaine for the experiences of the next few months. Only a week after her husband left for Manzanar, she was jolted by a radio interruption--an announcement that the Army had ordered all those of Japanese ancestry whose breadwinners were at Manzanar to be evacuated by noon on April 2, 1942. Elaine knew the edict affected her because Japanese blood flowed in the veins of her three year old son. She points out that such an order amounted to the rescinding of a "promissory note" authorities had given the nearly nine hundred early volunteers:

> They were told that _their_ families would be the last ones ordered out of military area number one because it was such a rush thing. They didn't need to worry about their property--about their personal wealth. Their families who were remaining behind would have ample time to take care of it, and no **doubt** by that time the government would have set up storage warehouses--they didn't have storage for that first group. As a result, doctors left behind medical instruments. . . . It was expected their wives would be able to handle it. Then comes this edict a week later that they had to be out in seventy-two hours. It was mind-blowing![83]

In the cases of Elaine and Tommy, the betrayal of the "promissory note" was even more encompassing in its effect for she had never expected they would go.

---

[82]Elaine recalls, "They found me guilty and they also found the other men guilty, and the case was taken on appeal. As a result of that appeal--as a result of some of the material that I had introduced as evidence . . .--it became a factor in the appeal, that there was nothing wrong, and that in fact they were trying me as a Communist, which was

ELAINE BLACK YONEDA

When she appeared the next day to be processed by Army personnel
assisted by the Maryknoll Fathers, she resented the special treatment
accorded her. An officer, apparently because she was an embarrassment
standing in line with all the Japanese, hurried her into the building
for processing. She had earlier been assured that "It doesn't mean
you. It's the father's ancestry that counts. By international law it
affects only those with more than one-sixteenth Japanese blood." But
Elaine was determined that it meant her, if it meant her child. She
was now assured that Tommy would be put into a "Children's Village" to
be "manned" by nuns. She repeatedly reminded the fathers of her vows
of marriage, but only a blank form for her son was provided. She insisted that her husband would leave the camp as soon as he was permitted
to enter the Army, and she wouldn't think of abandoning their child to
an orphanage;[84] whereupon, she was handed two forms with no assurance
that both would be honored. When she found that only Tommy was to be
inoculated along with all Japanese evacuees, she demanded to be included. If she ever doubted, she was now convinced that the

> whole evacuation was on a racial basis. This was racism
> behind it. You scratch the surface a little bit and you see
> the hand of Hearst and all those "Yellow Peril" forces that
> we had in this state, just all coming out of the woodwork.
> They had been silent for a couple of years. In fact, some
> of them had applauded and supported Japan's invasion of China.[85]

When asked by authorities if she wanted to leave on the 1st or the 2nd,
she decided that April Fool's Day was appropriate.

Elaine relates that her husband was "ashen-faced" when he was
greeted with a shout of "Daddy, Daddy!" from one of the several Greyhound
buses heading toward him through a thick cloud of dust. "Are you bringing our child to be killed?" he fairly screamed. He had written her not
to come even for a visit, particularly since Tommy was severely asthmatic.
That night Karl wrote in his diary, "I shouted madly at her through the
window. After they got off the bus, Elaine handed me a copy of the
De Witt "Civilian Exclusion Order #3.'" He had assumed that her move
to camp was voluntary as his had been. He, like the rest, had not been
informed. Karl's diary goes on, "Only after . . . explanation was I
able to take her in my arms--together we shed a few tears. Happy are
my thoughts of my wife's love and devotion to me and our child."[86]

Their fears about their son's welfare were soon realized--a dust
storm blew all that first night, and the youngster had an asthma attack

---

not illegal. Therefore, there's no such thing as a "Thousand Dollar Vag"
charge now on the books of California." Betty E. Mitson, interviewer;
O.H. 1377a, CSUF, March 2, 1974.

[83]Elaine Yoneda/Arthur Hansen, op. cit.

[84]An orphanage was not established at Manzanar until after the
Yonedas left.

[85]Elaine Yoneda/Arthur Hansen, op. cit.

[86]Manzanar Diary, op. cit., April 1, 1942.

which became a way of life for him as long as he remained in the center.
Tommy was destined to see the inside of the camp hospital many times
before he left. Blowing sand and rock that aggravated his condition
became so bad at times, that "standing in line you couldn't recognize
the person in front or behind."[87]

Karl's diary entry of April 4 notes,

> No work today. An Army sergeant called me into his
> office and questioned me about my political beliefs. Evi-
> dently someone complained about my being in the camp.
>
> He had a thick file on me on his desk and I told him
> to read it. "You will find that I am a fighter for American
> democracy against Japanese militarism and have been for many
> years. I have nothing to hide." He thanked me for coming
> to his office.

Despite their son's deteriorating condition, the Yonedas did not
shirk what they considered their duties within the relocation center.
It wasn't long before Elaine appeared at the administration building,
pounding on a desk, declaring that there was going to be "either mass
suicide or mass hysteria," especially among teen-aged girls, if privacy
was not provided in the latrines which had ten toilet bowls in two
back-to-back rows, completely without partitions. The whole camp was
plagued in those early days with what came to be known as "the Manzanar
runs" and, to make matters worse, exterior walls had lots of knotholes
and wide cracks between the rough boards, so Peeping Toms were having
a field day. Her action brought improved conditions there--and no
back-to-back toilets were placed in other camps. She registered a protest again about the danger to children caused by the fast-moving trucks
ungoverned by any speed limit. Karl relates that many resented his
having brought a Caucasian wife into camp. "She had a right to stay
outside, so why come in and stick out like a sore thumb?" they demanded.[88]
Despite that, Elaine feels that she gained acceptance--doubtlessly, her
ready willingness to make demands at the administration office helped.
She also worked, along with other internees, in a war industry established in the camp, a camouflage net factory. She suffered miserably
from an allergic reaction to the dyes used there.

Through election confirmed by the administration, Karl became a
member of the Block Leaders' Council--not a policy-making body, but one
that determined how to implement policies that came from the administration and submitted complaints and suggestions to them. When the Manzanar
Citizens' Federation--whose purpose was to provide an open forum for
discussing such things as improvement of camp conditions, furtherance of
the United States' war effort, and the future of the evacuees--was formed,

---

[87]Elaine Yoneda/Arthur Hansen, op. cit. Blowing sand and pebble
conditions are known to become severe enough to make traffic prohibitive
through Owens Valley.

[88]Karl G. Yoneda, interviewee; Arthur A. Hansen and Ronald C.
Larson, interviewers; O.H. 1376b, CSUF, March 3, 1974.

he became a member and was instrumental in pushing a petition drive re-
questing President Franklin D. Roosevelt to utilize volunteer manpower
from the camps and to open a second front.[89]

The things that Yoneda did while in camp represented more than
cooperation, they represented dedication to a cause. His effectiveness
was well recognized by the dissident elements in camp, which is why he
was one of those singled out for intimidating treatment. By the time
he left permanently on Wednesday, December 2, 1942, his life had been
repeatedly endangered by "Black Dragons"[90] in the camp (who had been
stoning camouflage net workers, as well).

Yoneda was among the first fourteen to enlist and leave a relocation center to be trained for work in Army Intelligence.[91] Because of
their language skill, the fourteen were mostly Kibei. This was ironic
since Kibei as a group had earlier been subjected to discriminatory
administrative policies on the assumption that most were pro-Japan.
(Unlike the celebrated 442nd Regiment which later served in the
European theater, this largely unsung group saw active service in the
China-Burma-India theater of war.)[92]

---

[89]Roosevelt Library, President's Alphabetical File 197-A and
Official File 25 contain references to a letter of August 5, 1942
signed by Yoneda and Koji Ariyoshi that contained the petitions of
218 citizens of Japanese descent.

[90]In a letter to Roger Daniels, reprinted as "Corrections and
Omissions: Yoneda Checks Out Book on Evacuation," New York Nichibei,
June 8, 1972, Karl Yoneda states that the Black Dragons were "organized
by Joe Kurihara, Ben Kishi, Harry Ueno, John Umemoto, several judoists
of Seigo Murakami group and others. Most of them were Kibei and belonged
to a salvage crew except Kurihara, Nisei who was a foreman of field
carpenters and Harry Ueno, Kibei, cook of Block 4 kitchen. Every day,
they drove all over the camp in a salvage truck with a Black Dragon
banner, throwing rocks at those who worked on the camouflage net project, trying to run over those whom they considered 'pro-Americans'--
they tried this on [Tokie] Slocum and me several times--threatening to
put those who oppose them on 'death list,' shouting slogans such as
'Don't be Korean dogs by working on camouflage nets,' 'Japanese Imperial
Army will free us,' etc., and posting 'pro-Japan' handbills. They
raided our 'apartment'--10 coming inside and 14 on the outside--intimat-
ing that my mother in Hiroshima would face dire consequences and I would
be machine-gunned along with other 'pro-Americans' unless I retracted my
criticism of the Black Dragons which I had made at the block leaders
Council meeting. Their so-called 'protest against injustice' turned
into hooliganism of distorted resistance, while the administration took
a 'no-see' attitude."

[91]Ibid. Yoneda disagreed with the statements on pp. 145-146 of
Concentration Camps, USA., op. cit., that "The Language School Commandant,
Lieutenant Colonel Rasmussen, acting on War Department authority in early
July, 1942, had by-passed De Witt and Bendetsen and sent recruiting teams
directly to the Assembly Centers and Relocation Centers. As Bendetsen
later described it: Col. Rasmussen, from his school in Minnesota, sent a

After Karl left, the venom that had been directed at him now shifted to his child. When, four days later, matters came to a head in what has come to be known as the "Manzanar Riot,"[93] Elaine and Tommy were among the sixty-five evacuated in the dark of night by the administration to protect their lives. The boy's name, along with that of Togo Tanaka and a handful of others, had appeared on a death list.[94] In the wake of the riot, the sixty-five, including families, found temporary haven in an abandoned CCC camp in Death Valley.

When Elaine was permitted to return to the West Coast shortly there-after (December 18), it was stipulated that she report monthly to De Witt's office on the behavior of her Japanese son--now almost four! He was one of the first of Japanese ancestry to return--long before the ban was lifted.[95]

---

detail in to Manzanar to gather up a few enlistees. Four only enlisted at that time." Yoneda's diary shows that "Col. Rasmussen, Sgt. J. Masuda and two others first came to Manzanar on August 6, 1942, and spoke to us in the Block One kitchen. More than 90 Issei, Nisei, and Kibei were present. They expressed strong desire to join the school. Col. Rasmussen himself tested our Japanese language ability individually and promised to come back for official recruiting. Also Koji Ariyoshi and Karl Yoneda told Col. Rasmussen about the Manzanar Citizens Federation circulating a petition which asked President Roosevelt to utilize Japanese American man-power from the camps for war effort and he replied 'Good work.' On November 28, 1942 MISLS [Military Intelligence Service Language School] recruiting team headed by Sgt. Masuda came to Manzanar. About 50 evacuees showed up and 14 of us passed the Japanese language test and not 'four or five.'"

[92]Respecting this theater, there is a popular novel for young people: Frank Bonham, Burma Rifles: A Story of Merrill's Marauders (New York: Thomas Y. Crowell Company, 1960). Sergeant Stanley Uno was an adviser on the book. Uno is the American soldier of Japanese ancestry mentioned in f. 44.

[93]For a re-evaluation of the unrest at Manzanar, see David Hacker and Arthur A. Hansen, "The Manzanar 'Riot': A Perspective and an Explanatory Strategy," a paper delivered at the Western Conference of the Association for Asian Studies, Sept. 28, 1973. A revised version of that paper appears on p. 41 of this book.

[94]In respect to the "death list," see Togo Tanaka/David Hacker, Betty Mitson, op. cit., pp. 43-51.

[95]Herbert Nicholson relates his experience of observing two or three Caucasian women and six or seven children crying on one of the evacuation buses leaving from Covina, California. Outside, a husband of one told him that the women were sisters and their mother, who was a Russian, had married a Japanese man years earlier and they had two or three girls. "The old man died, and she married a Russian. The children grew up and didn"t even know their father; he had died. They didn't know they were half Japanese. They grew up and married Caucasians and had their families. One of the girls went to get a defense job where you had to have a birth certificate; they began investigating the thing

Karl eloquently sums up his sentiments respecting the whole evacuation affair:

> I had the future of the Japanese living here in my heart always. . . . I thought and tried to figure out what was best for us to survive in this war and when the war is over. I told them, "Suppose we resisted en masse, what would happen to us after the war?" They would be called all kinds of names: "Bunch of slackers, bunch of SOB's. Here we shed our blood to defeat Hitler, Mussolini, and Tojo and you sit on your asses and didn't do a damn thing." I also told them to remember Hitler's ovens and the Rape of Nanking.
>
> On the other hand, those who resisted being drafted in 1943 and '44, you know--I certainly condemn the action of the government. They had no business drafting those that were kept in the camps.[96]

In comparing the prewar and postwar status of Japanese Americans, Togo Tanaka adds, "We must have done something right."[97]

Oral historians can justifiably claim that they, too, are doing something right by going to informed people for the human side of the evacuation story. Interviews, such as those cited herein, not only corroborate or invalidate existing records, but they also fill in the gaps in those records and expose anomalies of the period.

Additionally, oral history is opening up new avenues of inquiry for students of Japanese-American history, particularly of the hegira period. Such subjects, as the conditions of detention camps for "enemy aliens," the disposition of Japanese farm properties, the conversion of Los Angeles' Little Tokyo into a black community--Bronzeville--and its postwar reconversion, the response of the Japanese-American Left to relocation, resistance movements within the camps, the reaction of towns proximate to relocation centers, are the kinds of topics currently being investigated with the interview approach. Moreover, the interview experience yields all kinds of auxiliary benefits such as old newspapers, letters, documents,[98] moral and (sometimes) financial support, leads to other potential interviewees and documentary material, lasting friendships around a common interest, and often a certain catharsis for both teller and listener. Five interviewees cited in this work are known to have kept diaries in the camps. Of those, two are scheduled for publication; one as a result of the oral history contact. An autobiography of Herbert V. Nicholson and a study of Manzanar--both relying heavily on the oral documentation cited herein--are also in preparation.[99]

---

and found that her father was Japanese." Nicholson took the men of the families to the officer in charge of evacuation of the San Gabriel area, Colonel Severance, who reacted, "This is terrible. This is out-Hitlering Hitler!" Severance flew to Washington, D.C., but it was six weeks before he could get the women and children out of camp. op. cit., pp. 24-25.

[96]Karl G. Yoneda/Arthur A. Hansen, Ronald C. Larson, op. cit.

[97]Tanaka, "How to Survive, op. cit.

Dealing with the banishment of a people through the personal
contact inherent in oral history brings rewards beyond mere historical
documentation--it yields understanding. And that, of course, is one
of the fundamental purposes behind all historical inquiry.

---

[98]Such items are deposited in the project: _Japanese-American
Relocation in California During World War II_, CSUF Library, Department
of Bibliographic Services, Special Collections Section, Linda E. Herman,
librarian.

[99]Herbert V. Nicholson, _Treasure in Earthen Vessels_, is to be
published by Geddes Press, Pasadena, 1974. Arthur A. Hansen is editing
the diary of Robert L. Brown for publication, and a study of Manzanar,
coauthored by Arthur A. Hansen and David A. Hacker, is tentatively
titled: _Manzanar: A Perspectivist History_. See also F. 75.

THE MANZANAR 'RIOT'

AN ETHNIC PERSPECTIVE

ARTHUR A. HANSEN and DAVID A. HACKER

In his recent book, American Historical Explanations, Gene Wise reproves American historians for naively assuming that "the real aim of historical scholarship is to discover just what happened in the past; that what happened has been recorded here and there in what historians call 'primary documents'; and that the only true scholarship in the field of history must be based directly on only those primary documents."[2] While granting that this approach has eliminated much flagrant bias and derivativeness, Wise nonetheless maintains that it has led historians into some profound epistemological fallacies. First, it has fostered the scholarly ideal that "objective history-- the whole Truth, nothing but the Truth--can be realized once historians learn to behave as "ideal observers"--i.e., cease viewing reality through existential frames of reference; secondly, this approach has promoted the correlative notion that the way for historians to attain this ideal is to devote themselves to an intensive examination of primary sources, for in these documents the original experiences inhere in pure and unfiltered wholeness.

To refute these wrongheaded nostrums, Wise explains that "objective" history is impossible precisely because the historian's mind is grounded ineluctably in experience, and therefore he observes through selected frames of reference; this same relativism obtains for primary documents since they too are merely commentaries upon original phenomena by similarly bounded minds. Accordingly, Wise suggests an alternative model of historical inquiry--the "perspectivist" model--which he believes more realistic and productive than the "ideal observer" one. This new model would ask different questions of its sources. Because the ideal-observer model is preoccupied with what happened in the past, its questions are designed to disentangle the objective truth of history from the snares and delusions of assorted interpreters. On the other hand, since the perspectivist model discounts what happened as its sole or even fundamental concern, it queries its sources in a different manner. Although mindful of what happened, its chief concern, according to Wise, "is with the question, 'How do particular people experience what happened?' And further, 'How do they put form on their experience?' And yet further, 'How do these forms connect into their particular locations in time and place?'"[3]

The present paper utilizes the perspectivist approach in studying one celebrated episode occurring within the internment experience of

---

[1]A revised version of this essay is scheduled to appear in the Amerasia Journal, II, 2 (Nov. 1974).

[2]Gene Wise, American Historical Explanations: A Strategy for Grounded Inquiry (Homewood, Ill.: Dorsey, 1973), p. vii.

[3]Ibid., p. 34. Unlike Wise, who derives his inspiration for

Japanese Americans during the Second World War, the so-called Manzanar Riot. We have given our study a tripartite division. The first section offers a brief summary of the event itself. The second attempts to delineate and account for the dominant perspective influencing the interpretation of this event in the past. The third and longest section offers a new perspective for interpreting the Manzanar Riot. Although this portion of the study adds considerably to the existing stock of information about the riot, we feel its major contribution is that it presents a strategy for explaining this information in a significantly different way.

On the evening of December 5, 1942, some unidentified evacuees at the Manzanar War Relocation Center assaulted Fred Tayama, a Nisei who had returned the previous day to Manzanar from Salt Lake City where he had served as the center's representative at the national convention of the Japanese American Citizens League (JACL). The beating administered to Tayama, formerly a Los Angeles restaurateur and chairman of the Southern District JACL, was severe enough to hospitalize him and prompt the camp authorities to arrest three Kibei. Two of these suspects were taken into custody at the Manzanar jail and released after questioning, but the remaining one, Harry Ueno, president of the Kitchen Workers' Union, was removed from the camp and jailed in nearby Independence, California.

Ueno's arrest aroused widespread hostility and resistance among the internees. Contrary to the War Relocation Authority (WRA) rationale for this action—that Ueno had been identified positively by Tayama as one of his assailants--many internees charged that Ueno was innocent and was being victimized due to his recent allegation that certain WRA officials were appropriating sugar and meat intended for the internees in order to sell it for profit outside the camp.

At 10:00 a.m. on Sunday, December 6, about two hundred internees assembled in the mess hall of Block 22, Ueno's block, to discuss his arrest and consider ways of effecting his return to the camp. This meeting, comprised of Block 22 residents and a sprinkling of Kitchen Workers' Union members, entertained several plans of action, including the imposition of a center-wide strike of kitchens. After about twenty minutes the meeting was adjourned and a second meeting of Block Managers, mess hall workers, and Kibei groups was arranged for

---

perspectivist history from the novelistic technique and from recent conceptual breakthroughs in a multiplicity of scientific and humanistic disciplines, we have been led to adopt the perspectivist approach in this study chiefly through our involvement in oral history. This tool of inquiry, with its emphasis on the taped interview, has confirmed our suspicion of "objective" history and directed us to seek answers to the very questions which Wise depicts as central to the perspectivist model of historical explanation.

1:00 p.m. in Block 22.

News of the one o'clock meeting apparently spread throughout the entire camp population, for the crowd that subsequently arrived was so large (estimates place it in excess of two thousand people) that the gathering had to be moved outside the mess hall to the adjacent firebreak area. Following the delivery of some fiery speeches over a hastily-constructed public address system, a Committee of Five was selected to negotiate with Project Director Ralph P. Merritt for Ueno's reinstatement. This committee included two Issei and two Kibei associated in some way with the Kitchen Workers' Union. Its principal spokesman, however, was Joe Kurihara, a Hawaiian-born Nisei and World War I veteran who, while a friend of Ueno's, was unaffiliated with the Union.

Director Merritt was so alarmed by police reports of the huge assemblage that he requested the military police to form outside the center's gate in case trouble threatened. To ward off this contingency, he then accompanied the center police chief to the meeting, which was just concluding. In fact, the Committee of Five had already left to confer with Merritt. Accordingly, he returned immediately to the staff area to await the members.

Presently the mob arrived in front of the Administration Building, where it was confronted by a massed rank of armed soldiers. When attempts by the authorities to disperse the crowd proved unavailing, Director Merritt agreed to hear its demands. Urged on by the large throng, the Committee informed him that he must immediately obtain release of Ueno from the Independence jail and return him to Manzanar. Merritt refused to capitulate, but he did express his willingness to air this and other grievances with the Committee, provided that the crowd disperse and return to its quarters.

The highly volatile mob was determined, however, to stay put until the officials had satisfied its demands. Perhaps sensing that it was no longer in control of the crowd, the Committee urged Merritt to concede before matters got completely out of hand. Although publicly the Project Director reiterated his earlier refusal to this demand, a private conference with the police chief and the commander of the military police convinced him that this concession was necessary in order to avoid bloodshed. Out of the crowd's earshot Merritt then met with the Committee and informed it that Ueno would be returned to the Manzanar jail within one hour after the crowd had returned home if the Committee agreed to certain conditions: (1) that Ueno stand trial before Manzanar's Judicial Committee; (2) that no attempt be made to release Ueno from the camp jail; (3) that the Committee would meet with Merritt to decide on any other matters it wished to discuss; (4) that there would be no more mobs or mass meetings of any sort until the center had resumed normalcy; and (5) that the Committee would help maintain law and order in the center, and would assist the police in apprehending Tayama's assailants. Merritt also announced that a subsequent statement pertaining to Ueno's return would be issued at six o'clock that evening at Mess

Hall 22.

That afternoon Ueno was returned to the camp jail. When the Committee appeared at Mess Hall 22 at six o'clock to affirm this fact, it encountered a crush of two to four thousand internees. Again the meeting was transferred outside. On the grounds that it had accomplished its objective, the Committee attempted to resign. This suggestion was shouted down by the crowd which felt that the administration had not gone far enough by merely returning Ueno to the Manzanar jail. Ueno should be unconditionally released, even if release required his enforced removal. Moreover, the crowd demanded that internees like Fred Tayama, whom they suspected of collaborating with the administration and informing to the FBI about pro-Japan activities in camp, should be killed. Having degenerated into an uncontrolled demonstration, the meeting broke up when a hurried plan of action was outlined. The crowd divided itself into two main groups, one to ferret out Tayama in the camp hospital and finish the job begun the night before, and the second to liberate Ueno from jail.

After failing to locate Tayama, the first group broke into splinter groups bent on searching out and killing Tokie Slocum and Togo Tanaka, two other JACL leaders reputed to be "stooges." This quest also proved fruitless. By now the second group was approaching the jail. At this point Director Merritt ordered in the military police, who immediately placed a protective barricade between the crowd and the jail.

From seven o'clock to nine-thirty the administration attempted to negotiate with the evacuee representatives. At first the crowd contented itself with singing Japanese songs and gesturing menacingly at the soldiers. But when some of the internees began throwing stones and bottles, the military police were ordered to fire tear gas into their midst. Shortly thereafter, for reasons never clearly established, the soldiers opened fire on the crowd, killing a young Nisei and wounding ten other evacuees, one of whom died several days later.

During the night, the camp remained in a turbulent state. Kitchen bells tolled continuously, beatings of alleged informers ensued, and military police units patrolled the camp, breaking up numerous evacuee gatherings. Those whose names appeared on the internees' blacklists and deathlists were spirited out of camp and placed in protective custody, and the administration began a roundup of those believed responsible for the disruption. Within the next few days, the first group and its families were sent to an abandoned CCC camp in Death Valley, while the latter group was imprisoned within local jails and then transferred to a temporary isolation center in Moab, Utah.[4]

---

[4]U.S. War Relocation Archive, Relocation Center, Manzanar, California, Special Collections, UCLA Research Library, Collection 122, Boxes 16, 17, and the Japanese Evacuation and Relocation Study project, Bancroft Library, U.C. Berkeley, Folders E2.332, 07.00, 07.50, 08.10, 010.00, 010.04, 010.12, 010.14, 011.00, R30.00, R30.10, S1.10, and S1.20 A,B,C passim. Collection 122 consists of the files

To date, most of the accounts of the Manzanar Riot have been filtered through what might be labelled the "WRA-JACL" perspective.[5] The appellation is apt because nearly all of the original documentation was prepared by WRA or JACL affiliates and because secondary compilers have almost without exception simply buttressed this official version. This perspective has allowed considerable variety of informational detail, but has imposed virtual uniformity with respect to interpretive contours. The reasons for this stylization of form inhere within the historical experience of its creators and custodians. But before tracking down these connections, let us first outline the most conspicuous features of the WRA-JACL perspective.

One dimension can be glimpsed through the language used to describe the event. As a general rule, the primary sources refer to it as an "incident," while the secondary works term it a "riot." Since the former denotes an "occurrence" and the latter signifies a "violent disorder," at first glance these designations appear radically different. This impression is reinforced when one encounters statements like the following, which appears in a recent account written from the WRA-JACL perspective: "The incident, properly called a riot, at Manzanar early in December, 1942, was handled quite differently from the Poston strike."[6] In perspectivist terms, however, the difference is more apparent than real. What places both words within the WRA-JACL perspective is that each trivializes the event's <u>cultural</u> significance. "Incident" accomplishes this effect by scaling down the affair to commonplace proportions, while "riot" achieves the same by inflating it to melodramatic ones. Because neither term allows for meaningful contextual inquiry, both invite descriptive treatment but discourage explanatory analysis.

---

collected and maintained by Mr. Ralph Palmer Merritt, Project Director of the Manzanar War Relocation Center. Hereafter cited as WRAA, Coll. 122. The Berkeley archives have been prepared and indexed by Edward N. Barnhart. Future reference to this material will be cited as JERS, Barnhart.

[5]The primary accounts are contained in WRAA, Coll. 122, Box 16, <u>passim</u>, and JERS, Barnhart, Folder 07.00 <u>passim</u>. Secondary treatment of the Manzanar Riot from this perspective includes: Allan R. Bosworth, <u>America's Concentration Camps</u> (New York: Bantam, 1968), pp. 152-6; Audrie Girdner and Anne Loftis, <u>The Great Betrayal</u> (London: Macmillan, 1969), pp. 263-6; Bill Hosokawa, <u>Nisei: The Quiet Americans</u> (New York: Morrow, 1969), pp. 361-2; Norman Richard Jackman, <u>Collective Protest in Relocation Centers</u>, unpubl. PhD diss., U.C. Berkeley, 1955, pp. 170-83, 211-19; Dillon S. Myer, <u>Uprooted Americans</u> (Tucson: Univ. of Arizona Press, 1971), pp. 63-6; and Thomas Brewer Rice, <u>The Manzanar War Relocation Center</u>, unpubl. M.A. thesis, U.C. Berkeley, 1947.

[6]Girdner and Loftis, <u>Betrayal</u>, p. 263.

A second, closely related, feature of this perspective is its tendency to view the "riot"[7] episodically. This myopia has stamped itself upon the literature in various ways. First, it has militated against sustained, in-depth analyses of causation. Most accounts practically ignore the causative factor, and even those aspiring to explain cause have confined their investigation within the parameters of the immediate pre-evacuation, evacuation and camp experience. Secondly, it has caused the riot to be misconstrued as a denouement rather than seen as one development along a continuum of internee resistance. Thus, for example, in direct violation of the available evidence, one account concludes that "the easing of tension, and a return to normal life [at Manzanar] came shortly after Christmas of 1942," and another posits that "events which [subsequent to the riot] occasioned conflict in other centers, such as [loyalty] registration, segregation and selective service, occasioned no conflict in Manzanar."[8] Thirdly, it has unduly parochialized the riot; that is, the riot has often been reduced to a purely local phenomenon instead of being related to the metapattern of resistance activity within all the internment centers.

Another distinguishing mark of this perspective is its chauvinistic orientation. As a result, the riot has been viewed as a microcosm of the Second World War. This outlook has hampered seriously an understanding of the event in its own terms. It has, for instance, dramatized the riot as an ideological confrontation between pro-American and pro-Japanese factions. This interpretation can be seen vividly in contemporary newspaper accounts like that in the Los Angeles Times: "Shouting 'Pearl Harbor, banzai, banzai' an estimated 1,000 pro-Axis Japanese, many of whom are Kibei, adherents of Japan, demonstrated in

---

[7]For convenience, this term throughout the discussion of the WRA-JACL perspective will be employed without quotation marks, though they should be understood.

[8]Rice, Manzanar Center, p. 69; Jackman, Collective Protest, p. 183. If anything, the year 1943 was even stormier than the preceding one. Manzanar was the only center, for instance, where over fifty percent of the adult male citizens answered "No" to the question on loyalty, qualified their response, refused to answer, or refused to register at all (by contrast, at the Minidoka Center these groups constituted only eight percent of the male citizen population). See Morton Grodzins, "Making Un-Americans," American Journal of Sociology, LX (May 1955), p. 577. Moreover, this period saw widespread resistance to the imposition of the draft for Nisei and a mounting number of applications for repatriation and expatriation. See WRAA, Coll. 122, Boxes 15, 26, especially the reports prepared by Morris E. Opler, the WRA community analyst at Manzanar. On the general unrest and internee resistance during this time, see WRAA, Coll. 122, Boxes 10, 11, and 31-9, which contain the Block Managers' reports.

a firebreak and hooted down Japanese-American Nisei . . . who protested their antics." But even the secondary work which dismisses
the Times' version as "fanciful or at least exaggerated," prefaces
its own description with the similar assertion that "trouble broke
out around the first anniversary of Pearl Harbor, between pro-American
and pro-Japanese factions."[9] The above quotations reveal two additional
by-products of this filiopietistic outlook. On the one hand, it has
confounded the aggressively patriotic posture of the JACL--a small
minority--with that of the Nisei as a whole (excepting, of course,
the Kibei, who have been represented indiscriminately as "troublemakers"). Secondly, it has displayed an incapacity to understand
ethnic identity in terms other than subversive. This fact explains
why most accounts of the riot minimize or ignore the massive participation of internees and instead focus exclusively on the actions of
selected groups like the Kibei and colorful personalities like Joe
Kurihara.[10]

With this picture in mind, we now must see how the WRA-JACL perspective connects existentially with its promoters. Our task is a
dual one. We must account for its origination in the primary sources
and explain its survival in the secondary literature.

It would be a pointless tautology to say merely because WRA and
JACL representatives compiled the original accounts of the riot, they
were written from the WRA-JACL perspective. More pertinently, we need
to inquire into the connection between their interpretation of the riot
and their overall attitude toward internment and to relate both to
their conception of American society.

Although different in some respects, the WRA and JACL viewpoints
on internment were fundamentally the same. Roger Daniels has summarized
the WRA stance: "Although some of the staff, particularly those in the
upper echelons of the WRA, disapproved of the racist policy that
brought the camps into being, the majority of the camp personnel . . .
shared the contempt of the general population for 'Japs.'"[11] Similarly,

---

[9]Girdner and Loftis, Betrayal, p. 263. One account of the riot
which shares some of the features of the WRA-JACL perspective, Togo
Tanaka's "An Analysis of the Manzanar Incident and Its Aftermath,"
deflates the ideological interpretation: "The impression given in most
newspaper accounts of the Manzanar disturbance, that the instigators
were all 'pro-Japan' or 'pro-Axis' . . . and that the intended victims
of violence were 'pro-American'--all of them--is not necessarily an
accurate picture. . . . Undoubtedly, differences in ideology and
position on the war played an important part; but these were . . . incidental to the riot itself." See WRAA, Coll. 122, Box 16.

[10]The inordinate attention paid Kurihara's role is reflected in
the Berkeley collection. See JERS, Barnhart, Folders 08.10, R30.00,
R30.10.

[11]Roger Daniels, Concentration Camps USA (New York: Holt, Rinehart and Winston, 1971), p. 105. Attitude, of course, is extremely

A. J. Leighton has divided the staff into those who were "people-minded" (i.e., regarded the evacuees first as people and as Japanese secondarily) and those who were "stereotype-minded" (i.e., regarded the evacuees as Japanese first and people secondarily).[12] For our

---

difficult to evaluate, but the documentation--both written and oral--pertinent to the Manzanar staff would suggest that perhaps "contempt" is too strong a word to label their outlook. The staff member most frequently cited by internees for his contemptuous attitude toward them is Ned Campbell, the Assistant Project Director. For instance, after the Manzanar Riot, Harry Ueno is quoted, in "Harry Yoshiwo Ueno," Board of Review report, Dec.-Jan. 1942-3, WRAA, Coll. 122, Box 16, as remarking that "Every time Ned Campbell speaks he thinks he talks to a slave." When an interviewer asked another internee, Togo Tanaka, whether he thought Ueno's appraisal of Campbell an accurate one, he replied, "Maybe that was the way he (Ueno) reacted. I just thought he (Campbell) was a loud, obnoxious someone who, you know, in another setting I wouldn't hire, period. But he was a bigshot." Arthur A. Hansen, interviewer; O.H. 1271b, Japanese American Oral History Project, California State University, Fullerton, August 30, 1973, pp. 28-9; hereafter all interviews from this collection will be cited as CSUF. Perhaps Campbell himself provides the clearest insight into why his manner may have been construed as contemptuous. The following exchange is drawn from an interview with him. Had you known Japanese Americans prior to taking this job? "If so, maybe one or two in my lifetime." You have been criticized by former internees for not having understood the Japanese psychology. Would you care to comment on that estimate? "Well, that is one hundred percent valid. . . . I went out there a real babe, believe me, a real babe. I went out there with the idea that here was a job to be done. I shall never forget how distressed I was when, because of being the Assistant Project Director there, I was assigned a big Chrysler--which I liked; everybody likes a big car to drive around. And I felt happy about it. But then to have a boy, a young man, come up one day and say, 'You know, you're driving my car.' He just wanted to look at it and touch it again. It was the first time I realized just how hard we were stepping on these people's toes. Not only stepping on their toes but rubbing it in their faces. And I think probably that was my first realization that I was dealing with people-- I mean, not my first realization; I knew they were people--my first appreciation that after all we were dealing with human beings, and this was just not a job to be done with so many bodies out there. Certainly I was very guilty of the fact of going out first with the notion that we have so many people--so many bodies, if you will--and we have a job to do: we've got to feed so many mouths, and we have so many people we have to get into the hospital, and we've got this and that and the other. But they were just numbers to me. And I think probably that instance was the beginning of my realization that I did have a human quotient to deal with." Arthur A. Hansen, interviewer; O.H. 1329, CSUF, August 15, 1974.

[12]Alexander H. Leighton, Governing of Men (New York: Octagon, 1964), pp. 81-9. Leighton's comments pertain specifically to the Poston staff.

purposes, the distinction is less significant than it appears. Whether or not an individual staff member possessed a humanitarian outlook significantly affected his day-to-day treatment of the internees, but it mattered little with respect to his overall perspective. For the decision to affiliate with the relocation program implicated one, at least tacitly, in upholding the policy objectives of the WRA.[13] These objectives were concerned with social control and social rehabilitation--i.e., with developing protective communities where the evacuated Japanese American population could be detained and imbued with American principles and practices. Staff members who resisted these objectives were eliminated.[14] For those who remained, active participation in the camp bureaucracy effectively internalized these corporate goals within them so that ultimately they came to measure their own worth in terms of their fulfillment.

The JACL posture complemented that of the WRA: while the JACL leadership assuredly was not contemptuous of "Japs," its identification with Americanized behavior and attitudes was complete enough to cause disavowal and depreciation of traditional Japanese customs, social organization, and values. This helps to account for what Douglas Nelson has described as the JACL's policy of "deliberate and calculated compliance" with the relocation program. JACL compliance, according to Nelson, began from the outset of the evacuation program. "JACL members assisted the FBI in the initial roundup of suspect Japanese aliens. They were usually among the first volunteers to go to the assembly centers and later to the interior concentration camps. [And] in November 1942, the JACL, meeting at Salt Lake City, resolved to endorse the administrations and goals of the War Relocation Authority."[15] In return for their cooperation, JACL leaders were accorded a measure of responsibility and influence in the camps. Not infrequently, they were selected for the preferred jobs, chosen to edit the camp newspapers, and granted other social, political, and economic perquisites. As a result of their integration into the WRA administration, however, they too came to evaluate their personal status in terms of the successful realization of WRA objectives.

---

[13]Recounting an occasion when he had sided with the internees against the WRA in a labor dispute, Ned Campbell has confessed that his action "might have been a mistake, a basic mistake in organization. If the boss tells you to do something, you either quit or go ahead and do what the boss tells you to do." Ned Campbell, CSUF O.H. 1329.

[14]One WRA policy was apparently for staff members to avoid "intimate" fraternization with internees of the opposite sex. According to Robert L. Brown, who was then Reports Officer, Ned Campbell's predecessor as Assistant Project Director was dismissed because "he got his 'relaxation' by shacking up with .... [an attractive Nisei secretary]." Letter to Arthur A. Hansen, dated August 13, 1974.

[15]Douglas Nelson, Heart Mountain: The History of an American Concentration Camp, unpubl. M.A. thesis, Univ. of Wyoming, 1970, pp. 103-4.

Behind the WRA and JACL's shared attitude toward the relocation objectives rested a common social ideology. Put simply, both subscribed to a "progressive" view of American history. Central to this persuasion was the idea that the American past made sense only if read as a triumphant progression toward the fulfillment of the nation's democratic potential. This view acknowledged the existence of a long line of reactionary men and groups who, for selfish ends, had attempted to thwart the advance of democracy. But it took succor from the fact that liberal, humane individuals always had emerged who transcended themselves and rallied the nation into overcoming antidemocratic challenges.[16]

Given these situational and philosophical considerations, we are better able to comprehend the WRA-JACL perspective on the Manzanar Riot. We can now appreciate, for example, why the original accounts chose to describe it innocuously as an "incident." Like all good bureaucrats, the administrators (a term which is used here to embrace the JACLers as well as the WRA staff) intuitively sensed the wisdom of the adage that "no news is good news." For them even to have intimated that what happened on December 6, 1942, was more than slightly non-routine would have been tantamount to admitting that WRA policies were wrong or unsuccessful.

In keeping with this psychological imperative, it followed that causal explanations were largely unwarranted. Interpreting the disturbance as the outgrowth of serious, underlying grievances would have called into question the administration's oft-repeated claim that Manzanar was a "model" American community. That a resistance movement could arise in such a "happy camp" was unthinkable. It made better sense, therefore, to perceive the "incident" as either a transitory release from unanalyzable "frustration" or, as was more often the case, the pernicious work of a small but committed minority of pro-Axis sympathizers.[17]

The latter explanation gained currency among WRA-JACL analysts because they could readily incorporate it into their Manichean view of history. Envisioning themselves as selfless inheritors of America's democratic heritage, they justified their complicity in the relocation program by the belief that their efforts furthered the democratic cause. The WRA could argue that the attendant loss of civil liberties was unfortunate, but that perilous times sometimes necessitated short-term undemocratic means to promote long-range democratic ends; the JACL could uphold relocation by the argument that it would provide

---

[16]For a more detailed explanation of how this "progressive" idea has manifested itself within American historiography, see Wise, American Historical Explanations, pp. 86-9, 97-100.

[17]Cf. Gary Y. Okihiro, "Japanese Resistance in America's Concentration Camps: A Re-evaluation," Amerasia Journal, II (Fall 1973), pp. 20-34.

Japanese Americans an opportunity to prove their loyalty, thereby
paving the way for the enjoyment of democratic liberties in the postwar world. Having thus equated the existence of the camps with the
cause of democracy, it is hardly surprising that the administration
should interpret the riot as engineered by an anti-democratic faction.[18]

Before considering a new perspective for interpreting the riot,
we must account for the persistence of the WRA-JACL perspective in the
secondary literature. The most obvious reason is documentary in nature: later writers had access to copious materials about the riot,
but practically all of it was compiled by WRA-JACL personnel. Nonetheless, this fact does not explain why these writers have not penetrated beyond the existing documentation and staked out different
interpretive frameworks. We need, therefore, to explain why their own
experiential situations caused them to be receptive to the established
perspective.

A caveat must be entered at this point: it must not be assumed
that because these writers have extended the WRA-JACL perspective this
derives from a similar attitude toward relocation. They have not, in
other words, acted as outright apologists for the evacuation. To the
contrary, most have bristled with righteous indignation at what they
consider a deplorable and unjustified departure from America's traditional democratic practices. Eschewing the official view that the
"relocation centers" were necessary security precautions, almost unanimously they have redefined them as "concentration camps" and attributed

---

[18]Such an interpretation occasions even less surprise when one
considers the Manzanar administration's relative unfamiliarity with
all internee groups except for the JACL group. Robert L. Brown,
who as Reports Officer supervised the heavily JACL-staffed Manzanar
Free Press, provides a case in point. "I might have been isolated
by the kids I had working on the newspaper, and the people that were
around me. The girls in the office, the Block Leaders, the guy
we finally made 'mayor' . . . an old Issei." You felt, then, that
you might have been isolated maybe from what was going on in the
population at large, so you couldn't account for, say, the people who
were in the Kitchen Workers' Union; they wouldn't have been people
you were in contact with in the camp. "No, I wasn't in contact with
that group; I didn't know a damned thing about them." Arthur A.
Hansen, interviewer; O.H. 1375, CSUF, December 13, 1973, p. 53.
And Ned Campbell recollects that "the young fellows around the newspaper office were the ones I was more frequently in contact with, and
I think they became more friendly to me, and therefore came to me
with, not tattletaling, but forewarning." Ned Campbell/Arthur A.
Hansen, CSUF O.H. 1329. The experience of these two men is especially
significant since Campbell also explains that, "The camp was a two
or three man operation. I mean, two or three personalities or phil-
osophies [ran the camp]: the police chief, Bob Brown, and me." Ibid.

their existence to public hysteria, virulent racism, and economic opportunism. In light of this condemnatory attitude, it seems paradoxical that these writers have been so obeisant to the entrenched WRA-JACL notion that the riot was inspired by dark, anti-democratic elements.

The paradox can be resolved, however, when we consider another factor. Earlier we noted that the primary accounts of the riot were grounded in the progressivist view of history held by their compilers. This same view, with slight modification, has also informed the secondary writers. While this view was heightened by the overarching wartime distinction between pro- and anti-democratic belligerents, it has continued to thrive in the "Cold War's" atmosphere of emphasizing the ideological juxtaposition of the American-led "free world" and the "communist bloc." One of the liabilities of this persuasion is its criterion that all historical experience emerge as democratic progress. The impossibility of seeing the incarceration of 112,000 Japanese Americans as consonant with the advance of democracy has caused the secondary writers to style the internees as the unsung torchbearers of the democratic mission. Thus, they have been depicted as one-hundred percent Americans who set aside their grievances, miraculously transformed their camps into models of democratic life, and contributed to the defeat of fascism by unstinting allegiance to the war effort at home and abroad. As a concomitant of this heroic portrait, however, secondary writers have been blinded to the existence of internee resistance. In cases where evidence of resistance is too blatant to be ignored, as with the Manzanar Riot, these writers have seen them either as highly atypical episodes or situations provoked by a handful of subversives.[19]

In contradistinction to the foregoing perspective on the Manzanar Riot, we propose an alternative "Ethnic" perspective. Whereas the WRA-JACL perspective, as we have seen, has interpreted the riot in terms of its _ideological_ meaning within American society, the Ethnic one focuses upon the riot's _cultural_ meaning within the Japanese American community (with particular reference to Manzanar's internee population). Although ours is a "new" perspective toward the Manzanar Riot, it conforms closely to and draws much sustenance from a small number of general studies--mostly recent and unpublished--on internment.[20]

---

[19]Okihiro, "Japanese Resistance," pp. 20-22.

[20]Three of these works have already been cited: Daniels, _Concentration Camps USA_; Nelson, _Heart Mountain_; and Okihiro, "Japanese Resistance." Two others are unpublished studies: an older doctoral dissertation--Toshio Yatsushiro, _Political and Socio-Cultural Issues at Poston and Manzanar Relocation Centers: A Themal Analysis_, Cornell, 1953--and a more recent M.A. thesis--Matthew Richard Speier, _Japanese-American Relocation Camp Colonization and Resistance to Resettlement: A Study in the Social Psychology of Ethnic Identity under Stress_, U.C.

We believe it a perspective which, unlike the WRA-JACL's, promotes analysis and understanding rather than dramaturgy and hobgoblinization.

As a first step in this direction, we replace the word "riot" with "revolt." Terming the event the "Manzanar Revolt" forces us to see it not as an uncaused and inconsequential aberration, but as one intense expression of a continuing resistance movement. This change also credits the participants in the action with a greater degree of purposeful behavior; for while a riot's members are momentarily conjoined because they do not like where they have been, those involved in a revolt have some sense of where they want to go.[21] Overall, then, this redefinition of the collective manifestation encourages us to view it in relation to social change within a larger structural framework, thereby affording a more sociologically meaningful analysis. Instead of dismissing the "riot" as an isolated, spontaneous, and unstructured phenomenon, we now must locate its causes or determinants in the social system.[22]

It will be recalled that while a few accounts written from the WRA-JACL perspective deal with causation, even these restrict their inquiry within the social system to the period bracketed by the immediate pre-evacuation crisis and the "riot." Because the Ethnic perspective is predisposed to see the "revolt" as an expressive moment within a process of cultural development, it is more farsighted. On the one hand, it looks backward to the prewar West Coast Japanese American community in search of explanatory antecedents for the revolt; on the other hand, it looks beyond the revolt to ascertain its connection to subsequent subcultural evolution.

First we must turn to the prewar community. A heretofore largely ignored study by Toshio Yatsushiro--Political and Socio-Cultural Issues at Poston and Manzanar Relocation Centers: A Themal Analysis[23]--is especially useful for our purposes. Its thesis is that prewar Japanese American culture contained a limited number of themes--i.e., dynamic affirmations controlling behavior and stimulating activity-- which were strengthened by pre-evacuation discriminatory practices, reinforced by the evacuation crisis, and found expression within the concentration camp culture.[24]

Berkeley, 1965. A final work is Jerome Charyn's American Scrapbook (New York: Viking, 1969), a fictional account of the events encompassed in this paper, which has deepened our appreciation for Gene Wise's insight that historians could profit by adopting the novelist's multi-faceted view of experience.

[21]In their study of the Manzanar Riot, "Riot and Rioters," Western Political Quarterly, X (Dec. 1957), p. 864, George Wada and James C. Davies provide a definition of a riot's membership from which ours is extrapolated.

[22]This dynamic conception of collective behavior stems from Speier, Japanese-American Camp Colonization, pp. 7-8.

[23]As cited above in f. 20.

[24]Yatsushiro, Themal Analysis, p. 40.

Yatsushiro identifies six basic cultural themes which define
the prewar community. Each represents an element of traditional
Japanese culture, modified by the American setting. The first four
themes relate to personal and collective obligation, the governing of
human relationships and conduct by precise rules, and the use of go-
betweens to avoid possible embarrassment in social relations. The two
remaining themes have special relevance to the present study. The
first is contained in the following proposition: "Society is an
ordered social hierarchy in which status is ascribed largely on the
basis of biologically determined factors of sex, age, and generation."
This theme was clearly manifest in every aspect of family and community
life. In the family, the male Issei wielded near autocratic power;
in the community, he controlled political, economic, and social activities by leadership in associations like the Japanese Association
and the kenjinkai. The second theme maintains that "the welfare of
the group is far more important than that of any single individual."
Diametrically opposed to the American cultural strain of individualism,
this theme promotes cultural homogeneity by granting the group omni-
potence. Thus, the Japanese American community tended to minimize
distinctions between personalities and social classes, to attribute
all accomplishments to the group, and to seek group aid and advice in
all social and economic undertakings.[25]

The importance of these themes lies in their influence on group
solidarity. From the time of their arrival in the United States at
the end of the nineteenth century, the Issei had experienced a series
of attacks--both legal and extra-legal--which necessitated the development of self-sufficient "Little Tokyos." Each anti-Japanese attack
forced the Issei to retreat further from American cultural values and
to depend increasingly on their traditional Japanese culture. This,
in turn, reinforced group solidarity. Thus, by the outbreak of World
War II, the two most significant characteristics of the Issei-dominated
Japanese American community were group solidarity and the predominance
of elements of Japanese culture.[26]

These characteristics prevailed less among their children. During
the thirties the Nisei generation was maturing and represented a potential challenge to the group's solidarity and to its cultural orientation. As citizens, Nisei came into greater contact with American
society and consequently underwent increased Americanization. Their
attendance in public schools led them to emulate activities of the
American teen culture, and not uncommonly they resisted their parents'
attempts to direct their lives in accordance with traditional Japanese
values and practices. Some Nisei, in their anxiety to be accepted as
typically American, began to resent their parents and to ridicule their
Japanese ways. All this served to widen the "social distance" between

---

[25]Ibid., pp. 209-95 passim.
[26]Ibid., p. 183.

Issei and Nisei.[27]

On the other hand, the usual picture of Nisei as thoroughly Americanized is far from accurate, for countervailing forces were diminishing the social distance and returning the Nisei to the Japanese American community. One form of pressure emanated from the Issei, who, in addition to asserting ordinary parental influence, mandated Nisei participation in cultural agencies--e.g., Japanese language schools, kendo and judo societies, and Buddhist affiliated clubs--which undermined the Americanization process.[28] Other pressures came from without: socially, the Nisei encountered barriers to their assimilation into the larger society and found it necessary to participate in social organizations, residential patterns, and marital arrangements along ethnic lines; economically, they discovered upon graduation from high school and college that the only available employment opportunities existed within their own communities. Therefore, while the Nisei returned to the community perhaps more from necessity than desire, the result was a partial restoration of their ethnicity and a consequent maintenance of group solidarity.[29]

Because of their influence upon prewar solidarity, as well as their later involvement in the Manzanar Revolt, two Nisei subgroups deserve special consideration. The first is the Kibei. Applied literally, the term "Kibei" denoted any Nisei who had gone to Japan, for however short a time, and had returned to America. In some instances it was employed to describe any Nisei, whether he had gone to

---

[27]By "social distance" what is meant is the degree of sympathetic understanding that operate between any two persons. See, Robert Howard Ross, Social Distance as It Exists between the First and Second Generation Japanese in the City of Los Angeles and Vicinity, unpubl. M.A. thesis, Univ. of So. Calif., 1939.

[28]The result for many Nisei was confusion. Sue Kunitomi Embrey recalls that during her youth in Los Angeles' Little Tokyo, the bilingual instructor in her Japanese Language School told her that "he thought that my direction in life was going different from the others, that he didn't think I would be too happy within the Japanese community." Arthur A. Hansen and David A. Hacker, interviewers; O.H. 1366a, CSUF, November 30, 1973, p. 10.

[29]Ross, Social Distance, pp. 113-14. Tamotsu Shibutani, in Rumors in a Crisis Situation, unpubl. M.A. thesis, Univ. of Chicago, 1944, p. 36, while emphasizing the cultural schism between Issei and Nisei, still allows that as "the Nisei came of age in large numbers, they did not go out into the American community. Rather they developed a society of their own." Togo Tanaka, in "How to Survive Racism in America's Free Society;" in series, Arthur A. Hansen, coordinator, Japanese American Internment During World War II (Univ. of Calif. Extension, Irvine; April 3, 1973; on deposit at CSUF), encapsulates the Nisei's prewar plight: "From 1936 (upon graduating summa cum laude from UCLA) to 1942, I immersed myself behind the walls of Little Tokyo, venturing forth into

Japan or not, who "spoke Japanese . . . preferably to English and who otherwise behaved in what the Nisei regarded as a 'Japanesy' manner."[30] But its usual meaning was restricted to those whose residence in Japan exceeded two years and who received a portion of their education there.

Many Kibei, especially those whose stay in Japan was brief, experienced little difficulty in adjusting to the American milieu, and their behavior was indistinguishable from that of other Nisei. Other Kibei chose to repress their Japaneseness and exhibited hyperbolic American behavior. But for those who had spent considerable time in Japan, the situation was somewhat different. Although Kibei studies customarily emphasize that those in this category were treated as "pariahs within the larger minority group of the Japanese Americans,"[31] this is at best a half-truth. True, the more Americanized Nisei often derided, even scorned, them for their linguistic and social ineptitude, but by no means were they considered "pariahs" by the Issei. After all, Issei parents originally had sent them to Japan precisely to allow them to absorb Japanese cultural habits deemed essential for economic and social success within the ethnic community. Their Nisei contemporaries might have found them strange and maladjusted,[32] but the Issei applauded them as "model" Japanese children. These Kibei were mostly non-assimilationists--they formed their own clubs and recreational groups, actively led Buddhist and other cultural organizations, willingly joined the community business structure, and Kibei women married either Kibei or Issei men--and for this reason they strengthened group solidarity.[33]

The same cannot be said of the second Nisei subgroup--the JACLers. Properly, this term applied only to Nisei affiliated with the Japanese American Citizens League, an organization formed in 1930 as "a reaction against the Japanese orientation of the Issei leadership."[34] Generally, however, it was applied to Nisei who most fully accepted the attitudes,

---

the wider community only as an advocate of equal rights or civil liberty and of the proposition that, although we may look Japanese, look harder and you'll find a good American." See p. 89 of this volume.

[30]WRA, Community Analysis Section, "Community Analysis Report No. 8, January 28, 1944: Japanese Americans Educated in Japan," WRRA, Coll. 122, Box 16, Folder 1, p. 2.

[31]Ibid., p. 8.

[32]One Nisei, recalling her prewar attitude toward Kibei, offered the following response in an interview. Were Kibei frowned upon by most of the Nisei? "They were considered odd, and I guess it was mostly because of their language problem. And they really didn't make an adjustment into the community." Sue Kunitomi Embrey/Hansen and Hacker, CSUF O.H. 1366a. On the other hand, another Nisei interviewee maintains that "Kibei more or less looked down on us because they enjoyed the privileges of American citizenship plus they were fluent in the Japanese language; so they could wear both hats and be comfortable in both societies, where many of us were just Americans, period." George Fukasawa/Arthur A. Hansen, CSUF O.H. 1336.

values, practices, and goals of the American culture. Matthew Richard Speier has observed that while the Issei "retained ethnic perspectives and took account of the dominant society only in the form of a valuation group (i.e., a reference group whose standpoint is not adopted as one's own). . . . Nisei took on caucasian American society as their reference group . . . and adopted its perspective as their own in the form of an identification group."[35] While this distinction is partly valid for Nisei as a whole, it is more valid with respect to the JACLers. They, to a larger degree, penetrated into the dominant society through social, political, and economic activities; emotionally, they moved increasingly away from their parents and community. Still, at no time prior to the war did they pose a serious threat to group solidarity. Like other Nisei, the JACLers were young, uninfluential, and almost wholly dependent upon the Issei-dominated Japanese community for their economic livelihood.[36]

With this sketch of the social-psychological makeup of the prewar community in mind, we must now see how it was altered by the combined impact of Pearl Harbor and the subsequent evacuation and incarceration of Japanese Americans. For the Issei, who were subjected to a barrage of restrictions, harassments, and indignities--including the precipitous internment of their leaders in federal detention centers--the effect of Pearl Harbor and its aftermath was a pronounced increase in social solidarity. For them, the repressive measures exercised by the government represented only the latest and most serious of a long series of discriminatory actions, and they responded in their customary manner--with cultural retrenchment.

The Nisei responded ambiguously. In a study centering on this period, Tamotsu Shibutani points out that while "there was increased social solidarity [among Nisei] in the sense that everyone recognized the cleavage between the Japanese and the out-group quite clearly . . . there was increased disunity among the Nisei after the outbreak of the war."[37] Put another way, we can summarize their dilemma by stating that the crisis forced them to choose between their identification group--as symbolized by their citizenship--and their ethnic group--as actualized by their families and community. Many were too traumatized by the swirl of events to choose one way or the other, though this proved less the case for the JACLers.

Even before Pearl Harbor, when war with Japan seemed all but in-

---

[33]WRA, "Japanese Americans Educated in Japan," p. 7. Although the data is drawn from this source, we have placed an entirely different construction upon it than that intended. To our knowledge, there exists no "sympathetic" study of Kibei; in fact, there seem to be very few Kibei studies of whatever persuasion.

[34]John H. Burma, "Current Leadership Problems among Japanese Americans," Sociology and Social Research, XXXVII (Jan. 1953), p. 158.

[35]Speier, Japanese-American Camp Colonization, pp. 4;43.

[36]For an amplification of the prewar JACL and its relationship to the larger Japanese American community, see Togo Tanaka, "JACL," JERS, Barnhart, Folder 010.16.

[37]Shibutani, Rumors, p. 114.

evitable, some JACLers zealously advertised their Americanism. Unfortunately, their patriotic boosterism sometimes included a repudi-
ation of Issei leadership. Togo Tanaka, a national officeholder in
the JACL and the English language editor of the Los Angeles-based
Rafu Shimpo, provides a case in point. As Roger Daniels has related,
Tanaka, in a speech early in 1941, "insisted that the Nisei must face
. . . 'the question of loyalty' and assumed that since the Issei were
'more or less tumbleweeds with one foot in America and one foot in
Japan,' real loyalty to America could be found only in his generation."
Moreover, according to a recent study of the Rafu Shimpo during this
period, Tanaka consistently voiced this sentiment editorially.[38] (By
way of foreshadowing their later involvement in the Manzanar Revolt,
it is interesting to note that Tanaka was joined on the Rafu's editorial board by Fred Tayama and Tokie Slocum.)

Bill Hosokawa, a prominent JACL figure, has written of how
JACL leaders were summarily seized and interrogated by federal authorities in the wake of Pearl Harbor. (Tanaka, for instance, was arrested
under a Presidential warrant and placed in Los Angeles jails for
eleven days.)[39] Such persecution, however, only prompted JACLers to
redouble their efforts to "prove" their loyalty as American citizens.
They fought their campaign on two fronts. On the one hand, they uti-
lized the limited political influence they possessed to alleviate per-

---

[38]Daniels, Concentration Camps USA, p. 27; Patricia Courteau,
"Rafu Shimpo: A Look at Japanese-American Press Reaction, 1941-2."
California State University, Fullerton, seminar paper, Jan. 11, 1973.
Daniels' assertion is not clearly documented. In an effort to
clarify this point, the authors, in a telephone conversation with
Tanaka on August 29, 1974, queried him about the reputed talk. His
response was that possibly he had said something of this sort, but
he very much doubted it and would like to be confronted with evidence
to allay his doubt. As to another action attributed to him by
Daniels, in Concentration Camps USA, p. 41, that "On the very evening
of Pearl Harbor, editor Togo Tanaka went on station KHTR, Los Angeles,
and told his fellow Nisei: 'As Americans we now function as counter-
espionage. Any act or word prejudicial to the United States committed
by any Japanese must be warned and reported to the F.B.I., Naval
Intelligence, Sheriff's Office, and local police,'" Tanaka absolutely
denies its truth, if for no other reason than the fact that he has
never been on radio.

Courteau's evaluation of Tanaka's editorial policy is also open
to question, especially since she mentions that on December 31,
1942, the Rafu ran an article entitled "What Of Our Issei?" which
covered half the width and the entire length of a page and was
printed in capital letters. In her own words, this article "dis-
claimed the American feeling that legally those people [Issei] were
'enemy aliens' and . . . spoke out for them as true Americans. . . .
[and argued that] the great tragedy was in assuming all were enemies."

[39]Hosokawa, Nisei, pp. 223-41. For Tanaka's arrest, see Togo

sonal hardship and to exonerate the Japanese American community from irresponsible charges of subversion being levelled against it. More ominously, they cooperated with the authorities as security watchdogs; in this connection, an Anti-Axis Committee was established in Los Angeles, headed first by Fred Tayama and later by Tokie Slocum (and also including Togo Tanaka as a member), to serve as a liaison with the FBI to help flush out "potentially dangerous" Issei.[40]

However well-intentioned its efforts and helpful its services, the JACL came under heavy fire from the Japanese American community. Issei resented the manner in which JACLers, whom they regarded as young and irresponsible, seemed to arrogate the role of community spokesmen. They were angered further by the JACL's apparent complicity with the FBI in Issei arrests. Nor were the Kibei kindly disposed toward the JACL. The Kibei were disturbed that the JACL apparently had forgotten that they too were citizens. They also believed that JACLers were informing on them as well as Issei, a suspicion which hardened into conviction after the JACL undertook a Kibei Survey in mid-February, 1942.[41] There even existed widespread dis-

---

Tanaka, "How to Survive Racism," on page 93 of the present work.

[40]On December 13, 1942, Chairman Fred Tayama of the Anti-Axis Committee issued the following statement: "The United States is at war with the Axis. We shall do all in our power to help wipe out vicious totalitarian enemies. Every man is either friend or foe. We shall investigate and turn over to authorities all who by word or act consort with the enemies." Anti-Axis Committee circular given to authors by Karl Yoneda.

Tokie Slocum's anti-subversive activities were pursued with such vigor that even his JACL allies were offended. See Togo Tanaka, interviewee; Betty E. Mitson and David Hacker, interviewers; O.H. 1271a, CSUF, May 19, 1973, pp. 46-7; and O.H. 1271b; Togo Tanaka/ Arthur A. Hansen; August 30, 1973, pp. 2-7.

One interviewee, who served simultaneously as the Vice President of the Santa Monica JACL chapter and with the Santa Monica auxiliary police during the pre-evacuation period, maintains that the two roles of assisting the community and aiding the FBI and the military intelligence agencies were not mutually exclusive but compatible. Indeed, in the latter role he avers that he was able to exonerate many Issei from flagrantly irresponsible charges and spare them from being apprehended and sent to detention centers. George Fukasawa/Arthur A. Hansen, CSUF O.H. 1336.

[41]Nichibei Times, Feb. 15;20, 1942; Shibutani, Rumors, pp. 109-10. For information about Kibei chapters of the JACL and their policy differences relative to the pre-evacuation and evacuation period, see George Fukasawa/Arthur A. Hansen, CSUF O.H. 1336; and Karl Yoneda, interviewee; Ronald C. Larson and Arthur A. Hansen, interviewers; O.H. 1376b, CSUF, March 3, 1974.

satisfaction with the JACL among certain Nisei elements. Leftist groups, for example, "looked upon the J.A.C.L. as a large organization controlled by a small minority of 'reactionary' businessmen who used the body as a means of getting business connections and personal prestige."[42] Other Nisei were disgruntled that the JACL should presume to "represent" the community: in Los Angeles, the JACL totalled 650 members out of a total community population of 20,000.[43] Whatever their grievances against the JACL, Issei, Kibei, and Nisei generally believed that it was sacrificing the community's welfare for its own aggrandizement.

During the period from President Roosevelt's issuance on February 19, 1942 of Executive Order 9066 (which authorized the Secretary of War to establish "military areas" and exclude therefrom "any or all persons") until March 21, when the first contingent of Japanese American voluntary internees arrived from Los Angeles to the Manzanar Reception Center, the Japanese American community was rife with rumors about the complicity and duplicity of the JACL. For example:

The J.A.C.L. was instructed by Naval Intelligence to send questionnaires to all members to report on their parents.

The J.A.C.L. started their survey on the Kibei in order to turn in information to the F.B.I. They are taking this as a protective move to whitewash themselves by blaming others.

The J.A.C.L. is trying to be patriotic and they are supporting the evacuation program. They do not have the welfare of the Japanese people at heart.

The J.A.C.L. is supporting the idea of cooperating with the government and evacuating voluntarily because then they could go in and buy up all the goods in Japanese stores at robbery prices and make a substantial profit.

The J.A.C.L. big shots have their fingers in the graft. They are getting something out of the evacuation.

The J.A.C.L. is charging aliens for information that the aliens could get anywhere.

The J.A.C.L. is planning the evacuation with the officials. They are

---

[42]Shibutani, Rumors, pp. 114-15.
[43]WRA (written by Janet Goldberg under the supervision of Robert L. Brown, Reports Officer, Manzanar War Relocation Center), "The Manzanar 'Incident', December 5, to December 19, 1942," WRAA, Coll. 122, Box 16, and JERS, Barnhart, Folder 07.00.

mixing with high government officials.

All J.A.C.L. leaders are _inu_ [dogs; informers].[44]

Important about these rumors is less their content (many had little
basis in fact; others were clearly apocryphal) than their function.
As Tamotsu Shibutani has observed, rumors function as mechanisms of
social control (i.e., they keep errant individuals in line) and social
definition (i.e., they disseminate a common mood).[45] At a time when
governmental actions threatened the very existence of the community
and government policies were fraught with ambiguity and inconsistency,
the shared belief in rumors about the JACL buttressed group solidarity
and provided some certitude within the confusion. The community's
branding of the JACLers as "deviants" therefore must not be construed
as a simple act of censure, but rather as a cultural rite by which
the community attempted to define its "social boundaries"--what Kai
Erikson has denoted as the symbolic parentheses a community draws
around its permissable behavior[46]--vis-a-vis a hostile world, thereby
insuring its cultural integrity.

JACLers (i.e., aggressive pro-American Nisei) themselves employed
rumors during this critical time, though for contrary purposes. Iden-
tifying with the larger American community, they guarded its cultural
boundaries by uncovering "deviants" in the ethnic community. At times
they cast Issei in this role, but more commonly it was Kibei, whom
they distrusted as hot-tempered, pro-Japan enthusiasts who were
"willing to do almost anything, even at the risk of their lives, for
the emperor of Japan."[47] Rumors about the Kibei reflected and under-
scored this suspicion, as the following reactions illustrate:

I hear those god damn Kibei bastards botched up our chances in
the Army. If those son of a bitches like Japan so much why did
they come over here in the first place? I never did like those
guys anyway. They came over here with their Japanesy ideas and
try to change all America to suit themselves. They don't seem to
realize that 130,000,000 people might be right.

I really don't blame the Army for booting the Kibei out. I

44Shibutani, _Rumors_, pp. 115-16.

45_Ibid._, pp. 162-6.

46Kai T. Erikson, _Wayward_ _Puritans_: _A_ _Study_ _in_ _the_ _Sociology_ _of_
Deviance (New York: Wiley, 1966), pp. 3-29 _passim_.

47The collective indictment of the Kibei and the reasons behind
it are implicit in the following remark by one JACL official,
George Fukasawa (see f. 40): "We had most of our opposition (to the
JACL strategy of cooperating with government officials in the evacuation) from a group who called themselves Kibei, that were educated
in Japan and who, of course were indoctrinated in Japanese propaganda and culture through their formative years over there."

wouldn't trust those guys either. Some of them are O.K., but a lot of them don't belong in this country. You can't tell what they'd do. They might shoot the guns in the wrong way. But Jesus Christ, they didn't have to wreck everything for us Nisei by burning the [U.S. Army] barracks.

Those Kibei are the guys we have to watch. They're so damned hot-headed they will do anything. Then all the rest of us have to suffer just because they happened to be technically American citizens. It'll get so the hakujin [Caucasians] won't trust any Nisei.

I hear those Kibei ran wild after December 7. I'd like to castrate some of those bastards.[48]

Again, like rumors concerning the JACL, many of these were patently untrue. The important point, however, is that, if the JACL rumors seemed logical from the community's perspective, these Kibei rumors seemed equally plausible from a JACL perspective.

Having examined the prewar community and charted the changes undergone as a result of the Pearl Harbor and evacuation crises, we now must focus upon the situation that unfolded at Manzanar. In keeping with our Ethnic perspective, we need to connect prewar and camp developments and determine their cumulative impact on the internee population. More particularly, we must ascertain the extent to which, in cultural terms, the Manzanar Revolt represented a logical, even a "necessary," outgrowth of these developments.

First, however, we will relate some basic facts about the Manzanar Center. Situated in the Owens Valley of east-central California not far from the Nevada border, Manzanar was the first of the centers to be established. From March 21 to June 1, 1942 it was known as the Owens Valley Reception Center, controlled by the military Wartime Civil Control Administration (WCCA) and administered by a staff[49] drawn predominantly from the Works Progress Administration. After June 1, when it came under the jurisdiction of the WRA, its name was changed officially to the Manzanar War Relocation Center. Its population was chiefly urban in background; out of an approximate total of 10,000 internees, the bulk, 88%, originated from Los Angeles County--with 72% from the city of Los Angeles. Built on 6,000 acres of land (the smallest acreage of the ten relocation centers) leased from

---

[48]Shibutani, Rumors, pp. 66-7. Shibutani does not attribute these rumors specifically to JACL sources; our imputation here, therefore, represents merely historical inference, not factual information.

[49]Morton Grodzins, in "Making Un-Americans," p. 577, describes Manzanar's WCCA leadership as "a generally unfriendly staff." For a markedly contrasting estimate, see Robert L. Brown/Arthur A. Hansen, CSUF O.H. 1375, passim. This recollection of Brown's is confirmed by his diary entries during the WCCA tenure at Manzanar. This diary is presently being prepared for publication by Arthur A. Hansen.

the City of Los Angeles, Manzanar sat between the small communities
of Lone Pine and Independence (whose residents expressed considerable
hostility toward the evacuees).[50] Climatological conditions at Manzanar
were poor: in the summer, unpleasantly hot and dry; in the winter, for-
biddingly cold; throughout the year, owing to light surface soil and
high winds, subject to severe dust storms. Its physical accomodations
were substandard; in the first months it was not uncommon to find two or
three families occupying the same room, and as late as nine months after
its opening, in some 925 cases two families were obliged to share a
single twenty by twenty-five foot compartment. To make matters worse,
the administrative personnel were badly splintered: some members refused to "fraternize" with the evacuees. Moreover, between the time
of its opening and the Manzanar Revolt, the camp directorship changed
four times.[51]

       More pertinent to this study than any of these outward conditions
was the internal struggle waged over control of the internee community.
From the outset it was clear that the cultural division that emerged
during the evacuation period had carried over into the camp. In line
with their decision to accept relocation as their contribution to the
war effort, JACLers readily volunteered to assist in the establishment
of the camp. (In this enterprise they were joined, actually preceded,
by a cadre of left-wing Nisei--and some Kibei--intellectuals who, for
ideological and strategic reasons, chose to pursue a similar brand of
superpatriotism.)[52] Because of their early arrival and their avowed

_____

[50]David J. Bertagnoli and Arthur A. Hansen have interviewed extensively among residents of the Owens Valley communities and attempted
to assess their reaction to the camp and its internee population. See
O.H. 1343, 1344, 1345, 1346, 1347, 1378, 1379, 1384, 1385, 1393, 1394,
1395, 1396, 1397, 1398, 1399, 1401 (which is reproduced in its entirety
in this volume on pp. 143-160), and 1402. Additional information is supplied by Robert L. Brown/Arthur A. Hansen, CSUF O.H.
1375 and Ned Campbell/Arthur A. Hansen, CSUF O.H. 1329. While these
interviews reveal little "hostility" toward the Manzanar camp, concerted local opposition is registered in the entries of Robert L.
Brown's diary (see f. 49). In addition, a local businessman and poli-
tician, Rudie Henderson, in Final Report: Manzanar Relocation Center,
I, (February 1946), unpubl. mss., appendix 26, pp. 217-18, describes
the reaction of his fellow Owens Valley residents as one of "almost
unanimous . . . resentment and open hostility." Henderson also describes a vituperative petition, signed by 500 local merchants and
citizens, to prevent the internees from shopping in the nearby town
of Lone Pine.

[51]Rice, Manzanar Center, pp. 25-8; Yatsushiro, Themal Anal-
ysis, pp. 342-3; Kiyotoshi, Iwamoto, Economic Aspects of the
Japanese Relocation Centers in the United States, unpubl. M.A.
Thesis, Stanford Univ., 1946, p. 13.

[52]We have in mind here individuals such as Karl Yoneda, Koji
Ariyoshi, Chiye Mori, James Oda, Tom Yamazaki, and Joe Blamey. For
a description of the composition and objectives of this group, see
Tanaka, "Analysis of the Manzanar Incident," Togo W. Tanaka/Arthur A.

pro-Americanism, the administration rewarded JACLers by granting them the white-collar, supervisory, and generally favored jobs, according them what little power was available to internees and allowing them a voice in shaping policy. In addition, they were placed in control of the camp newspaper, the Manzanar Free Press, which afforded them an opportunity to influence public opinion.

This administration-sponsored JACL hierarchy was deeply resented by Issei and Kibei who were relegated to subordinate and menial jobs. It was bad enough to witness the JACLers' usurpation of community authority, but worse to see the purposes for which that authority was used. One can imagine how galling it was for Issei and Kibei to read in the Free Press of April 11, 1942 the following "appreciation":

> The citizens of Manzanar wish to express in public their sincere appreciation to General John L. DeWitt and his Chiefs of Staff, Tom C. Clark and Colonel Karl R. Bendetsen, for the expedient way in which they have handled the Manzanar situation.
> The evacuees now located at Manzanar are greatly satisfied with the excellent comforts the general and his staff have provided for them. 'Can't [be] better,' is the general feeling of the Manzanar citizens. 'Thank you, General!' (Emphasis ours)[53]

Nor could the JACL's flaunted citizenship and unctuousness toward Caucasian authorities have pleased Nisei. As Yatsushiro has noted: "The mass evacuation that resulted in the Nisei citizens being confined in 'prison-like' centers along with their alien Issei parents, provided the Nisei with a unique opportunity to examine their past hostility towards the ways of their 'Japanesy' parents, and to reflect upon the long years of hardships suffered in [their] behalf . . . [and] they became extremely respectful of the Issei, their judgment, their advice, and their ways."[54] Thus, a growing number of Japanized Nisei increasingly viewed the JACLers' behavior as "patricidal" and "treasonable."

Notwithstanding the JACLers' ostensible authority, the Issei managed quietly to resume the leadership they had occupied within the prewar community. There was, for example, a gradual ascendency of Issei-dominated Block Leaders over the JACL-headed Information Center throughout March, April, May and June. Initiated at the re-

---

Hansen, CSUF O.H. 1271b, pp. 14-20, and Karl Yoneda/Ronald C. Larson and Arthur A. Hansen, CSUF O.H. 1376b.

[53]Quoted in Yatsushiro, Themal Analysis, p. 509. Robert L. Brown says this editorial was a gambit, like the name Free Press, designed to circumvent possible resistance by DeWitt to a camp newspaper. According to Brown,"Larry Benedict [a public relations man employed by the WCCA] said [to him], 'I don't want to ask, because I know that the old general won't let us do a newspaper, so why don't you just print a newspaper anyway? And on the front page, in a little editorial,

quest of two JACL leaders, Roy Takeno and David Itami, the Information Center emerged in late March in order to answer perplexing questions and supply basic services for new arrivees. It developed branch offices and subsections, eventually numbering fifty-three persons on its roll. In early April, the system of Block Leaders came into existence, whereby each block selected three men, one of whom was appointed Block Leader by the Camp Manager; for the most part, those selected were Issei. It soon became apparent that the internees preferred to query the Block Leaders rather than the Information Center, which by the end of June had been displaced by the Block Leaders. Moreover, instead of being appointed by the Administration, it was determined by the camp authorities that now the Block Leaders should be directly elected. At the grass-roots level, then, power was gravitating back into Issei hands.[55]

Just as the Issei were beginning to consolidate their power in the Block Leaders Council in late June, a disquieting directive arrived from Washington declaring that only citizens could elect and serve as block representatives. Naturally, the Issei saw this action as another attempt to undermine their leadership and subordinate them to Nisei. Fortunately, Project Director Roy Nash, recognizing the Issei's important role in Manzanar's government and fearing the consequences of stripping them of that role, obtained a stay on the ruling. Nonetheless, as Community Analyst Morris E. Opler pointed out, "considerable damage had been done by the debate and the division which had followed the announcement of the ruling."[56]

The damage was compounded on July 4 by another policy decision from Washington. In a memorandum to Ted Akahoshi, Temporary Chairman of the Block Leaders, Assistant Project Director Roy Campbell made the following request:

---

why don't you put a little thing thanking the general for allowing you to do it, and he won't remember whether he allowed you to do it or not, and that will make him feel good.' So we did that. We put a little box and thanked General DeWitt for permission to print the paper, because it was such a necessary item. And I remember the old general was tickled to death. He said, 'That's fine. That's fine. That's what they need to do over there; they have to have communication.'" Robert L. Brown/Arthur A. Hansen, CSUF O.H. 1375, pp. 19-20. While this anecdote explains the reason behind the item, it must nonetheless have rankled the Issei and Kibei.

[54]Yatsushiro, Themal Analysis, pp. 356;310.

[55]Morris E. Opler, "A History of Internal Government at Manzanar, March 1942 to December 6, 1942," WRAA, Coll. 122, Box 12, Folder 1, pp. 4-30. Although this report issued from a WRA source, it was consistently critical of the WRA-JACL perspective and adopted a line of analysis closely conforming to what we have termed an Ethnic perspective. This situation did not endear Opler to the Manzanar administration. When a copy of this report was forwarded to the head of the

> Will you please get over to all Block Leaders that it is against
> the policy of the War Relocation Authority to allow meetings
> to be conducted in Japanese. We have no objection to having
> meetings held in English interpreted so that all can understand,
> but we feel that all meeting[s] should be primarily conducted in
> English.[57]

Again the Issei, and many Kibei, interpreted this measure as a device
to render them politically impotent. In the following week, the
Council registered its displeasure by passing a motion that "when a
meeting is attended by more Issei then Japanese will be used and brief
translation in English be made."[58]

More important, however, was the debate which preceded the motion,
for it depicts vividly the evolving Issei-Kibei frame of mind. Chairman Akahoshi, an Issei graduate of Stanford University known for his
cooperation with the administration, set the tone with his opening
remarks:

> I think this letter [Campbell's memorandum] is very important,
> because majority of those who come to the meetings are Issei and
> they want to conduct the meetings in Japanese. When I saw this
> letter I told Mr. Campbell 'that the Japanese people are greatest
> nation in the world for sacrifice'—many of us are day laborers
> and in spite of low income are able to send our children to uni-
> versity. No nation sacrificed as hard as Japanese. We have, I
> think, no saboteurs among us, why restriction on Japanese speaking?

Among the following speakers, only two—an Issei and Karl Yoneda, a
Kibei Communist who aligned himself with the JACLers, outdoing them

---

Community Management Division in Washington by the Manzanar representative of this division, she felt obliged to append the following
message: "Mr. Merritt [the Project Director] has read it and has
some question in his mind about the material. He feels that the
presentation is one-sided in that it criticizes but does not attempt
to explain WRA policies and the action of WRA personnel, while, at
all points, it attempts to vindicate evacuee attitudes and actions.
He feels that some of the events are capable of interpretations
which are not suggested by Dr. Opler. . . . I don't have the same
questions . . . but I realize, after talking with Mr. Merritt, that
the impression given to an outsider might be very one-sided. Mr.
Merritt has asked Mr. [Dillon] Myer [WRA Director] to look over the
material and let us know whether he thinks it is desirable to continue
with this type of interpretive, historical study." Letter dated July
26, 1944, to Dr. John Provine, from Lucy Adams (for Ralph P. Merritt).

[56]Opler, "Internal Government," p. 30.

[57]Memorandum dated July 4, 1942, to Ted Akahoshi, Temporary Chairman of Block Leaders, from Ned Campbell, Asst. Project Director; sub-

in his chauvinism--approved the policy. The rest, all Issei and
Kibei, dissented with emotion.

[An Issei] I am in favor to conduct meeting in Japanese, because
we cannot express ourselves ably in English. (3 or 4 people clapped
hands)

[A Kibei] I believe all block leaders are very responsible
people and they should be trusted by the Administration. You know
that once we, the Japanese, decide to carry certain duty, we do
accomplish it, that is the nature of us Japanese. (Big applause)

[A Kibei] Mr. Yoneda said that he is an American citizen, but
he have to give up that right. Same thing true to me too, I am
American but I cannot use my citizenship, therefore we must depend on Issei for leadership and certainly I am in favor for
Japanese meeting. (big applause)

[An Issei] My son is in U.S. Army and when he obtained furlough
and came home, he was arrested by the FBI in spite of fact that he
is American. (Spoken with tears in his eyes) We are always dis-
criminated against here and only one who protect Nisei is we the
Issei. I can speak only Japanese and if it must be English, I
must resign as block leader. Don't forget we are Japanese and we
are the people who can unite to do anything. (Big applause)

[Chairman Akahoshi] I think, we, the Issei, know what's bad and
what's good. Some Nisei have stool-pigeoned on us--some Nisei is
boasting that he turned in 175 of us Japanese to the FBI. Other
is boasting that he turned in so many and they are boasting each
other. I am quite sure that only 2 or 3 out of the 175 are guilty.
Roosevelt spoke about national unity--these Nisei are the ones who
disrupt national unity and they are the traitors to this country.
(Big applause)

[An Issei] Those Nisei are lazy bunch and they are no good. We,
the Issei, are doing everything. Look at those janitors. None of
Nisei are cleaning toilets. We Issei have to do all the work.

Equally interesting is that this debate was recorded by Karl Yoneda

---

ject: meetings conducted in the Manzanar Relocation Area, WRAA, Coll.
122, Box 12, Folder 1, pp. 4-30.

[58]Letter dated July 10, 1942, to Roy Nash, Project Director, and
Ned Campbell, Asst. Project Director, Manzanar War Relocation Center,
Manzanar, Calif., from Karl G. Yoneda, Block 4 Leader, 4-2-2, Manzanar,
Calif., WRAA, Coll. 122, Box 9.

and offered to the administration in a confidential report. The rec- ommendations which Yoneda appended and his cautionary advice also deserve attention since they reflect an opposing JACL viewpoint:

. . . may I suggest the following: 1. All meetings in camp must be held in English. 2. Stenographic minutes be made of Block Leaders Council Meetings unless some one of the Administrators attends meeting. 3. Qualification for Block Leader should be that he must understand English and preferably Nisei. (Some Nisei are just as pro-axis as Issei but one can argue with them easier because of their knowledge of American institutions.) 4. The instruction that all meetings are to be conducted in English should be widely publicized.
    If we allow another meeting such as was held this morning, the block leaders meetings will be turned into germinating nest for undersirable [sic] elements and pro-axis adherents. Crystalliza- tion of pro-Axis sentiment is getting stronger every day and if we don't guard against it, eventually there will be a clash between pro-axis and pro-America groups in camp such as occured [sic] at Santa Anita.[59]

This issue was resolved temporarily by the administration's in- terpretation of the WRA policy as allowing Japanese to be spoken at meetings if followed by an English translation. But a legacy of ac- rimony and widened division between Issei-Kibei and JACLers resulted.

These feelings were exacerbated by the announcement on July 27 that a new Manzanar Citizens Federation would meet the following evening. The leaders in the meeting were Karl Yoneda, Togo Tanaka, Joe Masaoka, and Hiro Neeno, all closely allied with the JACL, who spoke about "educating citizens for leadership," "participating in the war effort" and "preparing evacuees for post-war conditions." As Project Director Ralph P. Merritt later observed, the meeting represented "an attempt to organize American citizens into a federa- tion which would aid the administration and which probably would also help the Nisei get more power and political strength in opposition to the Issei."[60]

This strategy ultimately backfired. The meeting itself, packed with pro-American Nisei supporters of the JACL leadership, turned into a rally. Following the general meeting, an open forum took place in which Joe Kurihara, who would later figure prominently in

---

[59]Ibid.
[60]Letter dated Jan. 7, 1946, to M. M. Tozier, Chief, Reports Division, WRA, Barr Bldg., Wash., D.C., from Ralph P. Merritt, Project Director, Manzanar War Relocation Center, Manzanar, Calif., WRAA, Coll. 122, Box 16, Folder 8. Since the JACLers were not "electable" as block leaders because of their general unpopularity with the evacuees, the Citizens Federation was conceived as a counterorganization to mobilize support for their objectives.

the Manzanar Revolt, took the floor: "I'm an American citizen; I served under fire in France [during World War I], and now I'm in this prison. You are all American citizens. You're here with me. I've proved my loyalty by fighting over there. Why doesn't the Government trust me?" Then Tokie Slocum, a self-styled patriot, former Chairman of the JACL's Anti-Axis Committee, and World War I veteran also, shouted down Kurihara, to the accompaniment of loud cheers from the audience. He explained that he was "doing his part in this war by obeying his commander in chief and staying in camp."[61]

Customarily emphasized about this meeting is that it provoked Kurihara into accepting the Issei point of view, but more significant is its conversion of many other Nisei as well. Kurihara declared that "he was a Jap and not an American, and . . . [that] he wanted to go . . . to Japan where he belonged,"[62] while other Nisei, "who had had their patriotism dampened by evacuation . . . [grew] cynical over the Federation's petition for a second front and for the drafting of Japanese-Americans."[63] Increasingly, the Issei-Kibei point of view

---

[61]Merritt to Tozier, letter dated January 7, 1946. For a description of this meeting by a principal participant, see Karl Yoneda/Ronald C. Larson and Arthur A. Hansen, CSUF O.H. 1376b. Another account is offered in George Fukasawa/Arthur A. Hansen, O.H. 1336. Fukasawa, second-ranking member of the evacuee police force, attended the meeting to provide internal security. Because Tokie Slocum was "targeted for elimination," Fukasawa accompanied him to his quarters after the gathering. Fukasawa describes Slocum, a special officer in the internee intelligence agency, as "a superpatriot type of person. . . . He was very vocal . . . he'd get up at these meetings and he was quite an orator. I think, he was the type of person that would engender a lot of hatred from anybody who would be opposed to his views."

[62]Merritt to Tozier, letter dated January 7, 1946.

[63]Opler, "Internal Government," p. 40. The following excerpts from an interview with Karl Yoneda shed light both on the purpose of the Manzanar Citizens Federation and the petition drive for a second front, as well as suggesting that the real moving force in both was the leftist faction in the pro-American coalition, not the JACL leaders. You mean the (JACL) didn't have much input into the Block Leaders Council and so they really set up an alternative organization (the Citizens Federation) that would be able to have some policy statements voiced at the camp? "That's the way, I guess, they started, but when we came in--Jimmy Oda and myself--we turned it around and made it into an entirely different organization altogether, which they didn't like. As soon as we got in, we took over the leadership-- Koji Ariyoshi, Jimmy Oda, and myself. Togo Tanaka, Joe Grant Masaoka (who was the brother of JACL executive secretary Mike Masaoka and, along with Togo Tanaka, the Manzanar documentary historian for the WRA), Kiyoshi Higashi (the evacuee police chief), and Fred Tayama, they didn't say 'boo.'" What were the differences in philosophy

was expanding into an Issei-Kibei-Nisei point of view.

From the beginning of August until the Revolt in December, the Kibei formed the spearhead of the opposition to the JACLers. Once again, a ruling from Washington galvanized underlying discontent into retaliatory action: Bulletin 22 was issued, which excluded all Kibei from participation in the leave program. This discriminatory measure further debased the depreciated value of Kibei citizenship and robbed them of an important economic perquisite. When Kibei leader Ben Kishi announced that a meeting of Kibei would be held on August 8, the Nisei secretary of the Block Leaders voiced the fear that they might

---

with respect to the Citizens Federation? How did the JACL look at its purpose? And how did the people in your group look at its purpose differently? "Our purpose . . . one of the purposes was to push this petition drive (to open a second front). This was not done in the name of the Federation. But through the Federation we saw that we had more support among the evacuees. . . . (We wanted) to open a second front and utilize manpower of the Japanese Americans in the camps. I think that we obtained only about 214 signatures, among which were about 40 women." And what was the JACL's philosopy? How did that differ? What do you think they wanted out of the organization? "Well, the JACL people . . . you know, actually, they didn't know what to do. Many times they asked us, 'What do you think?' Because we were the real driving force within the Manzanar Citizens Federation. Although opening the second front, that's actually the Communist Party line. You know, there was no such physical condition existing . . . the United States was just getting up to their armed strength. It was impossible to open the second front in 1942. So they have to open it later in '44, two years later. . . . In our way of thinking, this is the way to help the Russian front, because the Russian front was being beaten by Nazis, and the Russian people were retreating. If we open the second front, why Hitler will divert most of the force toward the European front. This will help the Soviet Union. That was our thinking, and that was also the Party line too." So you in a sense maneuvered the JACL into certain policies through the Citizens Federation. They really didn't know what they were doing at this point. "Yes, that's why even Togo Tanaka and Joe Grant Masaoka signed our petition. 'That's a good idea,' they said. Of course, one of the driving forces was Koji Ariyoshi (the President of the Citizens Federation)." Karl Yoneda/Ronald C. Larson and Arthur A. Hansen, CSUF O.H. 1336. For an analysis of the overall differences in background and philosophy between the JACL leadership and their leftist affiliates in Manzanar, see Togo Tanaka, "An Analysis of the Manzanar Incident," and Togo Tanaka/Arthur A. Hansen, CSUF O.H. 1271b, pp. 14-20. The contrast between these two groups, in spite of their shared views on evacuation, camp objectives, and the war, was so extreme that Tanaka, for lack of a better word, labels individuals like Yoneda, Oda, and Ariyoshi the "Anti-JACL" group.

"try to find [a] scapegoat among Nisei Leaders and blame them for descriminating [sic] against Kibei and [that] this [would] . . . further aggravate sectional strife among Japanese." In response to Kishi's idea that "if the government do not recognize the citizenship right of Kibei and continues to treat them as dangerous element it might as well revoke citizenship of Kibei," the secretary reasoned that "this line of thinking is very dangerous and goes to show that at least some Kibeis are more inclined to forfeit Citizenship and would rather be regarded as aliens."[64]

The proceedings of this famous Kibei meeting were recorded by Fred Tayama in another JACL "confidential" report directed to the administration. In Mess Hall 16 gathered approximately 400 of the camp's Kibei population of over 600, augmented by a large contingent of Issei and roughly seventy Nisei. Five speakers were scheduled. The first was Raymond Hirai, who outlined internee complaints concerning medical care, educational facilities, food, housing, wages, and self-government. We concern ourselves only with his remarks on the last two subjects:

> Look, for example, [at] the rate of pay for Camouflage workers. Camouflage is a war production. They are using minors; many around the ages of 15 and 16. . . . I demanded many more things of Nash. And Nash told me, 'I am the Project Director here and I can do anything the way I want it to be done'. So I told Nash, 'You are like Hitler and Mussolini combined, and Nash replied, 'I am.' So I demanded what he had said in writing and immediately Nash turned around and said that he had never said such a thing. That's the type of Director we have here. I got so mad that I told him that I'd get a rock and hit him right on his bald spot (his head). (Laughter and applause from the audience.)

> We must demand re-election of all Block Leaders. We have people now in control who are unable to say anything and are just taking orders from the Administration. This is our Camp and the Japanese people should decide for themselves how this Camp should be governed; we should not listen to those prejudiced white. (great applause) [Emphasis ours]

The next speaker, Kiyoshi Hashimoto, entitled his talk "Kibei Nisei no tachiba" [The Stand of the Kibei Nisei], but confessed that he was unsure of what he wanted to say. Several persons in the audience shouted "wakkateoru" [We understand]. Then Joe Kurihara exclaimed: "I was born in Hawaii. I have never been in Japan but in my vein flow a Japanese blood; a blood of Yamato damashii. We citizens have been denied our citizenship; we are 100% Japanese" (a roaring applause and

---

[64]WRA, "Information Regarding Kibeis taken from Block Reports, Activities of Town Hall, and Special Meetings, Aug. 4-8, 1942," WRAA, Coll. 122, Box 16, Folder 8.

stamping of feet). The third speaker, Bill Kito, directed his commentary to the Manzanar Citizens Federation, charging that certain Nisei had completely disregarded the Issei--which remark provoked someone in the audience to demand that those Nisei ought to be struck down and precipitated great applause. The fourth speaker, Karl Yoneda, was greeted by sustained booing and cries of "Sit down! Get out! Shut Up!" The last scheduled speaker, Masaji Tanaka, received more sympathy:

> I am a Kibei Nisei, but the Kibei Niseis are not Americans; they are Japanese (big applause). The Kibeis are not loyal to the United States and they might as well know about it (roaring applause). But the Kibeis should use their citizenship rights for their own benefit (everybody looking around the room; no applause). I cannot understand why there are a few Niseis who still talk about their citizenship rights; and about American democracy. I have heard that there are a few who even send reports outside (boo and down with those rats). Those fools can holler all they want but in the eyes of the American people they too are Japanese and nothing but Japanese.

Following some extemporaneous speeches from the floor, Chairman Ben Kishi, declaring that he would assume personal responsibility for the meeting, adjourned the gathering by stating, "We may never be able to hold a meeting like this again and Japanese soldiers will be here soon to liberate all of us."[65]

Several factors about this meeting command notice: the stress on nativistic themes, the aggressive criticism of the camp's administration, the intolerance of dissenting viewpoints, and the heightened determination to punish suspected informers. The circle around the group was drawing tighter.

August witnessed further in-group solidarity. As a result of the

---

[65]Fred Tayama, "Brief Report of the Kibei Meeting held at Mess Hall 16, Manzanar Relocation Center, August 8, 1942," WRAA, Coll. 122, Box 17, Folder 1. Karl Yoneda has provided a graphic profile of Ben Kishi. Who was Ben Kishi exactly? "I describe him as a Mejii-samurai type . . . he says something very exciting that the people go for. For instance, when he opened the Kibei meeting, he didn't say, 'Men are dying in Asia,' but 'Men are dying, let's stand up and have a one minute silence.' He put it in such a way that everbody, even myself, wondered 'My god, what the hell's this guy trying to prove?' Later I figure out, my gosh, this guy is really pulling this pro-Japan stunt." Did you think of him as pretty intelligent? "No, he isn't; he's one of those 'ghetto-boss' type guys. Oh, yeah, he knows how to maneuver: 'You follow me. You listen to me. I'll take care of you.'" Did you see him as the major leader of any pro-Japan sentiment within the camp? Did you think that Kishi was the leader? "Oh yes, definitely." Karl Yoneda/ Ronald C. Larson and Arthur A. Hansen, CSUF O.H. 1376b.

KARL G. YONEDA

Kibei Meeting, Director Nash issued an official bulletin reinstituting
the WRA ban on the use of Japanese in public meetings.[66] This decision revitalized earlier Issei grievances, and further aroused the
Kibei's anti-administrative stand. This month also saw the "enforced"
resignation of those Block Leaders deemed cooperative with administrative policy.

The Issei-Kibei coalition had developed an effective organization.
On August 21 when elections were held to select Block Leaders in those
blocks whose incumbents previously had been appointed, JACLers were
ousted and supplanted by Issei or Kibei. In Block 4, for example, Karl
Yoneda was defeated by an Issei who amassed 93 percent of the votes. Yoneda
correctly evaluated the reasons behind his defeat in a communication to
the administration, explaining that the Issei-Kibei bloc had criticized
him on the following grounds: " 1) Circulated petition for Second
Front and wanted to send all Japanese American soldiers on front line
duty and let enemy shoot them first; 2) for America's war effort and
urged many citizens in the block to work on camouflage nets; 3) That
he is dangerous 'red'; 4) Married to white woman and does not follow
Japanese customs. He washes son's clothes, while wife works on camouflage, let's wife go to meetings, etc.; 5) Stooge for administration and also informer because he has been seen with [Tokie] Slocum
on many occasions; 6) Spoke at Kibei meeting against them; 7) Spoke
at Citizens Federation meeting for America; and 8) Responsible for
all meetings, in camp, to be conducted in English."[67] Viewing himself
as a scapegoat for pro-Japan elements, Yoneda believed this opposition
to him _politically_ significant. The overriding significance, however,
is _cultural_; from the perspective of the internees in his block, Yoneda
was a quintessential deviant, representative of all those characteristics
the subculture abhorred. A cultural anti-hero, he symbolized for the
evacuee population its need of social cohesion.[68]

This need grew urgent when on August 24 the WRA, through Administrative Instruction No. 34, began enforcing the ruling that only citizens could hold office (though aliens might vote and fill appointive
posts). The full impact of this ruling occurred in September when the
Block Leaders Council learned that it was to be supplanted by a Community Council structured along the above lines. Issei were incensed,
arguing that "they had lived long in the United States and that denial

---

[66]Official Bulletin dated Aug. 10, 1942, from Roy Nash, Project
Director, War Relocation Authority, Manzanar, California, WRAA, Coll. 122,
Box 16, Folder 1.
[67]Report dated Aug. 24, 1942, to Roy Nash, Project Director, Manzanar, from Karl G. Yoneda, 4-2-2, Manzanar; subject: Block Leader's
Election in Block 4, WRAA, Coll. 122, Box 9, Folder 3.
[68]The point here is not to contradict Yoneda's assertion that
while in Manzanar he had "the future of Japanese in America always at
heart." Karl Yoneda/Ronald C. Larson and Arthur A. Hansen, CSUF O.H.
1376b. Rather, it is merely to suggest that most internees, at
least by the summer of 1942, were inclined to believe the very opposite.

of the right to naturalize was unjust [and] to prevent them now from holding office in their own evacuee community was simply to emphasize this injustice."[69] Moreover, they charged that JACLers had inspired the decree and had poisoned their case with the WRA. That is, here was another attempt to diminish their influence. "As a result of evacuation they had lost heavily in property and in prestige. Their places in the old Japanese community were gone. Now they feared that they would be entirely at the mercy of the less sympathetic among the nisei and of the American government."[70] Their worst fears materialized, therefore, when the Project Director appointed a seventeen man Self-Government Commission composed entirely of Nisei to draft a charter for the new government. Their tolerance disappeared completely on September 25 when the new Acting Project Director, Harvey Coverly, announced that at the end of the month the Block Leaders would become Block Managers, exchanging their legislative functions for administrative ones. A rash of resignations followed. Indeed, by mid-October the position of Block Manager had become so undesirable that the administration could hardly find substitutes for those who had resigned.

Another threat that alarmed Issei was the formation of the Manzanar Work Corps. Designed to include a Representative Assembly and a Fair Practices Committee, it aroused their suspicion because the same JACLers who had formed the detested Citizens Federation also were sponsoring the Corps. Thus, when the election of Representatives took place in late September, Issei registered little interest in the proceedings.

But it was the Kibei, smarting from their recent exclusion from the Charter Commission, who emerged as the Corps' most vociferous opponents. At the Assembly's first meeting Harry Ueno, a Kibei representing the kitchen workers of Mess Hall 22, clashed with Fred Tayama, the Corps' chairman. Upon questioning Tayama regarding the Corps' functions, Ueno became convinced that it represented an administrative tool which would not fully protect the interests of kitchen workers. Consequently, Ueno organized the Kitchen Workers' Union to "wring concessions from the administration, rather than have the administration wring more work out of the evacuees, as they believed would happen under the Work Corps."[71] Since most Kibei

---

[69] Opler, "Internal Government," pp. 56-7.

[70] Ibid., p. 58.

[71] Robert Throckmorton, "Biographies of Riot Participants in the Lone Pine Jail: Harry Ueno," [Jan. 1943(?)], WRAA, Coll. 122, Box 17; Opler, "Internal Government," pp. 72-3; Rice, Manzanar Center, pp. 36-7. Karl Yoneda's recollections on Ueno and the Kitchen Workers' Union deserve careful attention. "He (Ueno) is such an unknown figure. He talks about organizing Kitchen Workers' Union. To me, through my experience of organizing, he just had a handful [of followers] in his kitchen and among the strong pro-Japan kitchen crew in my block, Block 4. . . . Actually, they don't have

were employed as mess workers and approximately 1,500 of the Manzanar work force of 4,000 were kitchen employees,[72] the Kitchen Workers' Union provided Kibei a powerful base for mobilizing community action.

If the formation of the Kitchen Workers' Union represented one index of rising anti-JACL sentiment, another was the swelling opposition to the JACL-dominated Charter Commission, headed by Togo Tanaka. One form of resistance was passive: few bothered to register for the Charter's ratification vote on November 9. When an "educational" meeting on the Charter was held, outraged speakers assailed its citizen-alien distinction and cast aspersions upon the Commission members. The same evening an ominous message appeared on mess hall bulletin boards:

> Attention: We do not recognize any necessity for a self-government system. We should oppose anything like this as it is only drawing a rope around our necks. Let the Army take care of everything. Stop taking action which might bring trouble to our fellow residents.
>
> Blood Brothers Concerned About the People[73]

The administration, responding to the cumulative pressure, rescheduled the ratification election for November 30. The postponment did not have the desired "cooling" effect, however, for the Charter had come to symbolize the deep cultural division between the para-administrative JACLers and, in effect, the rest of the camp population. Using their subsidized press, the Charter supporters attempted to mollify the internees' widespread fears and convince them of the advantages of a speedy ratification. To counter the influence of the Free Press' campaign, the oppositional forces established what Morris Opler has termed the "Manzanar Underground."[74] Soon the community was inundated with posters, bulletins, and other communiques, variously signed "Manzanar Black Dragon Society," "Southern California Blood Brothers Corps," and "Southern California Justice Group." Primary attention was given to undermining the self-government scheme by including intimidating letters to each member of the Charter Commission, but in time the Underground branched out to criticize every aspect of Manzanar life.

---

an organization such as the Kitchen Workers' Union; they merely name themselves." You mean few kitchen workers really identified in any strong sense with the Kitchen Workers' Union. "I don't think so, because I was there. If they had such a strong force, I am sure I would have detected it right away."

[72]Iwamoto, Economic Aspects, p. 28.

[73]Opler, "Internal Government," pp. 74-5.

[74]Apparently neither the camp internal security nor the FBI, who frequently came into camp for investigations, were able to penetrate the organizational structure of this group. George Fukasawa/Arthur Hansen,

As the date of the ratification grew closer, it became apparent that the Charter was doomed to defeat. Seeking to rid the self-government plan of its JACL stigma, the administration disbanded the Commission and announced that "before a final charter was submitted to the people, a city-wide election was to take place on November 22, and two persons from each block were to be elected to a committee to study the Charter and make adjustments."[75] (At the same time, the administration called in two FBI agents to investigate the Manzanar Underground, thereby hoping to eliminate a major source of opposition to the Charter.) Once again, however, the administration was confronted by passive resistance, for on November 22 the turnout of voters was embarrasingly meager.

Nonetheless, on November 30 the new Project Director, Ralph P. Merritt scheduled a meeting of the elected block representatives. This meeting proved even more embarrassing for the cause of the Charter; indeed, only about half of the representatives attended. As a first item of business, the group decided to poll how many opposed the self-government plan; all but one--Togo Tanaka, the JACL head of the Commission--raised their hands. This lopsided division was mirrored by the subsequent discussion, which deserves our attention for its representation of the general mood of the camp population:

[Harry Ueno (who was in attendance as an interested visitor)] In my block we didn't even elect delegates; we see no necessity for this thing. Instead of such a joke of a thing, we should organize a strong Japanese Welfare Group in this camp. It will furnish the representation for us. I think it is a plot of the government to use those who can be used when they talk about self-government.

[Togo Tanaka] I do not feel that we have any body capable of speaking in support of 10,000 people. The self-government arrangement would fill that need.

[The Chairman, an Issei Block Manager] I wish to differ with Mr. Tanaka. We do have a body capable of speaking for the population and representing them. That is the Block Managers. We can do everything that any Council of Nisei can do. What have you to say to that?

CSUF O.H. 1336. The clearest insight into the membership of the Manzanar Underground is supplied by Karl Yoneda, in "Manzanar: Another View," Rafu Shimpo, Supplement (Dec. 19, 1973). Herein he explains that the membership consisted of between 25 and 30 members who "constantly disrupted things by spreading false rumors and threatening the lives of evacuees, thus keeping the camp in constant turmoil." Most of the group, in Yoneda's opinion, were "kamikaze-type supporters of fascist-militarism," not "truly 'genuine protesters' against evacuation." In his diary entries quoted in this article, there is

[Tanaka] The Block Managers have their role to perform. They are important in the scheme of things. But their job is administrative. You do not represent the people so much as you do the Administration, at least in theory. The Managers have no power to legislate. That is the difference. [Emphasis ours.]

[The Chairman] There is one question that I would like to put before Mr. Tanaka, if he will be good enough to answer. I don't know whether it's rumor or not, but I have heard that the reason why the W.R.A. decided on the policy of discriminating against the issei in holding office in the proposed Council is because Mike Masaoka [Executive Secretary] of the National J.A.C.L. got together with Dillon Myer [WRA National Director] and had that discriminatory clause put in. What do you know about that?

[Tanaka] Now that you tell that to me, I've heard it too. Why don't you write to Washington, D.C. and Mr. Myer and ask him?

[Another Issei] I would like to ask Mr. Tanaka why it is that the nisei seem to want to control this camp? Why is it that they are out to persecute the issei?

Another vote followed on the self-government question--this time with a unanimous negative response.[76] The circle had all but closed.

Two interesting sidelights to this meeting are the role of "spokesman for the people" assumed by Harry Ueno and the attribution to JACL leaders of influence in shaping WRA policy. Ueno had emerged as a cultural hero. In part, this development stemmed from his formation of the Kitchen Workers' Union. More specifically, Ueno's public stature resulted from his charge that two administrators--Assistant Project Director Ned Campbell and Chief Steward Joe Winchester--were misappropriating and selling internee sugar supplies for personal gain. This charge had led to a full-scale investigation by the Block Managers. Although insufficient evidence was uncovered to implicate the two, the investigation did expose the fact that the internees were being shorted in their sugar allotment.[77] This finding alone guaranteed Ueno's popularity, for it confirmed the internees' deep-seated conviction that the administrators were capable of the most unscrupulous behavior.

JACL-WRA collusion rumors had been commonplace, but their

---

mention of their pressure-tactics as early as June 16, 1942: "Scavanger truck with Kibei crew, bearing Black Dragon flags (skull painted white on black cloth), appears in front of Block Leaders Council and Camouflage Net Garnishing Project telling everyone not to work on nets." An entry of July 22 indicates that pressure had given way to terrorism: "Very hot, 114 degrees. While Tokie Slocum (WWI vet) and I were talking in front of Block 4 office, a Black Dragon truck suddenly charged us at full speed. We managed to jump onto top step. Truck busts lower step and speeds away."

[75]Rice, Manzanar Center, p. 53.

credibility became intensified by a recent development. While the meeting on self-government was in progress, Fred Tayama and another JACL leader were serving as Manzanar's delegates to the JACL National Convention in Salt Lake City. Tayama's departure for that city in mid-November had irritated the internees, for he, even more than Karl Yoneda and Togo Tanaka, typified the antithesis of the "Japanese spirit." During the evacuation period, as the most prominent JACL figure in Southern California, he consorted with government officials and played the role of spokesman for the community. It was rumored that he had sought to exploit beleagured Issei businessmen during the period when it appeared that Nisei were to be spared evacuation. His cheerful cooperation with the evacuation also was resented. He seemed to be accorded special privileges by the camp staff: "Rumors circulated freely about the sugar, canned foods and fine furniture with which his home was filled, and . . . it was assumed that the sugar said to be in his home was a portion of the amount the kitchen workers claimed had mysteriously disappeared."[78] Virtually everyone in camp suspected him of being an FBI informer. Nor did his role as a leading spirit in both the Citizens Federation and the Work Corps endear him to the internees. And now he had the audacity to name himself Manzanar's "representative" at the Salt Lake City meeting where WRA national leaders would gather and policy decisions would be made. Indeed, word had filtered back to Manzanar that Tayama and other JACL delegates, "in the name of the Japanese people in and out of the Centers, had asked that nisei be inducted into combat units of the U.S. Army."[79] He had "stabbed his people in the back" and now was arranging to have their sons slaughtered. The mere mention of his name evoked profound disgust; if anyone endangered the group's existence and threatened its solidarity, it was Fred Tayama.[80]

It will be recollected that Tayama was beaten upon his return to the center, thereby setting in motion the Manzanar "Riot." What must be emphasized is that there is strong reason to believe that the overwhelming majority of internees fully endorsed this beating. Historians writing from the WRA-JACL perspective may see the attack on Tayama as the unwarranted work of a few pro-Axis Kibei troublemakers, but such an analysis construes the action too restrictively. Even if one concedes pro-Japan terrorism as the basis for the assault, and accepts the idea that only a small band of hooligans participated in it, one still has to account for the thousands that protested the

---

[76]Opler, "Internal Government," pp. 111-16.

[77]Throckmorton, "Ueno," pp. 3-10.

[78]According to Sally Slocum, the wife of Tokie Slocum, after Tayama's post-riot evacuation to Death Valley sacks of rice and bunches of bananas were found in his apartment. Joe Grant Masaoka, interviewer; UCLA Japanese American Research Project, No. 2010, Box 385; Research Library, Special Collections.

arrest of Harry Ueno and who were willing to defy the administration to have him released from jail. Nor did they simply believe him innocent of involvement in Tayama's beating. Indeed, one might say that Ueno was lionized because of his alleged connection with the attack. For the internees--Issei, Kibei, and Nisei--the time had come when something had to be done to prevent the corrosive effects of the JACLers. Seen through the ethnic perspective, the beating of Tayama was both necessary and good.

So too with the entire Manzanar Revolt. What happened on December 6 must not be seen in isolation or ascribed to ideological motivations. What transpired was of a piece with the Japanese American community's continuous struggle to preserve its cultural heritage and determine its identity, both of which were jeopardized by the administration's decision to bypass natural Issei leadership and deal instead with its own artificially erected JACL hierarchy. When the WRA moved the JACLers out of the camp after the Revolt, the Issei had taken a step toward restoring the dominance they had enjoyed before the evacuation.[81]

---

[79]Opler, "Internal Government," pp. 122-6.

[80]The best account of the social psychology of the Manzanar camp at the time of the Revolt, especially the attitude toward Fred Tayama, is Morton Grodzins, "The Manzanar Shooting," JERS, Barnhart, Folder 010.04. Written immediately after the disturbance, it makes no attempt to judge ideology or morality but merely to reflect public opinion. In so doing, it too is written from an ethnic (i.e., community) perspective.

[81]The restoration of Issei dominance and community ethnicity is a theme taken up in Yatsushiro, Themal Analysis and James Minoru Sakoda, Minidoka: An Analysis of Changing Patterns of Social Interaction, unpubl. PhD diss., U.C. Berkeley, 1949. The present authors are applying this same theme to the Manzanar Center in a study tentatively titled Manzanar: A Perspectivist History.

PART TWO: ORAL DOCUMENTS

TOGO W. TANAKA

HOW TO SURVIVE RACISM IN AMERICA'S FREE SOCIETY

A Lecture by Togo W. Tanaka   April 3, 1973

INTRODUCTION

In the spring 1973 term, Arthur A. Hansen coordinated a lecture series in the University of California, Irvine, Extension Program, dealing with the evacuation of Japanese Americans during World War II. While innovative instructors at all levels of education have in recent years begun to introduce the subject into classes, particularly those in history, the Irvine series was one of the first specifically titled as a class on evacuation and, perhaps, the very first to rely mainly on ex-internees and members of the Japanese-American community as lecturers. Ten of the eleven lectures were tape-recorded and are listed in the bibliography herein on pages 210-212. Togo W. Tanaka was third in the series, and his lecture, including a spirited question and answer session, is reproduced in its entirety.

Tanaka's words are particularly significant because they challenge those who would make the Nisei the scapegoats of the evacuation. The second generation were victimized by the relocation, and today they have to face their children who ask, "Why didn't you resist?" It is not an easy question to deal with, especially in this day of widespread militancy over rights. Tanaka makes no pretence at clear-cut answers; however, as he draws a verbal picture of his own dilemma, it becomes apparent to the reader that he replies to that query as best anyone can.

Dr. Hansen, I thank you for inviting me here. Actually I am here by accident. I was in Jamaica last December when a person in my office accepted your invitation on my behalf. She notified me on my return. The fact that the individual happened to be a person named Mrs. Christine Omura and also, incidentally, the fact that she happens to be a daughter who works for me made it a commitment that I found difficult not to keep, since I have been trying to keep her in our employ for some time. She felt that there might be some purpose in my doing this.

I find myself somewhat at a handicap here, however, because it has been some three decades since I have had occasion to do anything like this. I have not until recently recalled the incidents of the prewar years that I have been asked to speak to you about. Last week I was asked to substitute for the publisher of the Rafu Shimpo at a dedication of the UCLA Research Library celebrating the completion of their microfilming of all the old issues of the Rafu. And I suddenly realized, when I was asked to do this, that I had actually been on the staff of the Rafu Shimpo for only six years, and that there are members of that organization who were there at the time I worked there and who are still there today. The UCLA officials asked me, nonetheless, to take part in the dedication and, in doing so, I concluded that they wanted someone who really could sit on the sidelines and do it, because the short period that I worked with the Rafu was during the period of the 1930s.

I've been asked here tonight to speak on a subject, the wording of which eludes me a bit, but I'm going to try to keep as closely to the subject as I'm able to do. In addressing myself to the topic of "How to Survive Racism in America's Free Society," a review through the eyes of a Japanese American of what happened on the West Coast during the decade before Pearl Harbor, I hope you will allow me to start off with some biographical information.

The first words that I learned to speak were Japanese, unlike, I think, most of those of you here who are of Oriental descent. To me, English was a foreign language until, at the age of six, I was enrolled at the Los Feliz Elementary School in Hollywood. I was a year older than the other children, and as I recall we had two teachers in that kindergarten: one tall and thin and the other short and plump. One of them kept referring to me as "that Jap boy." Now my father, who was proud of his race and of his samurai heritage, had said, on leaving me in the care of my teachers, "Honor and respect your teachers." But he had also taught me to challenge and correct anyone calling me a Jap. Correct a teacher? I was confused. My confusion bothered my father, but he could offer me no satisfactory explanation. I think that this marked the beginning of an ambivalence about my status as an American that must have stayed with me until Pearl Harbor thrust upon some hundred and ten or twelve thousand of us the necessity for an unequivocal choice.

But the 1920s--and this is the period to which I am now referring--

were still turbulent years for Orientals in California. The Exclusion
Law had slammed tight the gates of immigration, and "Beware of the
Yellow Peril" was virtually still the slogan of the very powerful Hearst
newspapers, and they reached then from coast to coast. In Northern
California, the newspapers of McClatchy echoed the fears of organized
labor, and in Southern California both Hearst (of the Los Angeles Tribune
and Examiner) and Chandler (of the Los Angeles Times) joined as one in
the great crusade to keep California white. To this the beleagured
Japanese truck farmers, aided by a very thin line of defenders, responded
by saying, "Keep California green." But their's was not a successful
battle. That we should lose the campaigns but win in the end a place
on the American soil was a goal not yet in sight.

I look upon the twenties as a decade of trial, although the historians say it was relatively peaceful in the history of anti-Oriental and
anti-Japanese agitation in this state. The indignities that were thrust
on my parents in their quest for a home in this land were daily and
chronic. They were barred from most sections of the city. By law, they
could not own property. They were ineligible for citizenship, again by
law. They could not pursue any trade or business of their own choosing
on the same basis as the parents of my fellow school pupils. Many public
places excluded them. Legally, then, they were kept out of the mainstream
of our society. They cheerfully sought accommodation to these circumstances by keeping their eyes and that of their children on the future.
It would get better, they said, because it could not get much worse.

My mother found some strength in religion. She had been raised a
Buddhist, but she sent her children to a Christian Sunday school. She
finally made her own commitment to Christ and, when the outrageous slings
of racism struck, she turned the other cheek. But my father did not. He
was a self-taught Confucian scholar, and he disdained the English language
as a means of communication for the white man.

My lessons at school taught me about the lives and character of
George Washington, Thomas Jefferson, and Abraham Lincoln, but at home my
father taught me Shushin, the Japanese code of ethics, and he instilled
in me the values of honor, loyalty, service, and obligation that had been
taught to him by his forebears in Japan. He was proud of his race and
of the culture and the civilization it represented. He told me over and
over again that race discrimination, which was typical of the American
West Coast of that day, was merely a perpetuation of white imperialism
which, by force of arms, had brought most of Asia under the yoke of
Europe. Nevertheless, he really believed that education--to use a
latter-day term--meant upward mobility. "Study hard," he said, "and
learn. Don't expect equal treatment; you're not going to get an even
break. Accept the odds, and when times are better you can learn to compete in this society. But you're not going to stay here." My father
was something of a racial chauvinist himself. He had encountered
physical violence from white hoodlums, he said, in his early years in
this country. But for his children he drew a line at engaging in violence.
"Hating," he said, "is legally permissable, but hitting is punishable."

My parents owned and operated a small retail vegetable store in
Hollywood. My father did the buying at the downtown wholesale market,
and my mother did the selling. My brothers, sisters, and I all helped.

My mother learned to speak English and got along famously with her customers, all of them "white barbarians," as my father observed.

In 1923 when I was a first grade pupil, I was told by my mother to solicit relief for earthquake victims in Tokyo. I walked all day Saturday and Sunday one weekend, ringing doorbells and knocking on doors, asking strangers to give. I will always remember that walk. I learned suddenly, to my amazement and in spite of what my father had taught me, that human compassion and sympathy can transcend the barriers of race and reach out with loving kindness. The nickel, dimes, pennies, quarters, and dollar bills that I brought back in my big shopping bag destroyed forever my childish belief that only a Japanese could be trusted to be decent, kind, honest, and good, for had I not, I asked my father, been the beneficiary of an outpouring of goodwill and kindness from complete strangers, every one of them a white barbarian?

In my own case, as it must have been for thousands of my Nisei contemporaries, we entered the American experience through the public schools. We found the fabric of racial prejudice strong and closely knit, but somewhere around the thin edges the threads were coming loose. The friends we made at school encouraged that hope. One day, when I observed to my father that his own lack of Caucasian friends put him in a virtual ivory tower, he said, "You are beginning to think and talk like the enemy." At Thomas Starr King Junior High School in Los Angeles, I learned the value of fair competition through sports. You didn't have to be five times better, only a wee bit better. I won a handball championship, and our class football team placed second. We won a pennant in softball. And on the playing field, as in the classroom, it really didn't matter whether you were white, yellow, red or black. At the school I attended, it was usually ninety-nine percent white, one percent yellow, and there were neither red nor black. The discovery that in dealing with racism in our free society we were not alone was to come later.

Last Tuesday I lunched with a man who recently retired as a justice of a California appellate court. The law firm of O'Melveny and Meyers had persuaded him to join their staff. He is a retired colonel in the U.S. Army and a distinguished American jurist, a graduate of Brown University and of Harvard Law School, and a recipient of honorary degrees from several American institutions. As a teenager, I remember him having been elected by his peers to be student body president at Le Conte Junior High School in Los Angeles. It was still the decade of the twenties. The parents of his fellow students protested so heatedly that he was forced to resign. At Hollywood High School, where he preceded me by six years, John Aiso won first place in the constitutional oratorical contest. He was scheduled to go to Washington, D.C. to compete in the national finals. But it was still the decade of the twenties, and Southern California simply could not be represented by a "Jap boy," so they sent runner-up Herbert Wenig, and he won the national finals. Disappointment? Yes. Adversity? Yes. Injustice? Yes. But bitterness? No. Multiply this in one form or another by a hundred and ten or a hundred and twelve thousand, and I am sure that we will find in the lives of the Issei and Nisei of the West Coast, during the decades of the twenties and thirties, a resilience to bend with the blows of unequal treatment and neither break nor shatter in the face of threats of total exclusion.

Some years later, as I served as head of the publications department of the American Technical Society in Chicago among my staff of editors was a delightful Notre Dame graduate, Robert J. Sullivan, to whom I had assigned the task of editing a textbook, United States History: The Story of Our Land, by Merle Burke. Bob, in what I regard as a typically relevant Irish-style question, used to ask me, "How in the world could you, if you were healthy American citizens with youth on your side, allow yourselves to be herded into a barbed-wire concentration camp without putting up a fight? They would sure as hell never get a hundred and twelve thousand Irishmen to go--there would be bloodshed!" I really never found an answer. We went because there really was no other choice. We cared enough about our parents, who were legally defenseless and totally exposed. Some of my children, listening to the activists and militants, contemptuously refer to what they regard as the "spineless docility of the Nisei"--that is, of our generation--in acquiescing to governmental injustice. I find myself disagreeing. The late Robert Millikan, Cal Tech's Nobel prize winning scientist, told a small group of us trying to make our evacuation less painful to believe in God and the ultimate triumph of good over evil. Naive? Yes, perhaps. But we did, and I think we went on to fight another day and ultimately to achieve our goal, a place in this society, however changing. And even by today's pragmatic standards, we must have done something right.

I have always felt close to my father and mother. Through the agonies of the World War II years, behind barbed wire and watchtowers at Manzanar, and to the day my father died in Chicago at the age of seventy-eight, he was still an unreconstructed immigrant Japanese who, rejected by this strange land, never fully accepted America as his home. He asked that his mortal remains be buried in Japan. In death, we compromised. My parents' ashes rest at Valhalla, a cemetary in North Hollywood, and at his ancestral grave in Yamaguchi Prefecture on the slopes of a gentle hill overlooking the beautiful Inland Sea in Japan. When I visit there, I do not feel at home. When I place flowers on their grave at Valhalla, I do.

At Hollywood High School, on the urging and guidance of my father who envisioned a career for me in the diplomatic service of the Japanese government, I became the editor of the Hollywood High School News. He made me deliberately conspire to achieve every scholastic award in sight. He said, "It will not just happen; you must premeditate it." It took a lot of extra effort. I entered UCLA in the winter of 1932 and declared, in accordance with my father's plans and wishes, a major in political science in my junior year. I learned, incidentally, that all the dumb football players were in political science, and this was essentially most everyone there. (laughter)

At Hollywood High School I discovered a growing estrangement from the long-held ideals and objectives of my father. My progress in the Japanese language was halting and poor. "Spend more time studying Japanese," my parents kept saying. "If you have any ability, there is no future for you in this country." But I was beginning to question this. As I look back now, I think the reasons are numerous, and they are found in the associations that the Nisei generation made in the public schools.

A fortnight ago I had lunch at the Jonathan Club with an old friend from Hollywood High School days. We were together in what was called the Hollywood Hi-Y, and he recalled that one year, under the direction of our club advisor, Ben Alexander of TV fame, we both had danced in a chorus line made up of girls on the stage of the Memorial Auditorium. Rod Dedeaux went on to USC, where he graduated and where he later returned to become one of the all-time great baseball coaches while at the same time developing a successful trucking business. "In my den at home," he said, "I have a picture of all of us in those skirts, and you were the smallest."

By the time that I was a senior at UCLA, my father's cherished goal for me had, I'm sure, lost out. Yet he persisted. A compatriot from Yamaguchi Prefecture in Japan with whom he carried on an occasional correspondence had risen to prominence and power as Foreign Minister of Japan. His name was Yosuke Matsuoka and, as a young man, he had lived in Oregon and worked as a schoolboy in an American home while seeking an education here. He was now an architect of the Rome-Berlin-Tokyo Axis, and his memories were full of the racist slights and insults inflicted upon him in the United States. "The American credo," he said, "gives lip service to equality of opportunity and justice for all, but the performance verifies the hypocrisy of the white American. His treatment of Negroes, Orientals, and Indians proves it." My father read these letters to me at length and quoted Mr. Matsuoka. My only response could be that "White racism may be an affliction, and I do not deny its presence or its existence. But I know enough people of Caucasian extraction," I said, "who feel as I do and whose commitment to the same ideals are one with my own hopes. And I see no difference between the racist imperialism of Mr. Matsuoka's Greater East Asian Co-prosperity Sphere Program," which to me, then educated at UCLA, appeared nothing but a blatantly hypocritical disguise for a Japanese version of Mein Kampf. I was now debating with my father. "Furthermore, I added, "how can Mr. Matsuoka criticize white racism in America while aligning himself with the worst racist of them all, Adolf Hitler?" My father conceded the point, so we finally resorted to playing the Japanese game of go, and we agreed that world politics would be taboo. He then started on religion and sex, (laughter) on Robert Burns and Tagore (Indian poet), and we found common ground in discussing Kakuzo Okakura's remarkable little volume, The Book of Tea.

But my father was right in reminding me that racism, USA-style, deeply scarred its victims. When I first entered UCLA, I walked with two friends into a barbershop in Westwood. While they were quickly served, I was told I should go to a Japanese barber. Years later, during the war, I was in Salt Lake City to meet with Roger Baldwin of the American Civil Liberties Union. And he said, I thought with remarkable understanding, that he could measure the reception that Nisei servicemen in uniform would receive in small towns by whether or not the barber would cut their hair. The militant activists of the third and fourth generation of Japanese descent have seldom if ever experienced much of the subtle forms of indignity that the Issei and Nisei have found the prevailing ingredient of their lives. I've asked myself, "Is it any wonder, then, that my generation—in common with blacks and chicanos—should find subconscious inhibitions in their responses to their environment?"

In 1934, while I was in my junior year in UCLA, I applied for and was hired as an English section staff writer for the Kashu Mainichi, which is the California Daily News. Sei Fujii, the publisher, used me to put down his ideas in his English section. I remember him as a fighter and a longtime campaigner to seek equality in the California law for the permanent Japanese residents.

In my senior year I was offered a job as an editor on the larger Rafu Shimpo and, with Mr. Fujii's blessings, I went on to work for his rival. At that time, I found myself also working as a reader in the Department of Political Science at UCLA, making maps on weekends for Dr. Malbone Graham, and being paid fifty cents an hour by the National Youth Administration. From 1936 to 1942, I immersed myself behind the walls of Little Tokyo, venturing forth into the wider community only as an advocate of equal rights or civil liberty and of the proposition that, although we may look Japanese, look harder and you'll find a good American. But when war came, it simply didn't work.

Throughout the years that I was privileged to edit the Rafu Shimpo English section, the discomforting shadow of William Randolph Hearst and his newspapers lay heavily over Japanese Americans. In Los Angeles, Hearst had two dailies, the morning Examiner and the afternoon Herald. I remember them because I used to sell them on the corner, and I thought they had the best funny papers in town. But as I grew older and read them, they never failed to leave me with a terrible feeling that some foreordained doom lay ahead for me, as the terrible Yellow Peril would descend one day upon our beaches.

I thought of this one noonday as I sat in a dining room of a Santa Monica Beach mansion of Marion Davies, Mr. Hearst's mistress. Across the table, at its head, sat the aging tycoon, hosting a Japanese publisher from Tokyo in the company of my publisher, the late H. T. Komai of the Rafu Shimpo. They told me that Hearst had Japanese servants at his baronial castle at San Simeon, and he was said to be a good and generous employer. They also said, from what I read in those days, that Hearst's frenetic brand of journalism had helped spark the Spanish-American War, and he just might do that with Japan. So, feeling the electric tension generated by the Examiner and Herald columns in those prewar days, I developed a genuine fear of this man who printed the Stars and Stripes across his masthead and daily proclaimed his definition of what an American was. I learned that day that he truly and personally regarded the Japanese residents of California as sojourners, as an extension of the Japanese nation, and not as permanent residents, entitled to the same treatment under the law as white Anglo-Saxons. Mr. Hearst, as I remember from that brief encounter, was a somewhat cantankerous aging old white racist whose public display of what my Chinese friends would call a "concubine" made him, in my post-adolescent judgment, somewhat more "Oriental" than I regarded myself, with my acquired notions of a Puritan ethic and fidelity in marriage. But he had the power, and waved the red, white, and blue flag. He spoke for and to millions of Americans, but when I wrote a column, how far could it reach? When I had shared thoughts such as these with my fellow Nisei editors, however, we seldom felt either helpless or hopeless. I believe then that our academic pursuits in the halls of learning had equipped us to be patient.

I remember once quoting historian Charles Beard, who wrote in 1936,

"Unless we are to believe in the progressive degradation of the American nation, we are bound to believe that Hearst's fate is ostracism by decency in life and oblivion in death. Odors of his personality may linger for a time until his estate is divided and his journalistic empire is dissolved. But they will soon evaporate in the sunlight of a purer national life." These were strong words indeed, and perhaps in the light of the mellowing years too harsh an indictment of one of the most colorful Americans of this century. But for those of us whose lives were so threatened by his influence in the thirties, what recourse had we except to print such words in our papers and to stand hopefully and say, "Time surely must be on our side."

In 1936 when I received my B.A. from UCLA, I had no illusions about what it meant to be an Oriental in a predominately . . . what is called a WASP society. No illusions--but many dreams. One dream was to begin early to own my own home. My father had never been able to do so. The law forbad it. The law defined him as an "alien ineligible for American citizenship." But it conferred right of citizenship on me. When I became twenty-one, I asked my employer, who owned his home in his son's name, how you go about it. "Simple," he said, "save your money." So I did.

To buy a home, I inquired into, looked at, and tried to see some 119 houses. I had logged the record systematically. In 114 instances I had been told, "You cannot live here. Your money is not good enough. The deed has a racially restrictive covenant, and only members of the Caucasian race may reside here, except perhaps as a guest or a servant." This circumstance was a fact of life. It seemed to me then, as it does to me now, patently unfair, but I had been trained, it seemed, not to turn inward with bitterness, but to meet the challenges as postively as I knew how. "Turn the negative into a positive," my father had said, and experience simply deepened my resolve to seek through the courts of law and appeals to the consciences of fair-minded people everywhere that this custom, this practice embedded in our laws, ought one day to change. And to that end, I found purpose in devoting my energies to the editing of the English section of the Japanese daily newspaper that employed me.

In 1940 in my fifth year as an English editor of the Rafu Shimpo, an opportunity presented itself. A gentleman named Edgerton, a land developer, and a builder from Buena Park named William Cannon came to Little Tokyo and opened an office. At that time, I had established a program in the newspaper called "The Nisei Business Bureau," and we funneled through it all the good news about job and housing opportunities that would lower the barriers that penned us into a segregated community. Edgerton's firm, known as Pacific Development Company, had purchased a large tract on the west side of the city, at Jefferson and La Cienega. Knowing of the great demand for housing among the Nisei, they opened an office, hired an agent who was a friend of mine, and asked us through our newspaper to promote the sale of new homes in Jefferson Park, where FHA financing would significantly upgrade the level of housing for Japanese Americans in Southern California. "No race restrictions?" I asked. "No," they said. And so we went to work.

In a short time deposits had been collected on more than two square blocks and plans moved ahead for building. There was considerable

excitement about the venture in Little Tokyo and our newspaper. It was
billed as a three million dollar Nisei subdivision, and thirty-three
years ago that sounded like thirty million would today. But the word
spread swiftly in the larger community, and fear ripped the entire west
side. Mass meetings were held; petitions were circulated; and rumors
flew. The Los Angeles City Council then became a battleground when
the flat map for the subdivision was submitted for approval. Councilman
Harold Harby, who I remember well, represented the district in which
it was located, and he fought tooth and nail against it. A protesting
resident told me at one of the mass meetings: "This is nothing but an
advance landing for the Imperial Japanese forces to invade our shores."

One morning Mr. Edgerton called me and said, "Will you go to a
meeting this evening at the Calvary Methodist Church on West Avenue and
talk to a neighborhood gathering and explain to them that this is an
American citizen development? Allay their fears and tell them that the
rumors of unpainted shacks with goats tied to the posts are untrue."
And he went on, but I interrupted and said, "I understand the fever is
like a Southern lynch mob, and I'm not really cheered by the thought of
going there." But he said, "Get someone to go with you." So I phoned
Freeman Lusk, then director of public information of Los Angeles City
Board of Education, whom I regarded as a good friend. He had been on
radio; he was an eloquent speaker; he was an officer in the Naval Reserve;
and he was in good physical shape. (laughter) So when I explained the
situation he said, "Okay."

We faced a rather full audience that looked extremely tense and grim,
and I did the best that I knew how, but the vibrations were not friendly.
The minister of that church, a young man named Reverend George Warmer,
seemed to be embarrassed by the intemperance of the more vocal members of
his congregation. When Freeman Lusk was called upon to answer questions,
a hostile resident asked, "What would you do, if you didn't care to have
them live near you and one moved in next door?" Freeman looked at me and
said, "Why, I'd move." The local newspapers had a banner field day with
that quotation. Jefferson Park died before it was born.

It seemed to me then, as I look back over three decades, that the
stage was indeed being set for our removal from the West Coast. While
Imperial Japan's brand of yellow racism rampaged from Shanghai to Nanking
across China, and as Hitler's Aryan hordes overran Europe, California's
historic brand of white racism took careful aim at this numerically in-
significant and politically impotent minority. They would drive us out
of the West Coast and they would herd us behind watchtowers, but it would
not destroy our faith, nor would it prevent us from eventually making our
way back. We--the Issei and the Nisei--had been nurtured in a crucible
of constant heat, and we would not wilt nor die easily. As Robert Millikan
told me just before the evacuation, somehow we would endure punishment
without crime and prove the durability of what he called the "American
Dream."

I thought that, since I am recalling some of the highlights of the
great years that I had with the Rafu Shimpo, I would record this evening
the fact that in 1941, in the few weeks before Pearl Harbor, I had the
experience of meeting Eleanor Roosevelt at the White House. I remember
her as an extraordinarily gracious, thoughtful, and sensitive person with

a simplicity of manner and genuineness that won my personal and lifelong admiration, so much so that my recent reading of Elliott Roosevelt's memoirs about his parents saddens me.

I had been sent in October and November of 1941 to Washington, D.C. by my publisher to ask Attorney General Francis Biddle for advance permission to continue publishing the Rafu Shimpo when war came. I had gone to the public library at his instruction and researched the provisions of the Espionage Act of 1917, under which newspapers owned or controlled by citizens of enemy nations but permanent residents of this country might function. Mr. Biddle seemed a bit surprised by the request, but he was courteous and sympathetic, it seemed to me. I explained to him the terrible dilemma faced by the Nisei, American citizens pledged to this country, living in most cases under the same roof and sharing the responsibility of protecting their loved ones who would, by the inequities of American law, be regarded as enemy aliens if war came. Like my father who years earlier could not answer me when I said the teacher kept calling me "that Jap boy," Mr. Biddle simply shook his head. He said he did not really know what he would do in our position, except he reiterated that "the course of justice would, in the fulfillment of American constitutional rights, prove that decency and fair play would triumph over brute force and violence." Comforting words, yes, but they did not resolve our dilemma.

The next morning I got the surprise of my entire career as an English editor of the largest Japanese daily newspaper in Southern California. When I look back I wonder if it wasn't the series of traumas that I suffered which drove me from the profession. There was a note awaiting me at the Wardman Park Hotel where I was staying: "Report at 10:00 a.m. at the Munitions Building, War Department." When I arrived at the door, I was given a kind of guarded security clearance, pinned with a badge, and escorted to a large room where two generals in uniform greeted me-- Major Wallace Moore and Lieutenant Colonel Sumpter Bratton of War Department G-2. "You told Attorney General Biddle," Major Moore began, "that you would like to continue publishing when war came. Is that right?" I said, "Yes." "How do you know war is coming?" For six years I had been writing the Domei news dispatches from Tokyo taken by our newspaper short-wave wireless operator. The dispatches came in a form called Romaji, which is Japanese written in English, so the question seemed to me rhetorical. I told him, "Everyone knows it's coming. I've been on Capitol Hill, and I've met or interviewed over fifty people, senators and congressmen and their staffs, and I read the papers as well as anyone else. And everyone says war is coming; it's just a matter of time." But they didn't seem convinced that I was not privy to something special from Tokyo.

They interrogated me skillfully, pleasantly, and in a relaxed manner all through the morning and part of the afternoon. Then they asked me to identify some printed pages. The room was darkened, and on the screen they flashed page after page of editorials from the English section of the Rafu Shimpo. "Did you write these?" I was asked, and I said, "Yes." The substance of what they were showing me was "Should war break out between Japan, the land of our fathers, and the United States, the land of our birth, then our loyalty and allegiance, especially by the

Japanese samurai code, would be completely, totally, and absolutely with the United States." And they thought this was some kind of convoluted reasoning, that we should be good Americans by Japanese standards. But this then had been and was the position of the English section. They kept asking, "Do you really believe this?" And I kept saying, "Yes."

Then they said, "How about your father? Where would his sympathies be?" So I said, "The question is unfair, because it implies that if I said his sympathies would be with Japan, an unthinking and unknowing person would conclude that he constituted a threat to this nation, and he does not. He has always been a law-abiding resident who suffers taxation without representation, who has been unjustly excluded from the privileges of American citizenship, while he has cheerfully assumed all the responsibilities of a citizen." But Colonel Bratton interrupted me and said, "Major Moore didn't ask you to make a speech. He simply wanted your opinion of where your father's true sympathies would be if war broke out between the United States and Japan. Now which is it, in your opinion?" "My father would be sympathetic to Japan," I said. "And you?" "I would fight for the United States, and my father would expect this and be proud of it."

Then came the blockbuster. "How do you explain these editorials in the Japanese section?" They darkened the room again and they flashed on the screen articles and opinion columns from the Japanese section. Some quoted Japanese military officers in Japan, stating that the dual citizen Nisei in the United States would be useful to Japan in the event of war. "Your newspaper," I was told, "is either schizophrenic or is engaging in transparent doubletalk, and how can you explain this?" I couldn't even read the Japanese on the screen. True, I could understand Romaji, but the Kanji was beyond me, and in all the years that I edited the English section of the Rafu Shimpo I never mastered the written language enough to understand, much less read, the major part of this newspaper. The G-2 men appeared unimpressed--polite, but I'm certain unconvinced.

I talked to myself and said, "Togo Tanaka, UCLA '36, tutor to all those football players at Sigma Alpha Epsilon house, reader for Professors Ordean Rockey and Melbone Graham, pride and joy of your father, you're a stupid dum-dum. You've just blown it. You're as good as dead. From here on it's all downhill." They sensed my discomfort, and I had lost my poise. I was truly confused and troubled. I could rationalize, but I had no explanation. I was then twenty-five; I had been married a year, and we were expecting our first child.

I flew on to New York in the company of Gongoro Nakamura, president of the Central Japanese Association, and we participated in a citizenship program at Columbia University. I returned to the Rafu Shimpo, and early in December I addressed an Orange County service club. My picture appeared in the Santa Ana Register with the caption, "Jap Editor Sees War Coming." On December 5 with my publisher, I attended a giant rally at the Biltmore Hotel where Henry Luce addressed a United China Relief dinner, and on December 7 I learned from Wagner White, on the staff of Hearst's L. A. Examiner and a writer for the Saturday Evening Post, that war had burst over Pearl Harbor. We put out a special edition that day, and on December 8, 1941 I was taken into custody by the FBI on a presidential warrant, arresting me and holding me incommunicado.

For the next eleven days I shared cells in three different jails with dope addicts, drunks, thieves, wife-beaters, and scores and scores of my friends, mostly Issei, the Who's Who of the Los Angeles Japanese community. There were two of us who were citizens, myself and Eiji Tanabe, a bilingual Kibei and Nisei born in the United States and raised in Japan. He was an executive of the Japanese American Citizens League.

We were shunted from the old City Jail at First and Hill to Lincoln Heights and then to the County Jail on top of the Hall of Justice. Rumors were rampant. A Gardena M.D., a Dr. Honda, who had been prominent in the affiars of the Imperial Japanese War Veterans Association had hanged himself in his cell at Terminal Island jail. Some said we were held as hostages, and others feared that we would be shot. After all, it was war, wasn't it? So, stripped of our worldly belongings in the prison yard, and eating out of tin plates with bent utensils, I think we asked ourselves a number of things, Eiji Tanabe and I. I kept try-ing to recall the first ten amendments to the Constitution and the Bill of Rights. I got nowhere with the guards when I asked, "Could I call a lawyer?" Then, "Could I call my wife? I'm worried. She's pregnant." And I wondered about my parents and my brother and sisters. Never having been really churched, I found myself inexplicably turning to prayer in the quiet of the long night in those cramped jail cells, and discovered the meaning that when all else fails, truly, what else?

Some years later when Francis Biddle sent me a copy of his book on Justice Holmes, he inscribed it, "With greetings and best wishes to Togo Tanaka who cherishes the secret of happiness--freedom." For whatever he may have meant, my recollection of those days in those dark cells impressed on me that it indeed must be a time of testing.

On the twelfth day, as I remember, I was released. No hearing, no notification, no nothing. A guard came up to me and said, "Get your clothes and go. You're free." In five minutes I was out of that cell and downstairs in the lobby of the Hall of Justice. To my total amaze-ment, my wife was standing there waiting. No one had notified her; she really did not even know where I was. I was about to phone her when we met. I am not a believer but, if there is anything to ESP, I go back to that moment.

I returned to the Rafu Shimpo, an ex-jailbird. Our publisher was also in custody, and there was no one who had heard that he had been released. Permanent wartime camps for the Issei at Missoula, Montana and Santa Fe, New Mexico were being set up.

In the months that remained before we were removed, there were a few, I think, rather revealing events. In February of 1942--Pearl Harbor still a vivid tragedy and air raid warnings a nightly fear--I received a telegram from Sacramento: "The Governor of California wishes to see cer-tain Nisei." I boarded a train and when I arrived I met a score of friends: Saburo Kido, Walter Tsukamoto, Mike Masaoka of the JACL, Yasuo Aibiko and Larry Tajiri of the Nichibei Times, Peter Aoki of the Hokubei Mainichi, Roy Takeno of the Kashu Mainichi, and many others.

We were received in the executive offices of Governor Culbert Olson. I wrote in my diary that the most memorable quotation of the day came from Governor Olson. "You know, when I look out at a group of Americans of German or Italian descent, I can tell whether they're loyal or not. I can tell how they think and even perhaps what they are thinking. But it is impossible for me to do this with the inscrutable Orientals, and particularly the Japanese. Therefore, I want all of you present here to pledge yourselves to make a sacrifice for your country, the United States of America. Promise to give up your freedom, if necessary, in order to prove your loyalty." Then and now, to me that was an indefensible racist blow. I could understand it, but I could not accept it. And some of us present objected, and Walter Tsukamoto, then the national president of the Japanese American Citizens League, declared that this would be a betrayal of American constitutional principles. Governor Olson said, "It would be for your own protection. If we did not move to confine you, there would be violence and bloodshed and, in view of Pearl Harbor, many of you might be killed."

When I told this to Joe Shinoda, who was a member of our newspaper editorial board, he responded, "Tell that dumb jerk of a governor that, if I had my choice and had to be killed, I'd rather be killed by neighbors that knew me than by strangers regarding me from outside a barbed wire enclosure." Joe Shinoda never saw the inside of a relocation center. He beat the curfew and the deadline and fled with his family to the interior country, to Red Bluff and Denver, Colorado, from whence he continued to direct his multimillion dollar business, the San Lorenzo Nursery.

By way of closing my lecture, I would like to offer a final recollection. At UCLA I took a course given by Professor Charles Titus on "The Columbian Picture," a theory developed by a political science professor at Columbia University. He devoted six months of lecturing to what he said was the school of thought that believed in the inevitability of war between the United States and Japan. As I looked at my course notes during World War II in the confines of the relocation center, it seemed to me that some of the quotations I had copied sounded like a voice of prophecy. The quotations came from a book that was published in 1909 called The Valor of Ignorance by a white racist of that day-- Homer Lea--who gave substance to William Randolph Hearst's campaign. Though Lea was a racist, he saw the essential vice in our policy toward Japanese immigration. "By making the Japanese ineligible for citizenship, we had created caste in a republic. The secondary consequences were of even greater importance. The creation of an inferior caste by political disfranchisement soon permeates every phase of daily existence. Those who are disfranchised are treated by the populace, not alone with social unconcern but with indignities. Municipalities will direct restrictive ordinances against them so that they become the natural prey not only of the lawless elements but also of the police. Their status already being fixed in public opinion, their voice in protestations soon dies away in hoarse and broken whispers. When a class or race finds itself in a republic without political franchise, then as a race or class its rights are ground into broken dust. To expect the Japanese to submit to indignities is to be pitifully incomprehensive of their national character." Homer Lea saw clearly that the military in Japan were using the situation in California to lay the basis for war with the United States.

HANSEN: Now, Mr. Tanaka will field any questions that you have.

STUDENT: I was wondering if you plan to tell us about your experience in the camp.

TANAKA: Yes, I'd be glad to. My family was evacuated to Manzanar. We were given an opportunity to go to the Santa Anita Assembly Center and, in the process of making a pre-evacuation inspection, I ran into the glorious opportunity of occupying a place that was said to be the stall in which Seabiscuit, the famous racehorse, was kept. (laughter) But they hadn't cleaned it properly, so I declined the honor, and we went to Manzanar. We were there from April 23 until December 6, 1942. Initially my job there was . . . . Well, we arrived there after some of the earlier people had gone. We went on the assumption that they would give us jobs for which we thought we had some experience, but the experience of evacuation had made those of us who were identified with the "Establishment" within the Japanese community somewhat unpopular. And Joe Masaoka and I, who had applied for work on the staff of the Manzanar Free Press, were told that we could do two things: either sweep the floor or deliver the papers. So we opted for delivering the papers, and we did so for two months. Then the War Relocation Authority offered the job of becoming what they called "documentary historians," and this was a job that they said would entail writing daily reports about camp activities and turning them over to a gentleman in Washington by the name of Solon Kimball, who headed up, I think, a department called Community Services for the WRA. It was explained to us that it was really a part of a research project inspired by Dr. Robert Redfield from the University of Chicago, an anthropologist, and therefore Joe and I had an opportunity to continue our education. What we didn't realize at the time was that we would soon be identified as informers, spies and dogs, people who were abusing or invading the privacy of the evacuees. As a consequence, when the riot broke out on the eve of the anniversary of Pearl Harbor, both he and I were on the death list--not at the top of the list but about in the middle--and we were removed for our safety and placed in protective custody at an abandoned CCC camp in Death Valley.

This is altogether too brief a sketch of our life inside the camp. My personal recollection of being at that place was one of distaste and frustration and a belief that it was really an outdoor jail. However, I should say that while my eyesight was fixed on the barbed wire and the armed guards and the watchtowers, I had a father-in-law who was an artist, and he could see only the beauty of Mount Whitney and Mount Williamson, and he painted those things. Out of the experience of Manzanar came a great deal of beauty in his life. It seemed to me that there must be a lesson somewhere in the contrast between the way that we each reacted. But he was not a citizen; he was an alien afforded the privilege of spending the war years in safety and confinement at the camp, but I felt that there must be a place on the outside for me.

Camp experience was something that I think many people--the parents of many of you here--can tell you what it was like in different camps around the country. Recently, I was impressed by the conflict among some people who feel that we should call them "relocation centers" and others who feel they should be called "concentration camps." For those of us who equate concentration camps with the horrors of Belsen and

Dachau—I had the privilege of serving the American Friends Service Committee in Chicago after being released from the camp as a volunteer worker to assist in evacuating some refugees who had been in these camps in Europe—we find it extremely difficult to equate our experience with the horrors of people who were in European concentration camps. But since I am no semantic expert, I leave it to those who find meaning in whatever definition that they want to give to the words, and I have no quarrel with people who say we were in concentration camps. But they were not of the same variety as the contemporary European experience. I don't know whether I've given you an answer to your question.

STUDENT: Since you were a historian and you were in the position of observing events and recording them, would you amplify a little bit on the situation at Manzanar, in particular some of the forces that led up to the eruption that you discussed, the subsequent killing of two of the internees, the wounding of ten others, and the threats and counter-threats that went on within the camp?

TANAKA: Well, someone told me when I was gathering research data for Dorothy Thomas on the incidence of neuro-psychiatric cases among the evacuees—I was sent to the Illinois State Hospital at Kankakee and went to other places where some of the victims, the psychological victims, of evacuation were held in custody and confinement—that all of us, the ten thousand of us behind barbed wire and watchtowers at Manzanar, suffered from—I don't know, I've never studied psychology—an anxiety neurosis. They said we were all a little bit nuts, that confinement does this to you, life in that type of atmosphere. Here were people from various grades and backgrounds, from different economic levels. The only thing they had in common was the fact that the American government had chosen to say "You are Japanese." In the case of some men, even if they were one-sixteenth Japanese and were blue-eyed and blond—and this was the case at the Pomona Assembly Center—they still were regarded as Japanese. The rectifying of this type of Nuremburg classification, of what the blood made you, threw people who had very little in common other-wise suddenly all together.

There was a lack of privacy when we first went to Manzanar. The barracks were not actually completed. There were terrible windstorms that swept through the Owens Valley which brought dust through the cracks in the door. I think there were two months running when we suffered from diarrhea. The food was not properly prepared. However, as camp life settled down—and I think you'll find in the literature on the camps that it did become stabilized—then I think there were the more normal kinds of complaints: stealing of food, both by some evacuees within the camp, and particularly by Caucasian administrators who were accused, whether rightly or wrongly, of pre-empting food that should have gone to the evacuees. These were sources of trouble and grievances and, while the newspaper headlines reporting on the riots and the disturbances made it appear political, I think that there were really more elementary reasons for much of the unrest and disturbance. I think that the overriding factor was that people, like Joe Masaoka and myself and others who were given the job of reporting and recording, were then in the unenviable position of being regarded as informers and as people who were placed by the Caucasian administration to conduct surveillance. I think in most of the camps, when you had an active Japanese American Citizens League group telling the young men in the camps, "You are American citizens, and you owe it to your government to fight for the United States and to volunteer for armed service," you had a response that might be described, as you have probably noticed, as one either of disbelief or a qualified willingness to at least hear. But, by and large, this was not a popular thing to propose. I know that in the three months before we were driven out of the camp, Joe and I made it a point to speak at mess halls--this is what they called the cafeterias-- throughout the camp to small groups urging young men to volunteer, because this had been the policy of the JACL in Salt Lake City. I had a prewar friend (Joe Kurihara) who was convinced that Joe Masaoka and I were out of our minds, and he felt very deeply about this. He would follow us and, after we had made our presentations and told the audience, "The only way out of this place is to prove, we must go the second mile and prove that we belong here, and we must identify ourselves as Americans." This man would follow, and he would say, "I served my country, the United States of America, in World War I. I fought and bled on the battlefields of France, and I know what it means to sacrifice one's life and be willing to give my life for this country. But since this government, out of its lack of wisdom, has seen fit to regard me as a 'Jap,' by God, I'm going to be a good Jap, 100 percent! I will never do anything to fight for the United States. I am going to return to Japan. I've never been there, but I'm going to go to Japan, and if you listen to these young idiots who have just preceded me you're going to find yourselves in other camps like this because there are people in Washington today . . . ." And he quoted Senator Rankin of Mississippi and Senator Stewart of Tennessee who had proposed bills in the Congress of the United States to exclude forever any person of Japanese descent from American citizenship, so this was an argument against which no voice raised by any of us who believed otherwise could prevail. And I think ultimately as they conducted these riots, those of us who represented a minority opinion in the camp could do nothing but hold fast. We might get on the outside, where we might be able to at least rejoin an ideological majority. And I think the riots did that. They drove us out and gave us a chance to regain our wits in a more friendly environment.

STUDENT: After you left the camp, did you feel your life was threatened by people who were resettled in other parts of the country, since the animus was so great at the time? Did you feel a continuing sort of threat?

TANAKA: No, I did not. I had the most peculiar experience. I was rescued from Death Valley, because we had been trying to get out of Manzanar from the day that we were put in, and I began to write letters. I wrote letters to no avail. Then one day I got a questionnaire, a form signed, I think, by Lieutenant Colonel Karl Bendetsen of the Western Defense Command in which I was asked to renounce my allegiance to the Emperor of Japan, and by so doing could then gain at least consideration of an application or petition to get out. I wrote at the bottom of it that I refused to do so on the ground that I never owed allegiance to him. It got me nowhere. I think there were others living in the camp who said the same thing.

We were finally released, and there was a great deal of antagonism toward us individually. There must have been at least fifty of us who were removed for our safety to Death Valley, California. I had hoped then to go on the outside and support my family through whatever job that I could get which was identified with the war effort, and I was offered a position in Washington, D.C. with what was then called the OWI, the Office of War Information.

En route to Washington, D.C., we were allowed to stay at the Quaker hostel on Belden Avenue in Chicago, and there, for the first time, I encountered people who, in the midst of war and bloodshed and all of this hating, seemed somehow to have a tranquility and a serenity and a kind of peacefulness that impressed me so much that I volunteered to work with the Quakers for the next several years. I never did get to Washington, D.C. While in camp, I had tried to volunteer for the service and had been told that certain people could qualify for a commission in the Navy. All such thoughts then disappeared. I did not. So in consequence, my service in Chicago was to help the people that came out of Europe and also those who came out of the relocation centers to find jobs and housing as they were being relocated. Curiously enough, the man who had urged the death of persons like Joe Masaoka and myself, a gentleman named Joe Kurihara, this very eloquent man who spoke in the camps, who had gone to Tule Lake camp and had been repatriated—well, not repatriated, but shipped on the Gripsholm over to Japan—subsequently contacted me through the Red Cross and asked for some testimony as to the fact that he had at one time been a loyal American citizen and now sought to return to the United States (which was provided). This was still during the war. So I don't recall ever having been threatened as a result of what had happened in Manzanar. I will admit that I took out more insurance than what I would normally do. (laughter)

STUDENT: It seemed that one of Mr. Kurihara's complaints at the time was that the efforts of historians such as yourself were responsible for federal intelligence agencies that were present in the camps intimidating the Kibei agitators especially, and that information was passed on to the FBI, perhaps through the naiveness of the reporters. Could you comment on that a little please?

TANAKA: Yes. I think his apprehensions were justified. Right at the time, I didn't think so; but in the light of . . . . Well, let me say this. You know, when I had been jailed shortly after Pearl Harbor, I felt that, you know, I had been fingered by somebody. And I looked around for someone to blame, not realizing that, of course, much of it was due to circumstances for which I was partly responsible myself. I had been to Washington, D.C.; I had said things; I had seen people; but I nevertheless looked for people to blame this on, because it was a very unhappy thing for me to be jailed without due process of law. We used to meet with Joe Kurihara, and he would say, "Why don't you and Joe quit writing these damn reports, because they're going to use them in kinds of

ways that will be detrimental to us." At that time, we couldn't see it.
We said, "Well, you know, we have an obligation here to show our best
face to the public because we have a public relations function. If we
say we have a camouflage factory or we're growing, whatever, rubber
plants (guayule) for the war effort, these facts ought to get out, and
the fact that we're chronicling these events in no way hurts us in this
camp." We were accused of a great deal of activity that, you know, we
shrugged off because we knew they were not true. Yet we had no answer
to them because people could tell others . . . . We were not conversant
or fluent in the Japanese language. There was this terrible division
within the camp between those who spoke and thought in the English
language and those who spoke and thought in the Japanese. In the midst
of war, it was an impossible situation. I think that there will really
never be an objective judgment as to whether or not what we did was
producing results that we had intended. For myself, I don't think that
we did. But this is, you know, like the usual writing of an objective
history of the Civil War from the Southern point of view. (laughter)

STUDENT: Did you own property at the time, and if so was the property
returned to you when you returned?

TANAKA: Well, that's very interesting. I was involved in two pieces of
property at the time we were evacuated. Along with three partners, I
owned a corporation, the Osage Produce Company, which was a commissioned
brokerage house in the Seventh Street Terminal in Los Angeles. Back in
1940 and 1941, a business that did eight hundred thousand dollars a
year was a very substantial business, and I was one-fourth owner of that.
My three partners had enlisted my participation in the business because
I could easily obtain what was needed then to make it a going business--
a bond. It was then at the time rather difficult for people of Japanese
descent to get this from Sacramento. We had some twenty-two employees.
We had bought the business from an alien Japanese named Ozawa and, looking about for something that would be typically American, we picked an
Indian name in the same sequence in the telephone directory and said,
"Well, the Osages are Indians and they're American." So we named it
Osage Produce Company. In the year that we lost that business, we were
making about forty thousand dollars profit a year, which we split among
the four of us. When war came, it was very interesting. We would hear
one evening Mayor Fletcher Bowron on the radio saying, "We have a problem
in the City of Los Angeles. If you think that Pearl Harbor was a disaster
and the fifth column Quisling in Norway was a disaster, then ponder this:
We are sitting with the food on our tables being controlled by the Japs
in the produce industry. They could put arsenic in the tomatoes, and we
would all be dead tomorrow morning." This type of thought being aired
over the radio made it quite evident that things were on the way for our
removal. If all of us were evacuated and our employees were all of
Japanese descent, we were gone. So we sold our business for about ten
cents on the dollar. I am told that my share was bought either by the
fellow who was then head football coach at UCLA or a Los Angeles produce
man, Henry Rivers, and I think that my partners in the business, all sub-
stantially more affluent than I, never went to a relocation camp, but

they eventually lost their part in the business also.

We lived in a home in Glendale, and we left this in the tender care of a neighbor. But we were eventually forced to sell. I use the word "forced" advisedly. When we moved to Chicago, knowing that it would be years before we might be able to return--and by then quite thoroughly fed up with the West Coast and finding that America was a great deal larger than the West Coast--we decided to seek a permanent home in the Midwest. So we sold it; whether we sold at a loss or a profit, I've never really been able to decide.

STUDENT: I think it was Ellen Endo, English language editor of the Rafu Shimpo, who recently quoted you on your position with regard to the Japanese-American community as one of "involvement but not commitment." Do you have any ideas on that?

TANAKA: Well, I'll tell you, I was trying to be funny, and it wasn't very successful. They asked me to speak, you know, on behalf of Akira Komai at the UCLA Research Library, and I said, "I'm not really fit to do this because I was at the Rafu for only six years, and I ended my tenure as editor way back in 1942, which is a long time ago." And I said, "This reminds me of a story that Joe Blatchford tells. He said, 'I met a gentleman last night who was a kamikaze pilot, and he had flown twenty-two missions.' Joe asked him 'How come twenty-two missions?' and he said, 'Mr. Blatchford, I want you to know there's a difference between involvement and commitment!'" (laughter) You see, I have to confess, I don't get the Rafu Shimpo. They don't send it to me today, and my reading matter is somewhat limited in that regard, so I didn't know she had written that. But I did say that at this dedication because it is true. Mr. Komai came to Chicago in 1945 and asked me to return to help edit his paper. We had a long discussion and I told him that, if I were true to his ideals, we Japanese Americans should seek to widen our horizons and to find a niche outside of the narrow confines of the West Coast. He should allow me to stay in Chicago and experience more of a life where one wasn't a member of the Yellow Peril. And he agreed. So what I was trying to say then was that perhaps this, you know, tagged me as having been only involved and not really committed. I think that, at the time that I was there at the paper, I was committed, and I feel that here again we're involved in the meaning of words. Does that answer your question?

STUDENT: I have another question. During the time that you were at Santa Anita, there was a group of people who started a study of democracy. It was headed by Bob Fujii, now with the Chicago Shimpo, and I think another person was Joe Koide. I may be mistaken. Were you at Santa Anita at that time? If you were, what was your position with regard to that study?

TANAKA: Well, I know Bob Fujii quite well, and I know Joe Koide. My recollection of them was that belonging to a newspaper staff that represented . . . . You know, here again we use the word advisedly, the "Establishment" within the Japanese community regarded them as Communists.

And it turned out that they were. Not just Communists in the sense that people called them that; they were. I mean, Joe had been trained in Moscow, and he is one of the most fascinating people and a great teacher. In those days it wasn't revealed that he was, and he didn't acknowledge it. Today he does, because he served the United States and, by reason of this background during World War II, when Bob Fujii was under attack by some of the people in Chicago in the 1950s, he was hard-put to get people to sign petitions on his behalf, and I was one of those who did. Bob and S. I. Hayakawa and I used to meet for lunch from time to time during the year when the Japanese American Citizens League was seeking to have the McCarren-Walter Immigration Act of 1952 passed, and we happened to be among the dissidents who didn't believe that the JACl represented a wide enough view, that they had taken the position that, well, the most practical thing is to get this for ourselves. And so they had gone to bed, politically speaking, with people whom we regarded as racists and bigots. But in the long run they were right and we were wrong because, though we may not have been wrong, we weren't practical, and they obtained citizenship for the Issei where perhaps the course of action that we advocated might not have done so. But for Bob Fujii and Joe Koide, I have nothing but personal friendship for them and admiration for what they did during the war.

STUDENT: You started to mention Eleanor Roosevelt, and I wondered what was the occasion of you meeting her.

TANAKA: Well, it was this futile quest to get support in high places for the position that our newspaper had taken, and that when war comes surely there must be some measure of relief for our parents. Here they were, enemy aliens ineligible for citizenship. Does their permanent resident status mean anything? We Nisei assumed then that our position was unassailable, that we were citizens and that our citizenship rights would be protected. But we recognized that the Issei, our parents, were not protected. And I think this was the reason that we went to Washington, D.C. and talked to people so that we might share with them not only our concern but give them the facts about what this Japanese-American minority on the West Coast was and where we stood.

STUDENT: Was that just after the Second World War began or was it prewar?

TANAKA: No, no, this was before the outbreak of war. This was within weeks of Pearl Harbor.

STUDENT: You also said something about meeting or talking to or seeing William Randolph Hearst. I didn't quite catch the occasion of that.

TANAKA: The occasion was the visit of a Japanese publisher from Tokyo who Mr. Hearst was hosting. The publisher of the Rafu Shimpo accompanied him, and I went along to assist in interpretation.

STUDENT: Well, you indicated that he was rather racist in his attitude. Why would he host a Japanese person?

TANAKA: Well, you know, it's like "some of my best friends are."

STUDENT: Did he want to establish some type of relationship of understanding? I don't understand what the deal was.

TANAKA: Well, if you read the life of Mr. Hearst, he was a very gracious host. He regarded the people of Japanese descent in this country not as citizens or permanent residents but just simply immigrants who really belonged to Japan. But that didn't prevent him from being a gracious host to a visitor from Japan.

STUDENT: I'd like to hear you comment, please, about William Randolph Hearst and the coming of the war. I was a young child at the time, living in Glendale, and all of a sudden we were told . . . . Well, you said you were in a dark cell on December 8, but we were in a dark house on December 8 because we thought the war, you know, we were having "air raids," supposedly. Mr. Hearst's paper used to come out and say how clannish the Japanese people were, how the heart of the Japanese community knew the war was coming, that they were going along with the emperor, and that we had to get rid of them. You also spoke of an anxiety neurosis, and I and many another schoolchild had this same neurosis because every time we heard a siren we thought we were going into an air raid. I would just like to know if there ever has been a study made or if you know of any study on propaganda and the effects that it had on the West Coast just after Pearl Harbor.

TANAKA: No, I'm not . . . . I've done no writing for the last fifteen or twenty years. The only writing I do now is escrow writing. My being up here and talking to you university people . . . . I thought it was a little bit funny as I was coming down here, because really it's like a used car salesman coming in here and talking to you about theology. (laughter) It's true that I own a company called The School Industrial Press. I do none of the work. I happen to be in the area of real estate development and investments. I have a company called Gramercy Enterprises and our publishing company, which was organized in 1955 when I moved from Chicago to Los Angeles. It is largely in the field of trade publications. We still do some subsidized publication, but I don't spend five minutes in a month in that area, and it's very kind, but this is what surprized me when my daughter, who does that work, had signed me up to come here and said, "You have notes from the evacuation and resettlement and stuff. Why don't you get up and read them?" She thought this is what I could do. I don't know whether I am adequately answering your question, but I do know of one book written by a friend with whom I served on the university staff, and that was Tom Shibutani. He wrote a study of the evacuation called Rumors in a Crisis Situation, and I am sure that the literature is full of the effect of propaganda. I remember Morton Grodzins with whom I shared many years of pleasant exchange of opinions. Morton was on the staff of the University of California study. We were together at the meetings of that staff in Salt Lake City. He was a neighbor of mine in Chicago. When he came out with his book, Americans Betrayed, it brought the presidents of the University of Chicago and the University of

California, Chancellors Robert Hutchins and Robert Gordon Sproul, into an exchange of correspondence, because Dorothy Thomas had felt that Morton Grodzins had pirated this material and he was in her way. They had a falling out now that Morton had written this book to be published by the University of Chicago Press. The University of California had three books of its own that were to be published, and California tried to stop Chicago from publishing this particular book but they couldn't. Morton Grodzins wrote a book called The Loyal and the Disloyal, and I believe in that you would find references to what the impact of propaganda and the newspapers had, or their effect on public opinion.

STUDENT: What about your newspaper? Were you able to continue to publish until about May 1942, or not?

TANAKA: No, I think April 2 was our last issue.

STUDENT: Would the Rafu Shimpo have the prewar issues in their archives?

TANAKA: Well, I think Mrs. Patricia Courteau, who is present tonight, can tell you that. She's an authority on the Rafu; I'm not.

COURTEAU: I believe UCLA has them all the way back.

TANAKA: Well, then in that case they are microfilmed back to 1914.

STUDENT: Would it be possible to speculate as to what would have happened if there had been more resistance to confinement or evacuation?

TANAKA: Well, I've tried to figure that one out. Your guess is as good as mine. It's very possible . . . . I think the logistics, you know, the physical difficulty of imprisoning 112,000 resisting people would have been an enormous task, and if among those people there had been more of what the Japanese call "Yamato Damashii," that is, more of a kamikaze spirit that said, "You're not going to move us, so come in and shoot us or carry us . . . ." I really doubt it. If you read the literature from the Supreme Court decisions on down, if you look and if you think back, you see, even by the time we were ready to come back here--and I thought I would never be ready to come back to the West Coast--people were being shot at and killed, and there were a number of deaths, and I'm quite certain that other speakers, if they haven't already, will tell you of the violence. I think that public violence was being fostered and encouraged by the people at the top who ran this country at that time who certainly have . . . . I don't know whether we would have had an early-day version of the My Lai massacre here; some people said we could have had. The whole point is that I think those of us who had anything to do with it felt that the old Chinese adage, "He who fights and runs away lives to fight another day," this really must have been a part of the thinking. I don't really know. I have found that speculation on it leaves me nowhere, so I've stopped speculating.

STUDENT: This is a question on an aspect that I don't see mentioned in the books on evacuation, but I have come across it in doing some interviewing, and I just wonder what your opinion of it is. A couple of the people that I have interviewed told me that, during that period when there was no legal immigration permitted at all, their parents came in illegally, and naturally, if they wanted to come, that was the only way they could. In one instance the Nisei woman that I interviewed said that her father was always very worried about the fact that he had come in that way and was always willing to do anything that authorities wanted him to do. In fact, even after the evacuation was over, he still worried about it until he died. Do you have any opinion about the influence of that kind of thing, whether or not that was a factor? I realize that there can't be any statistics on it, but do you think that was a big factor with many families?

TANAKA: Well, no one ever made a head count of the people who were so-called illegal immigrants. I'm certain that as individuals, any of us who were related to people who were in here without a passport or visa certainly must have been affected by it. My son-in-law is assistant professor of engineering at UCLA and took his degree at MIT and Stanford and teaches there in the summer, and his father was an illegal immigrant. He tells me stories about how he had served in the Russo-Japanese War, and he found that he had his belly full of serving in the Japanese army, and nothing could be worse than that, so he jumped ship and landed in this country. A most enterprising man; he raised his children, and he has two sons that went to MIT and have doctorates, and his daughters are equally educated; I believe they got their degrees in education, and he worked long and hard and suffered and struggled, but he has always been, until citizenship became available, an illegal alien. So I'm certain that this must have been . . . . I don't know whether . . . are you referring to whether it had any effect on evacuation?

STUDENT: Yes, I'm just wondering if that situation might have also kept people from resisting who might have resisted.

TANAKA: Oh, I'm certain of that. But then at that point, when people were agitating, and this was a very prevailing point of view then: "Get rid of them." You know. "Get rid of them. Take them to some island and dump them and blow the island up. They don't belong here." And this was not an isolated opinion; it was almost universal. There was not a single voice raised on the West Coast of any responsible newspaper that said, "These are American citizens; they belong here. Their rights ought to be protected." You know, it was Pearl Harbor. People had died. Around the world the fear was that Japanese militarism was on the march and would one day shortly threaten this West Coast. You mentioned darkened rooms on the night of the air raid fears. This was the climate in which we lived, so we sat there, like the Japanese carp, that didn't wriggle when it was pulled up and were on the cutting block.

STUDENT: I'd like to get your views on rumors that the JACL members sold out the Issei leaders during the war, especially after they destroyed the records.

TANAKA: Well, I think this was a widely-held . . . . By destroying the records, what do you mean?

STUDENT: Well, like those records belonging to community leaders or members of certain organizations.

TANAKA: I have no opinion because I am no authority on the JACL. I was identified with the JACL at the outbreak of war, and throughout the years I have maintained my membership and have supported its policies. I think that the JACL, along with everyone who was identified in any way in the camps with the camp admistration, was an unpopular target of criticism because when you're miserable, you know, JACL in one sense represented privilege because of its access to people in high places. I once walked the streets of Chicago soliciting memberships for the JACL and ran into a very imposing array of arguments, why Japanese Americans who were being relocated in Chicago and now were reasonably well settled would have nothing to do with that organization. I think that this situation has changed, but if you're referring to all the adverse criticisms of that organization in postwar years, I wouldn't say anything that would hurt them, you know . . . .

STUDENT: This was during World War II, I guess just after the war began, that the Issei leaders destroyed all their records so that they wouldn't be picked up by the FBI. Rumor was that the JACL had sold out the Issei. So that's why I asked. What did you know about it?

TANAKA: Do you mean as to the relationship between the Issei destroying? They did more than that; they destroyed . . . .

STUDENT: No, the relation between the Issei being picked up by the FBI and sent to these detention camps like Missoula and . . . .

HANSEN: I think his question is about arrest of the Issei, isn't it? At the time of the evacuation, the JACL acted as informers not only in the camps but prior to the camps, by pointing the finger at certain Issei whose names were then given to the FBI, who thereafter put them into detention camps.

TANAKA: Well, you're right in thinking that this was the prevailing point of view among most evacuees at one time or another.

STUDENT: In fact, they said that they were getting twenty-five dollars a head or something. That was the rumor.

TANAKA: And you know, the truth of the matter is--if truth can be assessed--that we at the Rafu Shimpo had published a directory on the 2600th anniversary of the founding of the Empire of Japan, a very respectable book, and in it we published the pictures and biographies of every leading Japanese Issei figure in Southern California. In it we also ran the names and addresses and telephone numbers of just about every organization in that Southern California community. You know, this was a community that I think Frank Miyamoto, the sociologist from Washington, says was characterized by an in-group solidarity, the kind of which you seldom saw in American society, because we had been, as a result of California's long history of racism and anti-Japanese legislation and movements, that this was what we were. We knew everybody. We were one big club, and to say that it was necessary for anyone to point out Issei was patently ridiculous. But in the years after the war, long after it was a controversial matter, I had an occasion to meet with people in Washington, D.C. who had something to do with that kind of selection of Issei. My father-in-law, an artist who had worked for RKO, who was probably the most harmless kind of person, belonged to an archery club, and he was arrested by the FBI and, for the duration of the war, was sent first to Missoula, Montana and to Santa Fe, New Mexico and ultimately, through the representation of the Quakers, we got him back to the Manzanar relocation camp. But this was the basis on which people were picked up. And to say that, you know, if there were individual Nisei engaged in that kind of activity, then I would be glad to know. I know we did some research and said everyone in this situation accuses another, but it is pretty hard to make the accusation stick. But there were people that I thought fingered me, and this wasn't true either. That's the only comment I can make.

STUDENT: When you were in Washington before Pearl Harbor, was it ever indicated to you that the idea of a concentration camp was already a preconceived notion of the government, or did it seem to you more of a snowballing propaganda thing after Pearl Harbor?

TANAKA: I never heard one word. I remember being in the office of Senator Elbert Thomas of Utah, and I had an afternoon with members of his staff where I learned a good deal about--he had been a Mormon missionary in Japan for some thirty or thirty-five years, and I learned about Mormonism. He had two very wonderful young people on the staff who explained to me their marriage in the Temple in Salt Lake City. When you get married there, it's not just for this lifetime, it's forever. That just shattered my ideas about what Mormon marriages were. (laughter) But these people and many others, I was with Congressman Jerry Voorhis and his staff, and maybe I just saw the wrong people. I was trying to see Congressman Rankin; I didn't get to. But there were many people who told me that they regretted that our relations with Japan were so bad and nowhere did anyone give me any idea that we would be deprived of our rights, that we would be put into concentration camps or relocation centers, that we would be treated as enemy aliens. If there had been, it certainly would have been news, and I certainly would have reported it, but there was no such indication. It came after Pearl Harbor.

STUDENT: I'm not sure of the source, but I've heard that a document that you had turned in was used as prime evidence for, I believe it was, the Tolan Committee to justify the concentration camps. Can you comment on that particular document?

TANAKA: Well, that's news to me. I remember appearing before several commission hearings, and I also remember that State Senator Jack Tenney published a red book of subversive organizations--during and after the war, at taxpayers' expense--in which my name appeared several times as an enemy agent of the Japanese government or a special agent of such, but if the Tolan Committee did use anything that I wrote as a means for justifying evacuation, it comes as news to me now. I will say this, I had a very peculiar experience. In 1936 there was a congressional election, I think, on the west side of Los Angeles, and one of the candidates was a man for whom I worked as a reader in the Department of Political Science at UCLA, Ordean Rockey. He ran for Congress. And I, in my enthusiasm to help him, volunteered. The opposition--I think the gentleman's name was Dockweiler who ran and won--insisted that anyone with a name like Togo Tanaka only proved how subversive Rockey was, because Togo was a name of a Japanese admiral and Tanaka was the name of the famous Tanaka Memorial, and this was a Japanese version of Mein Kampf. Well, that was the first time I had heard that, but during World War II, when I had discovered to my relief that I was not going to be drafted because I was now a staff member of the Quakers who didn't believe I should make a contribution to the war, I met with Robert Walker King, who was in Chicago as a delegate for Henry Wallace at the Democratic National Convention. He called me and said, "You know, you're never going to get called by your draft board in Glendale because they don't believe you're for real, either. You've just got the wrong name."

What you tell me now comes as a--well, it doesn't come as a surprise because all through the years I have been confronted with statements which may have some basis in fact--but I think . . . . Well, this one may very well have, but I'm not aware of it.

STUDENT: When you went to talk to Eleanor Roosevelt, did any such activity ever make the newspapers? Did they ever come out or was this kept highly secret?

TANAKA: Well, as I remember, our paper reported it, but we weren't news.

STUDENT: I'd like to know what was happening in Japan in the twenties and thirties that caused Japan to march on China?

TANAKA: Well, I don't feel qualified to answer that because I've read probably no more and maybe much less than members of this class.

HANSEN: I think we'll have to rule that question somewhat, not irrelevant, but not tangent to the topic at hand. I don't think we can really go into a discussion which is more appropriate to a course on Japanese history. I don't mean to be abrasive about it, but I think that has to be the ruling.

STUDENT: Sir, were you present at the Manzanar Riot when the short period of actual rioting took place?

TANAKA: Yes, I was.

STUDENT: I've read several sources on that and most of them beg the issue. Was there provocation on the part of the internees that directly resulted in the shootings, provocation of the sort that would call out that sort of a reprisal?

TANAKA: When it happened, it happened near the Administration Center, and I was not a witness to it. I was at the far end of the camp in Block 36.

STUDENT: It seems like witnesses to it are short at hand, because nobody seems to say one way or the other. There seems to be some talk of a jeep being aimed at the guards, which may or may not have happened. I've always wondered about this.

HANSEN: You compiled a report that appears in Dorothy Swain Thomas's study that has your name appended to it. You certainly had access to some information. As I follow the story, you must not have been anywhere near it, as you say, directly, but you were apparently being hidden from . . . .

TANAKA: I was in the barrack of Reverend Ralph Smeltzer, a Brethren minister who obtained a car and took me out of camp. The shooting, I'm told, was accidental. Well, I thank you very much for the courtesy.

HANSEN: I'd like to thank Mr. Tanaka for a very, very enjoyable talk this evening. I think that he very graciously handled all the questions and answered them extensively, which is rare for any speaker.

A FRIEND OF THE AMERICAN WAY

AN INTERVIEW WITH HERBERT V. NICHOLSON

INTRODUCTION

Herbert Victor Nicholson was interviewed by Betty E. Mitson in his home at 1639 Locust Street, Pasadena, California on five occasions beginning on April 19, 1973.

Nicholson was born in 1892 in Rochester, New York, of Quaker parentage. At the onset of World War I, he was a graduate student in mathematics and economics at the University of Michigan. In 1915 he discontinued his studies and went to Japan to fill a secretarial role to Gilbert Bowles, a Quaker missionary who was then Secretary of the Japan Peace Society. In that capacity and, also, as Secretary of the Fellowship of Reconciliation, Nicholson met many Japanese officials, both civilian and military. In 1920 he married Madeline Waterhouse who was a Congregational missionary, and they continued teaching English and working with farm boys in the Mito area. Attempts to enlighten the local Japanese about the adventures of their army in China caused Nicholson considerable harassment by local police. Largely due to international tensions, the family, now including a daughter and two sons, returned to reside in Pasadena in 1940.

The series of interviews with Nicholson cover the whole spectrum of his work with people of Japanese ancestry, from its beginnings in 1915 to date. But the main focus in the present selections is upon an aspect of the Japanese-American wartime evacuation which most publications have dealt with only as incidental to the main story. Beginning with Pearl Harbor and continuing in subsequent days and weeks, several thousand Issei, both female and male, were arrested and placed in Department of Justice detention facilities. Classified as "potentially dangerous enemy aliens," they are largely a forgotten group. Nicholson's narrative is particularly important, therefore, because it illuminates this neglected area in the historiography dealing with the evacuation; it provides considerable detail about the people arrested, places of detention, conditions of imprisonment, administrative personalities, and Department of Justice hearings. In addition, the last part highlights Nicholson's visits to the 442nd Regiment and an effective letter writing campaign which he launched to open the relocation centers and permit those of Japanese ancestry to again reside on the West Coast.

In order to illustrate the way in which they were particularly prepared for their wartime endeavors on behalf of interned people, the selections begin with the experiences of the Nicholson family just prior to Pearl Harbor.

MR. AND MRS. HERBERT V. NICHOLSON

N: We got back to America from Japan in summer, August 1940.

M: When you came back, did you have anything in mind that you were going to do?

N: We had nothing at all. We had been dropped by the Mission Board in Philadelphia. They were a little bit scared of me. They didn't have any money again; they were about broke. They told me in January that they were going to drop us that year. They had decided to pay our salary to the end of 1939, and then we were to be on our own. We came home without any prospect of any particular work, but we did want to work for the Japanese. So in the fall, various people were doing things to help us. A niece took us to see the principal of a Christian school in Los Angeles. It didn't take long to find out we wouldn't fit in with him. He was a very nice looking man with a nice beard-- looked like some of the pictures of Jesus. We happened to discuss war issues and, when he found out I was a pacifist, he was not interested in having me at his school. No pacifists teaching his kids! So that fell through, and I didn't want a teaching job anyway. So we spent the fall there.

. . . . .

Then we were looking around trying to find where the Japanese were, where we could get in touch with them.

M: Now, you speak the Japanese language?

N: We speak Japanese. There was a little group of Quakers in New Jersey where we belonged, this Quaker meeting in Haddonfield, New Jersey. They call it a quarterly meeting--they would meet four times a year-- and they continued to give us fifty dollars a month. They had begun that in 1915 when I first went to Japan.

. . . . .

So they continued this fifty dollars a month when we returned and that was our only visible means of support, with three children going to school and living here. Of course, dollars meant a lot more than they do now, but it was a remarkable thing that we never went into debt, and we always had plenty to eat in the house. We never starved. We didn't have any luxuries, but we lived through that period with fifty dollars a month assured income.

. . . . .

Then just after Christmas we had a telephone message from a very fine Japanese pastor of a Methodist church in Los Angeles. He said that the pastor of the West Los Angeles Japanese Methodist Church had had a stroke, and they needed somebody right away to fill in. Could I possibly go over there and take charge and preach in English and Japanese and run this church beginning in January 1941? I said, "I'm not a Methodist; I'm a Quaker. I've never had theological training. I don't know how to preach in either English or Japanese, and I'm afraid I can not do it."

M: Do you mean you don't know how to preach the Methodist way?

N: No. I'd had no training in seminary or anything like that. I was not a preacher for Methodists. I was what they call a Quaker minister. We have what we call the recorded ministers, people that we think have a gift from God to preach, who will preach when the Spirit moves them. See, that's the idea. You don't preach at stated times and for pay-- to do that is what we call a "hireling ministry." We must not preach at stated times and for pay. But you go to a meeting and preach if the Spirit moves you to preach; if he doesn't, you don't. See, you have the freedom, and seminary education is not necessary. That was what my background was, so I turned it down. But he said, "Mr. Nicholson, come over and see me. I'd like to talk to you." So I went over and met Reverend Yamaka for the first time, and he was a Christian gentleman. I fell in love with him right away. We became closely attached to each other, and we had such a wonderful visit that I decided to go to this little church the first Sunday in January and try out as a Methodist, to preach in Japanese and English.

When I got up there to preach in Japanese, I found I had a Romaji testament to use. I could read Romaji very well. That's the Roman characters instead of written the Japanese way, you see. I could read that pretty well, so I began to read in that. Just in the middle of it, in came Yamaka, this wonderful preacher, the best Japanese preacher in California, and my knees began to shake. I didn't know what I was going to do, but he sat way in the back and smiled at me. And you know, that he encouraged me so much with his smile that I gave a little sermon in Japanese and I had an English one. We had lunch together and they decided to call me to be their preacher, so I said I would undertake it.

. . . . .

The Sunday School superintendent there was a very fine lady. She had a concern to get back to Japan before the war came on, and she left. So Madeline became the Sunday School superintendent. I preached in English and Japanese, and my wife had charge of the Sunday School and together we got forty dollars a month. That was pretty good pay! (laughter) Anyway, we weren't concerned about money because we weren't preaching for money. We did preach at stated times which was not according to Hoyle. But we surely didn't preach for money because we didn't have it. But we made some wonderful friends, and it was the most remarkable thing, before the war came, that I became acquainted with the Japanese Christian church leaders. I was one of the Methodist preachers. I went to the Church Federation meetings. I went to the annual meeting of the Church Federation. I got to know all these Japanese preachers, and it was a wonderful thing. That thing and the fact that I could speak Japanese and knew the Japanese culture, the Japanese background, had prepared us in a peculiar way to help them in wartime. We were prepared for that work.

. . . . .

We were there a year and a half with the church and in May of the next year, 1942, they had to go to Manzanar, and the church was finished.

. . . . .

M: Before we go to the wartime period, I want to ask you more about this church experience. About how big a congregation was it?

N: At that time, they had a great big, old house, and the old folks met in the living room. The young folks had built a little barrack, about eighty feet long. And the attendance at each service was about thirty Nisei, thirty Issei, and we had about one hundred in the Sunday School. We had a very large Sunday School. It was very nice, and we enjoyed it so much. Among the Issei there were some grand old people. Oh, we just loved those fine old folks, and they became very dear to us. And among the Nisei there were some very brilliant people.

There was a young man named Lafayette Noda who was studying for his Ph.D in chemistry. He's now a professor at Andover; a wonderful fellow and he was brilliant. He was a pacifist like I was. And there was a fellow named Jackson Takayanagi who was one good fellow; he's now a preacher. He was a pacifist or he became a pacifist while I was there, perhaps with my influence, I don't know. There was another fellow, Johnny Nagayama, who was a cripple from polio, a young boy still in high school. He was an only son, and his mother and father were saints, wonderful people. We had close connections with them. Then there was a boy named Tommy Yamada who was a very brilliant fellow, bright, at the top of his class at University High School in West Los Angeles. He was valedictorian for the February commencement, but the parents got so upset about this--the war had come on--that they said, "If he speaks as valedictorian at commencement, we're not going to go, and we won't let our kids go."

M: That was in the February following Pearl Harbor?

N: Yes. They felt so upset, you know, and so Tommy was not allowed to give the valedictorian speech.

M: Now, by the parents, you mean the Caucasian parents?

N: Caucasian parents. The high school parents who said, "If you allow a Jap to speak, we won't come to the thing. We'll have nothing to do with it." So they had to . . . . The teachers were fair, most of them. They thought it wasn't right. The teachers were splendid, but the parents were emotionally upset, you see. In fact the teachers were so good all through, here at Pasadena City College, when things broke out. We were so proud of the teachers and the student body as a whole, but the parents were the ones that upset the apple cart. But you know, Tommy Yamada went into government, and he was at the Pentagon Building as head of all the finances. He had a very important job, a very busy man, with a big salary. Now, just after the election last fall, he was put into the White House as head of a department that was just started to try to cut out bureaucratic red tape. Tommy was put in that job, the same fellow that wasn't allowed to give the valedictorian speech.

. . . . .

Tommy's mother is very dear to us. That big picture we have on the mantel was given to us by Mrs. Yamada. See, they were up at the camp at Manzanar.

M: Did Tommy stay the whole wartime period in the camp?

N: Oh, no. He soon got out. He didn't go with the Army volunteers--he was of high school age. He went out to college. I've forgotten what Tommy did, but he didn't stay long in the camp. The young people got out pretty quickly, but the old folks wouldn't move. But that's getting ahead of the story.

. . . . .

M: I wonder if at this stage we ought to cover anything else about the period before the bombing of Pearl Harbor?

N: Well, like everybody else, we were getting very much concerned about the situation, and the FBI had sent a man over to see me--I remember his name was Gardner--Mr. Gardner came in to see if I would join the FBI and work for them. I said, "I'd be interested in helping in some way, but what would they require?" He said, "Well, you couldn't live in California. You would have to leave the state." I said, "I'm not interested." "And you can't have any Japanese friends." I said, "That's absurd. Here's where I am. I know the people. That doesn't make sense to me. I'm not going to work for you." So that settled it right there. And our son Samuel received a letter from a Naval School up in Berkeley. They were teaching the Japanese language to people because very few people knew Japanese. They began to teach Japanese for intelligence service in the Navy and Army. They sent letters to the children of missionaries that had been born in Japan and could speak Japanese, wanting them to come to this school. Samuel had a letter saying, "If you come up here, we'll make you a lieutenant in the Navy, and you'll have a salary of . . . ."--oh, I've forgotten what it was. It was a good salary. "If you will come to this school and take a course, then you'll be in the Navy," you see. At that time, Samuel was quite concerned. He said, "Now what shall I do, Daddy?" I said, "It's up to you to decide. You're eighteen years old. You'd better decide for yourself what you should do." And he didn't like that at all. He wanted me to tell him why he couldn't go into the Navy. Well, it was all settled--he went to a church here. In his

Sunday School class the teacher made fun of conscientious objectors, called them yellow, and so forth. He at once didn't like that, so he took a stand for the first time publicly, told them he was a C.O., and one boy backed him up. But he left the Bible class after that, and he took a stand and wouldn't take the Naval job. So later he was called up for military service and was sent into the Civilian Public Service. He was up at Mammoth Lakes and Coleville for three years working. I paid thirty dollars a month for his keep. He got no pay, and I paid thirty dollars a month for his keep until one of the fellows up at the camp said "Nicholson, you have no business paying that." I didn't have much income, but I have it entered in my little cash book here. I see where I sent thirty dollars to the Service Committee here for his keep in this camp.

M: This was alternate service?

N: Yes, the alternate service they had in those days; they called it CPS. Three years thrown away. We have a book here called The Lost Years, by Sue Kunitomi Embrey, and those three years were mostly lost years for Samuel.

M: About how long before the war did the FBI man come and offer work to you?

N: It was sometime in the fall of 1941, not long before Pearl Harbor.

M: Did he specify what work he expected you to do?

N: No, he didn't say. He just wanted me to work with them, that was all. I turned him down.

M: Do you think it was because of your adeptness in the language?

N: No. Because I knew the Japanese people, you see.

M: I see. He wanted you to cut off all contacts with Japanese people, and yet he was going to make use of you because you knew them.

N: I think that was absurd for him to say that. But, of course, I wasn't going to get involved anyway, because I love Japanese and they love me, and they trusted me completely. And I didn't want to get involved with the FBI at all in this situation.

Well, to get on, I'd like to tell about Pearl Harbor Day. We were over at the church preaching as usual on Sunday morning and Fujimori, the other preacher, was back now. That was an interesting thing. He came back in July, and he took over the Japanese part, and I kept the English part, and my wife kept the Sunday School.

M: Were you both delivering sermons then?

N: I was giving the English one, and he was giving the Japanese, and we worked together well. But Fujimori was not a pacifist like I was, and some of the other Methodists weren't. But anyway, the tension between Japan and the United States got worse and worse. On Pearl Harbor day, he preached and I preached, and we went out and had a little lunch. Sometimes they would invite us to their homes, but we just sat out in the car that day and had our lunch, then we went out and started visiting.

Mr. Niwa, one of our members, saw us passing along the road. He was on the sidewalk and he said, "Sensei, Sensei,--teacher--they bombed Pearl Harbor!" He had just heard the news. It was about twelve-thirty. That's when we heard it. So we stopped, and he told us what had come over the radio. So we said, "We'd better get together. You tell folks to come to the church, and we'll all meet there." So we got quite a crowd together at the church, and they were certainly upset. Oh, it was pathetic, to think this terrible thing had happened. They had been afraid something was going to happen but nothing like that. So we talked and I said . . . .

M: You mean nothing like Pearl Harbor?

N: Like Pearl Harbor, nothing that bad. We felt sure that war was going to come; it was getting worse and worse, but we didn't think anything like that would happen. So we were terribly upset. I said right away, "Now, you will be losing your jobs of gardening"--they were mostly gardeners--"and I don't need any salary anymore, so just forget me. I will keep on coming as long as I can." And Fujimori said the same thing, "You needn't pay us anything." Well, you know, at Christmas time they gave me a hundred dollars instead of forty!

M: Oh, my! Then, it was obvious to you, even on that first day, that the people were going to be subjected to problems because this attack was from Japan? It was obvious?

N: Oh, of course, trouble would come. Oh, we knew that right away, sure. But that evening I went to have supper with a lovely old man, Sakamoto Gisuke, an eighty year old gentleman. At supper he said, "I'm on the FBI black list because I was in the Japanese army." He hadn't carried a gun, he wasn't fighting. He was in the army in the Russo-Japanese War as a non-combatant. He said, "All the people that were ever in the Japanese army are on the black list of the FBI, and we're going to be picked up tonight. I'm sure we are." So I was quite upset about that. It was crazy to pick up this innocent old man just because he was in the army back in 1905 and 1906.

· · · · ·

Sakamoto Gisuke was picked up that night along with many other old veterans. Nicholson's response was to plead the case of the Japanese in the Los Angeles offices of the FBI and Naval Intelligence the following day. For details and analysis of those actions, see pp. 23-28 of this book.

N: The FBI should have had more sense than that, but they had to pick up somebody to make people feel safe.

Well, anyway, I got permission to go to the Church Federation. I went to speak to a committee that had been organized to deal with this Japanese situation. They said they would give me five minutes to talk. So I just went there with one concern, to get them to give some publicity. I told them that I had been to the FBI and I had seen Commander Ringle, and I felt that a lot of these were lies, these things that were coming out. We shouldn't get emotionally upset. We should be loyal to our Japanese friends about us, and we should do something about it. I told how the FBI and the Intelligence had refused to put anything in the paper, and I said, "I'd just like you to put a statement in the paper." I had talked about three minutes when the head man jumped up, a white haired Methodist preacher. He jumped up, very angry and shouted at me, "Shut up! After those skunks Kurusu and Nomura did what they did in Washington, we can't trust any Jap." Isn't that awful? I left the room and waited outside until the meeting was over. I waited an hour or two. When this old man came out, I went up to him and I said, "Dr. Martin, you have no business talking like that, you a minister of the Gospel. You ought to be ashamed of yourself." He didn't say a word and went off in a huff.

Seven years later I sat beside him at a dinner at the First Methodist Church in Hollywood where I showed a picture and asked for money to help send goats to Japan, and they gave me five thousand dollars that night. That was one of my biggest collections. (laughter) And he didn't mention that incident. I don't know whether he remembered it or not. I think he forgot it. He was the one that had laid me out.

M: And he was part of the group that raised money after the war to send goats to Japan?

N: Yes. And there's one other thing that I would like to tell here along this line. We have a very dear friend, Tamon Maeda, who while he was vice-mayor of Tokyo had . . . . For a year after the earthquake in 1923, a history professor, Charles Beard, was sent over by the United States to help reconstruct Tokyo. He and Maeda worked together for a year and were very intimate friends. But on that Sunday evening of Pearl Harbor, Tamon Maeda and his wife were in a restaurant having supper, and the history professor came in with his wife. He stalked over to Maeda's table and very abruptly said, "Maeda, we have been friends for many years, but after this dastardly thing, this Pearl Harbor, our friendship stops!" And he turned around and walked away. I went back to Japan in 1948, and I took a book with me written by this same history professor, Beard. He wrote a book called Roosevelt and the Coming of the War, and I took this book back with me to show to Tamon Maeda. He hadn't seen it, and he was thrilled to read it. But imagine a man who was so emotionally upset to talk like that to this friend of his! After he really studied the thing, he found out that Roosevelt was back of the whole business. That's the thing that book

shows. It's the most dastardly . . . . It's the most awful thing. A
man who was so upset to say that, after he really studied it as a historian, he could write a book like that. It's most amazing. Roosevelt himself was pulling strings all the time to get this to happen. He wanted
America to be so terribly upset that they'd go into the war. He knew
that America didn't want to go to war. In September he gave a speech to
some kind of women's group in Boston in which he said, "Never shall our
boys be sent abroad to fight again," or something like that.

M: "To foreign lands."

N: You remember that famous speech?

M: Yes.

N: See, and he had to get something pretty serious to overcome that speech.
(laughter) That's the thing that people in this country don't understand. You know, all through the war I was asked to speak in many
places. I went to speak in service clubs often. And you know at these
service clubs they would always say, "Nicholson, we don't know anything
about the Japanese point of view of this thing. We'd like to know what
it is. You just talk freely, tell it." I said, "I'm not pro-Japan.
I'm not in favor of Pearl Harbor." I didn't think it was right. But
I would do, and I gave them things. Never once did they report me to
the FBI for things I said--the service clubs didn't.

M: Now what period was that?

N: That was all through the war. But I talked in churches, and I completely
left politics out of the thing. I didn't want to get in an argument.
All I wanted was to get people sympathetic with these people in the
camps. I'd ask them for gifts. We took Christmas gifts, every
Christmas to these camps. One church here, the First Methodist Church,
gave us five thousand presents, at a dollar apiece, every year to take
where the Japanese prisoners were down in Gila River, Arizona. I would
talk in these churches, and nearly always afterward somebody would ask
some fool question. I was foolish enough to answer it honestly, and
they would report it to the FBI. Anything that was reported to the FBI
they had to investigate, so about once a month an FBI man would come
here to see me. "Did you say so and so?" I said, "I sure did. And
it's the truth too, but they got it stretched a little bit." They
said, "You'd better be careful or you'll land in jail." I said, "That's
okay. I'm ready to go to jail. A lot of better men than me have been
there." (laughter)

M: I wonder if you'd like to talk a little more about the people that were
picked up by the FBI in that early period?

N: Well, I became particularly interested in these "potentially dangerous"
people because I had so many friends amongst them, and I felt a concern
to visit their homes where they had been picked up, to see their wives

and their relatives, and then follow them to where they were going to be taken. At first we didn't know what would happen to them, but we knew they wouldn't stay long at Terminal Island. That was just temporary. So I began visiting in homes around this area and then the Friends Service Committee asked me to join them to work with them. They were going to give me fifty dollars a month and pay my travel expenses. So I went in my car down to Imperial Valley with Gurney and Elizabeth Binford who were also Quaker missionaries. We visited all the homes down in Imperial Valley where we heard that people had been picked up by the FBI. We got the names of the people from Japanese in each community, and different facts about them, why they thought he was picked up. We made quite a record. Then we went all the way down near to Yuma and then back over to San Diego and visited some down there and then up the coast to Los Angeles.

Then soon after that I took a trip up north with Floyd Schmoe, a Quaker professor at the University of Washington, and Tom Bodine, another Friend, in a little jalopy. We went up through Bakersfield and Fresno, stopping at Japanese centers. They were mostly churches. I remember one night, though, we went into the Buddhist Temple in Fresno. There were five or six Buddhist priests, mostly language teachers. They had come from Japan, and they were just frightened to pieces. They were sitting in front of the fire, it was cold and it was in January, and we got talking about different things. One of these young priests said, "There was a man over at Fowler who was picked up--a Christian Japanese who is an honest man. They had no business getting him. He was in the insurance business. He was quite active in the Japanese Association. I'd like to take his place, so they could send him back to his wife." And I said, "Well, I'm afraid you can't do that." Then there was an old Buddhist priest there, a very nice old man that I got interested in and got his name. But they hadn't been picked up yet; the Buddhist priests hadn't. Then we went up to San Francisco. We spent some time there, then up into Oregon and Seattle.

Then Floyd Schmoe and I took a train to Missoula, Montana. There was a fort there that had a lot of barracks in it they could use as a detention place for the Department of Justice. By this time, the six hundred people had been gathered in different places in San Francisco, Portland, Seattle and Los Angeles. They had all been sent by train to Missoula. Six hundred of these potentially dangerous men were there, so we wanted to go to see them, having been in the homes of a great many of them as we went up the coast. We got out there and found that Frank Herron Smith, the Methodist superintendent that I had been working under, was there also. We got there on Saturday, stayed in a hotel, and on Sunday we went to the fort and met Mr. Collaire who was the Department of Justice man in charge of the camp. It was a detention camp; not a prison at all. There were rough army barracks. Collaire said, "I'd like you people to go inside and have a service with the men. Get the crowd together and talk to them and try to encourage them, and then come out and tell me what you think of the situation." So the three of us went inside, and we got the whole crowd together--six hundred of them--in one barrack.

The acoustics were rather bad, but Smith gave a Methodist sermon. I gave a talk about the families that I had been to see, so I had some warmth in what I said, and the tears were really in their eyes as I told them, "I have a list of people I've seen, and I want to talk to each of you personally, you folks in whose homes I've been." They were really moved by this. Then we had a chance to talk personally. I met all these people in whose homes I'd been. We shook hands with them and had a lovely time.

When we got through with it, we went out to Mr. Collaire's office. "According to the letters that these people write--everything has to be in English--the letters that they write out to their children and their children write back to them," he said, "these are the most loyal people we have in America."

M: Is that right?

N: The potentially dangerous! He said, "Not one of them would do any harm." That was the judgment of this man who had known them for only a week or two. He judged by the letters they had been writing. And he handed out a letter from a Nisei boy writing to his father: "Now, Dad, keep your chin up and keep the faith." (laughter) That sort of thing, you know. It was really good.

Well, then he said, "Say, you people speak Japanese. We're short of interpreters. Would you like to stay to interpret?" Smith said he had to go home.

M: Did he speak fluent Japanese, too?

N: Yes, he was a missionary from Japan. He spoke Japanese pretty well, I think better than I did. But anyway, Floyd Schmoe and Smith left. I said, "I'll stay here and help you with interpreting, and I want to witness in the hearings for some of my friends." A Department of Justice man was in charge of the hearing, and they had three people that were brought in to act as judges. Then they'd have an FBI man present, and they'd have a secretary to take everything down verbatim. Then the "suspicious character" was brought in, and he was allowed to have a friend. But way up there in Missoula they had no friend to come so practically none of them had friends to sit with them. So, since I was there, I was friend for quite a few of those I knew from Los Angeles, at the same time as I was interpreting. Between interpreting, while they were deciding what to do with this particular man, I would go out and be a witness at another hearing.

I would just like to tell how these hearings worked. In our hearings, the man in charge--I've forgotten his name--was a very fine gentleman and I got to really like him. He was the Department of Justice man running it. There was Dr. Johnson who had been a Baptist minister and was a professor of philosophy at the University of Nevada. Then there was a man named Smith who was head of the Falcon newspaper in Carson

City. And the other man was a lawyer. I've forgotten his name. They were all very nice gentlemen, and the FBI man was alright too. And then they had a woman who was taking everything down. They started the hearing by the Department of Justice man asking the victim "Why are you here?" They all answered, "I don't know. I don't know." "Well, you are here." And they thought they were going to get why it was. "You are here because we suspect you of being a dangerous character." That is all they got. They didn't give the reason at all. I was interpreter there in fifty-two hearings. Fifty of the hearings were for unmarried, sake drinking, gambling laborers at a copper mine in Nevada. And in the other two cases, one was a man from Las Vegas who was in the chicken business, and the other was the boss of this gang of fifty laborers.

M: They weren't West Coast people at all then?

N: No, this was Nevada. These were the Nevada hearings. Each hearing was done by different groups. These were all from Nevada; there were only fifty-two of them.

M: Do you mean that the hearings were divided according to states?

N: Yes.

M: I see. But at Missoula they had hearings for people from other areas. It just happened that you were handling the Nevada hearings?

N: They were short of interpreters, so they asked me to take this. I said that I thought I could stay for four or five days, and they thought they would get through in that time. The "judges" were all busy men and wanted to get home. Well, you know, at noon our team would go in and have lunch together. We became good friends, and had a wonderful time at lunch. They would ask me questions, and I'd tell them different things. "Oh," they said, "we're really learning something about Japan. This is wonderful." And they were the most sympathetic people before they got through with these poor old fellows. But, you know, what was the matter with the fifty men? Once a month this foreman would take fifty cents out of their pay and send it to Japan to help with the orphans and widows of men who had died in war. They had a society that collected money to help the orphans and widows of soldiers who had died in the Japanese wars. And the fellows didn't even know it themselves. They didn't have any idea why, and they had all come over as young fellows before they could be taken in by the Japanese army. There was a sort of obligation to pay this fifty cents because they hadn't served in the army.

M: And they didn't have any idea that was the reason they were brought in?

N: They had no idea. Those fifty were identical. The chicken man was entirely different. He had been a preacher here in Pasadena. He was a good man; he was alright, nothing at all. But he had done something that they were suspicious of, and why they put him on the list, I don't know. Then the head man deserved it because he actually sent this money. But wasn't that absurd? They always asked the same question. The professor of philosophy would always ask, "What's your philosophy of life?" Asking these poor uneducated "sake" drinking gamblers, "What's your philosophy of life?" I said, "Don't ask them that question." But once one man was talking too long. He would talk on and on and on, and I said, "Say, Ojisan--grandpa--you'd better quit." And they said, "Oh, no, you can't stop him. He can talk as long as he wants to." (laughter) The whole thing was a farce, an absolute joke. I didn't see how these reasonable intelligent university graduates and professors with Ph.D.'s, how they could carry on a thing like this, I just couldn't understand. It was absurd.

Well, anyway, I was witness in several hearings. One was for Mr. Hiraiwa. He was an eighty year old man who had been in the Sino-Japanese War. The man in charge of this said, "Well, Mr. Nicholson, what do you think we ought to do with this man?" I put my arm around his shoulder and I said, "Send the old man back to his wife in Pasadena as soon as you can--the sooner, the better." He said, "Okay, we'll do that." It took them six weeks to get him back. Six weeks! He arrived in Los Angeles on a train at nine o'clock in the morning with a lot of other fellows from Missoula that had been sent back. And his wife had left at six o'clock in the morning for Turlock for an Assembly Center. He was taken to the Santa Anita Assembly Center, and I went there to take a birthday cake to him in a Van de Kamp box, all done up properly in a box. I said, "I want to give this to this old man for his birthday." The tough examiner had a rusty knife, and he jabbed it through the cake. I said, "You crazy fellow! What do you think you're doing?" "There might be a bomb in it," he said. (laughter)

M: Oh, my!

N: "It was made at Van de Kamp's, nothing to do . . . . What do you think this country is anyway?" Wasn't that crazy? That's the way they acted out there at Santa Anita. It was terrible! But anyway, it was six more weeks before I could get the old man out of there and transferred to Turlock where his wife was. I said, "I'll be very happy to drive the old man up to his wife." They said, "You can't do it. It would be dangerous. We'll have a military guard take him." So they took that old man one evening to Los Angeles and put him on a bus alone and sent him up to Turlock. He got there at two o'clock in the morning with nobody to meet him, and he didn't know where to go. He sat around in the the bus station till morning. He didn't know English very well. They finally got him over to the camp. Wasn't that crazy? That's the kind of things they did all the way through. It just didn't make sense. It made me so exasperated.

M: And you had offered to take him!

N: Well, anyway, I'd been keeping pretty busy. We worked until ten o'clock at night to get these hearings through. When these four days were over, we went to the station in the evening to take a night train. The others were going back to Reno, and I was coming back to Pasadena. I walked toward the rear of the car, as the train came in, to get on a coach. And one of them said, "Why, Nicholson, what are you doing? The sleepers are all up front." I said, "I don't have money for a sleeper." "Well," he said, "isn't the government paying for this?" I said, "All I got out of this is this pencil the secretary gave me and a few free lunches." I had to pay for the hotel at night.

M: Oh, my, for all your interpreting work you got not a penny?

N: For all my interpreting, that's all I got. I said, "No, I'm not taking anything from the government for this work. It's a lot of foolishness.

M: But they didn't offer you any either, did they?

N: They didn't offer me any, no. Going up it hadn't cost me anything. My fare back was fifty dollars. I charged that to the Service Committee. But, you know, I was in the hearings as a witness in, I think, about fifteen or twenty cases. One lady whose husband I'd been in the hearing for--I think it was this Mrs. Hiraiwa--asked how much the trip cost me. I said, "Fifty dollars." She gave me fifty dollars. In each case, I could have gone to them, and I would have received fifty dollars from each one, but I returned the fifty dollars to her. I said, "It's all paid for." That dear lady died, and we were at her funeral last Monday night. And yesterday I heard that she has left money in her will for us. These people were so grateful for what we've done.

Well, anyway, I got on the train and sat up all night. About four in the morning, at Ogden, my friends changed trains, and I got out on the platform to say goodbye to them. They were so friendly, just like long lost friends. It was a wonderful experience, and I met Mr. Edward J. Ennis [Director of the Alien Enemy Control Unit] up there. I met him later on, too.

I went back then to the homes of the people I'd met from this area.

I didn't go up the coast again. I went in this area and visited them again and reported. And I kept that up then all through the war while they were interned. I kept going to detention camps, and nobody else did it. Frank Herron Smith never went again. I was the only one that followed these people up and went in with them. That's why I know more about it than anybody else.

M: Yes.

N: I'd like to just tell now what happened from that time on. When Mr. Collaire told about these being loyal people, he said, "This is all caused by the pressure of public opinion--public opinion given by the enemies of the Japanese, their competitors down here. The people that were working in the same businesses, nurserymen, and so forth. And the Sons of the Golden West, these extremely anti-Japanese folks are doing this thing."

M: He was aware of that?

N: He was aware of that. That was when we first came he said, "This is all caused by public opinion." And you know those fifty men that were identical? I forgot to say that the authorities asked me, "Nicholson, what do you think we ought to do with these men?" I said, "I'll go out and ask them what they prefer." They said, "Alright. They'll stay here, they'll go back to the mine and work, or they'll go to one of the relocation centers. Which will they do?" So I went out and asked them. They were unanimous. They wanted to stay here. (laughter) They never had such good food and such nice quarters in their lives. They didn't have to work. They could just play cards all the time, and they didn't have any sake to get drunk on. They didn't have money to gamble with.

N: They were all single men, anyway.

N: Oh, all single men. Unmarried old men. They didn't have anybody to go to, no relatives anywhere in the country. They said, "We'd rather stay here." So I went back to the court and they just roared. After all the effort, half of them were sent to one of the relocation centers and half were kept at Missoula. Does that make any sense?

M: Do you think it was just an arbitrary choice, who went and who stayed?

N: If they sent them all out, the public would be alarmed. They had to keep some.

M: Oh. And so there was no rhyme or reason as to who stayed?

N: No rhyme or reason. The whole business was a farce. Absolutely crazy! I was ashamed of a government that would do a thing like that. But isn't that something? Well, then they began collecting more people because public opinion brought more pressure, "Take these Japs out of here." And the stories that were told the FBI: "This fellow has a short-wave radio. He's in touch with a ship out in the ocean." And every time the FBI heard these stories they had to investigate them. Oh, they were kept busy investigating stories that weren't anything at all. (laughter) The bomb in the house was a tin pan. It was absolutely absurd, but more and more people were picked up all the time.

M: Now, let me ask you about the period when you were at the hearings. Do you remember what month that was?

N: That was in January, I think, soon after . . . . It was perhaps January 20, or somewhere around there. But here beyond La Crescenta in Tujunga

Canyon, they opened an old CCC camp that would hold three hundred people, and they began bringing people in **there** instead of taking them down to Terminal Island. When they would get three hundred, then they'd ship them out, a whole train load of them, up to some other place. Missoula had six hundred. Then they sent them out to Bismarck, North Dakota, to another camp out there. I never went to that one.

M: These are specifically those who were taken in for detention?

N: These were "potentially dangerous" people. They were continuing to take in more as public opinion demanded it. The man in charge at Tujunga Canyon was Mr. Scott. He was a Methodist and an Immigration Service man. Mr. Scott was a lovely man, a real gentleman, and he had charge of this camp. I got to know him very well because I was there many times. He just thought these were wonderful people. For instance, he told me, "Nicholson, I could open this camp at any time and say, 'Gentlemen, you may go home to your wives and your families. Come back tomorrow evening by five o'clock.' They'd go home and have a good time, and they'd all get back by five o'clock, and they wouldn't do any damage while they were out. And I have Sarge . . . ." There was an old man, an old retired soldier in a uniform with a pistol at the gate. (laughter) "And they insisted on building towers with a fellow with a gun on top for these perfectly loyal Americans." Mr. Scott and Mr. Collaire understood. If the authorities had just taken their advice! But they couldn't take their advice, because of public opinion. These emotionally upset people were still bringing pressure. It was an awful thing.

Well, Mr. Scott was a Methodist, supposedly, but a man came in there, Rev. Kenji Nakane, who was an Issei preacher from Coachella. He was picked up because he had been teaching Japanese. Nakane was a lovely fellow. He became very good friends with Mr. Scott. In fact, Mr. Scott was converted by him. He had been a nominal Methodist; he didn't know what religion was all about. But before Nakane was through with him, he became a Christian. When Nakane was finally taken out to one of the relocation centers, Scott promised him faithfully, "Nakane, I'll keep on with the Christian services here when you've gone." So he called on me many times to come and preach to them. The Christmas of 1942 Scott phoned me and said, "Nicholson, will you come out, and we'll have a Christmas meeting. We want you to preach, then we'll have a turkey dinner." My wife and I went out and had a wonderful time with just a few people who were left then. Most of them had gone out to other places, and the hearings were nearly over.

At the party, Scott said, "I've been accused of desecrating the flag." He went to a United States flag, and on one of the white borders there was some Chinese characters written. He said, "What does that say? They say I've been writing on the flag." I said, "That's the first language school down in Little Tokyo. It says 'Daichi Nihon Gakko.' That's where the flag came from. They got it from that school. They were being patriotic, and that's all it is on there." He said, "Well,

I'll explain that to them."

Mr. Scott would take those people just a short distance away where there was a sanitarium with a hundred and fifty TB patients that were in there with a guard out front, a sheriff out there with a pistol. Nobody was allowed in unless they had a pass. He would take some of his men, like Nakane, up to the sanitarium. There was a Japanese pastor in there sick, a dear friend of theirs. He was so nice to them, oh, he was a lovely fellow. I've lost track of Mr. Scott. I'd like to see him again.

M: About how old a man was he at that time?

N: Oh, at that time he was about forty-five or so, a very fine man.

M: You've been on visits to that hospital too, haven't you?

N: Yes, but that's another story. They decided after the hearings to put these men in Army camps. So the first six hundred were sent to Louisiana.

M: From Missoula?

N: From Missoula. The whole six hundred were shipped to Louisiana. I followed them down there perhaps in February or so, soon after that. Missoula was closed. That was a prisoner of war camp in Louisiana under the Army. I was down there about four days and went out to visit the camp. There was a little Jewish colonel in charge. I met him first thing and I said, "I've come here now to visit certain people." I had a long list of those I wanted to see. I'd been to their homes. He said, "Boy, that's going to take a long time. You're only allowed to see one at a time, and you have to have an official with you, and you can talk only in English." I said, "I've got only four days here. Mr. Collaire in Missoula let me go in and talk to them freely." "Oh, you can't! These are dangerous men!" I said, "Now, just wait a minute, Colonel. There's not a single dangerous man there. They're all loyal Americans. They would be citizens if they were allowed to be. They picked the cream of the Japanese, the leaders of the Japanese community, and they're wonderful people. Have you noticed--haven't they organized already? Don't they have a mayor? Don't they have a city council?" "Sure," he said, "they're well organized. They got together on their own, and they have a little town of their own inside." They had a mayor and a vice-mayor, and they had different officials doing things. They divided up the work, and they were all doing their part. I said, "Don't you see that?" He said, "Yes. That does sound interesting. Well, you can go and see as many as you can this morning and then have lunch with me." So I had lunch with the colonel, and we talked more. He said, "You can go in the hospital and visit all of them in there." So I did that and then came back the next day. He didn't actually get me inside, but he let me get a whole bunch together and talk with them freely before I got

through. So I saw all I wanted to see. Before we got through, he
shook my hand and said, "Nicholson, I'm so glad you came. I realize
these are decent people. They're not dangerous ." He said, "You're
right." Wasn't that great? It was just a wonderful thing.

Then I--I've forgotten whether it was that time or the next time I was
there--I got on a train. I didn't have money to travel. The Service
Committee did help me at first, but by then I was going mostly on my
own. I'd start out from home with thirty dollars on me. I'd buy a
ticket part way, and then I'd trust on some money coming in, or I'd
hitchhike, or get there some way. But I always got there. I got on
a train, again coach, down there in Louisiana and arrived at Dallas
at eight o'clock in the morning, sitting up all night. I asked how
to get to Seagoville. That's where the women were put in. About
fifty women had been picked up that first night, and I wanted to see
where they were and what they were doing. Oh, and I had been to
Philadelphia before that. Mr. Collaire had closed Missoula and had
moved to Philadelphia, Pennsylvania, and was in charge of this whole
business then. I went to his office and had quite a talk with him.
I told him, "I want to go to Seagoville," and that was all. He didn't
say anything more. He said, "That's fine. You'd better go." So I
got off the train and asked, "How do you get to Seagoville?" I was
told, "Well, there's no bus running out there. It's about twelve miles
out in the country and it's a long trip for a taxi." I said, "Well, I
don't have money for a taxi." They said, "Well, you get on this street-
car and then go to the end of the line. Then you will have to hitchhike."
So I went to the end of the line just outside the city limits, and I
stood thumbing by the road. An old ice truck came along with a colored
man smoking a big cigar. I got in and said, "Are you going toward Seagoville?" "I go right past the Seagoville prison. I'll take you out
there." I had a lovely visit with that old colored fellow. He was a
Southern Baptist. We had a talk about religion, about everything else,
and pretty soon he stopped when he came to this beautiful . . . . It
looked like a college campus, no fence around it, nothing at all. It
was a federal penitentiary for women. Beautiful two-story, brown brick
buildings. He let me off at the gate, and I went into the administration building and said that I wanted to see the head man. They said,
"That's Mr. O'Rourke." So I went in the office, and he jumped up and
came over and said, "Glad to see you, Mr. Nicholson. Mr. Collaire has
written me and said you were coming. I want to show you the works."
So he took me outside right away, and we walked across the campus and
he said, "Now the Italian women are in this building, and the German
women in that one, and this one has the Japanese women." As we went in
the door, Mrs. Wada, who had been teaching Japanese and was a pastor's
wife--a very dear friend of mine--and Mrs. Onodera who had been very
active in the Women's Society in Los Angeles, saw me coming. They rushed
up to me and threw their arms around me, "Mr. Nicholson!" And O'Rourke
said, "I can see I don't need to introduce you." (laughter) "I'll
leave you here with these folks and you spend the day. At four o'clock
you come back to my office and give me a report of what happened." The
FBI was watching these people all the time, and the rules were I could

see only one person at a time, with an official present and only speak in English. He turned me completely loose in this federal penitentiary for women, and Mrs. Wada took me to her room. It was on the second floor, a beautiful room with wall to wall carpeting, a beautiful Simmons mattress bed, a little writing desk, and a private bath--as good as any hotel you'd ever see. It seems that this penitentiary was built to make a good impression on women immigrants who had come in illegally.

M: Oh, it was always a penitentiary for illegal immigrants before?

N: That's what they used it for.

M: It wasn't ever used for criminals?

N: No, it wasn't really. Wasn't that something? We went down to lunch, and the dining room was beautiful. There were little square tables with linen on them, linen napkins, and four sat at a table. I sat with three old ladies. They had lovely chinaware, delicate chinaware and silver--as good as any hotel you ever went to. The lunch was delicious. It was swell. Then there was a great, big room with over-stuffed furniture, a beautiful room. We all sat around, fifty women and me. I told about the men I had seen and their husbands who were in Louisiana. We prayed, and we sang hymns, and we laughed, and we cried, and we had a wonderful time until four o'clock. Then I told them I had to leave. I said, "I'll come and see you again sometime, but in the meantime I must go and have a talk with Mr. O'Rourke." They said that Mr. O'Rourke was a wonderful man. He was so good to them. They were just having a grand time, no troubles, no problems of any kind. Anything they wanted Mr. O'Rourke would do for them. Wasn't that good? An Irishman. So I went to Mr. O'Rourke, and he said, "Well, how about it?" I said, "This is a wonderful setup." So he was tickled to pieces, of course. He said, "I'll write back to Mr. Collaire and give him a report." So I just told him what I had done and he said, "That's fine." So Mr. O'Rourke took me to the station in his own car and we became friends. Oh, he was a lovely man.

I got on a train, then, to go to Lordsburg, New Mexico. That's where there were some more of these prisoner of war camps. I felt in my pocket, and there was an envelope in it. I pulled the envelope out, and I opened it up, and it had forty-three dollar bills in it. While I was talking, those ladies had taken a collection. Forty-three dollars in the envelope, and on the outside it said, "The Widows' Mite." (laughter)

Well, then I got to Lordsburg the next morning. I had another night on the train. It saved hotel bills to sit on a train all night. I asked where this camp was, and they said, "Well, it's about four miles out in the country. There's no way of getting there. You have to walk. This was springtime, I think, and it was getting pretty hot. So I walked out to this camp. There was a major in charge of the camp, an alcoholic who was drunk most of the time. This was a regular prisoner of war camp. He had a lieutenant in charge, and I told this lieutenant that I wanted to see certain people. He was terribly strict; he was a little bit under the influence of liquor himself. He took me into a sort of waiting room, and they called in the men one at a time who I wanted to see. I had a notebook with everything written in it--very valuable. It had all the names and addresses of the people I'd seen. He took that from me and an account book I had. I had a testament on me, and he took that. He didn't take my purse, but he took everything else, and he said he was going to keep them. He threatened to keep me there, and I said, "That'd be wonderful. I'd love to come in here and stay with these, my friends." But he was really an obnoxious fellow. I did see quite a few of them, but there was always someone present. They couldn't talk to me and tell me what they really wanted to say. It was a very unsatisfactory visit. But I went again about . . . .

M: Did he give you back the books?

N: I got them back finally.

M: But you weren't allowed to see everyone in the camp, then?

N: No, just a few that I had on my list, and then I couldn't see all of them either. And there was one case . . . . There was a man who died at this camp. The wife was at Poston, and she wanted me to find out what was the cause of his death. They didn't tell her. He wouldn't say anything about that. But I was back there perhaps a year later, and they had stopped the Seagoville camp. The Seagoville women were taken to Crystal City where they started a family detention center, where the men and the wives could be together. The children, even, from the other camps were brought out. They had a family camp at Crystal City, right down near the Mexican border. That's where Popeye the Sailor came from--the spinach business. Half of the town was a ghost town. The spinach business didn't go as high as they thought it would, and it was overdone, and the town was half ghost. But there was this old CCC camp outside of the town. And out there, Mr. Collaire had come from Philadelphia and was there, the next time I went down. Mr. Collaire was there. So I had a nice visit with my old friend. I'd met him twice before, you see. He let me go inside the camp and visit freely with them. They had little cottages. All over the place were little cottages and there were Germans, and Italian and Japanese families living there. They had a shop where they had groceries and other things for sale. They gave them scrip instead of real money. They were allowed so much. They would go shopping and do their own cooking at home. It was a lovely spirit. Mr. Collaire was good to them.

M: Now this was a camp for aliens who still were not considered safe?

N: This was the family camp. They hadn't been let out. They had the hearings, and they kept them.

M: It included Germans and Italians?

N: Germans and Italians.

M: As far as you know, was this the only camp of its type at that time?

N: Yes. That's the only . . . . See, these women had been at this other place. There were Italian and German women at that place also.

M: But had all the other detention camps been closed by then?

N: Well, just the ones where the women were, but the other places . . . . The Louisiana thing was still going, and Lordsburg was still going. But they took the men from there whose wives were at Crystal City out. If they didn't have any relatives there, they didn't. But they took all these people to Crystal City. I don't know how large this town was. It was a lovely little town. Mr. Collair said, "Nicholson, I've gotten in trouble because on Hitler's birthday the Germans wanted to have a birthday party for Hitler, and so I sent out to the town and had a big birthday cake made and brought in. They got this birthday cake, but I didn't let them have any beer. But they had a birthday cake. They had a flagpole inside with the stars and stripes on it, and they pulled that down and put up a German flag. The people in the town saw the German flag go up, and they were critical. They came to see what was happening. They found out it was Hitler's birthday and that Collair had collaborated in it, so they were all against him. They wanted to have him put out of his job. He asked, "What do you think I had better do about this?" I said, "I think you'd better move that flagpole outside. The stars and stripes shouldn't be behind bars." So he said, "That's what I'll do. I'll move the flagpole outside."

I went from there for a second visit to Lordsburg, and this time the major was still drunk. He wasn't visible. But there was another lieutenant in charge, and he was a very nice man. He was friendly and cooperative. I had a very good time with him. He told me that on the emperor's birthday they tried to celebrate there. A lot of prisoners of war from Japan were there, which I didn't realize. They had been brought all the way from the Pacific area where they had been captured. They wanted to celebrate the emperor's birthday. They didn't ask anything about it, but they got a sheet, and they put a big red sun in the middle of it. Then they just got some sticks and held it up in the air, and all stood around and shouted, "Ten no Heika banzai! Ten no Heika banzai! Ten no Heika banzai!" They had to do it three times. The soldiers got so excited, they pulled in a machine-gun and nearly shot the crowd down. They fortunately didn't shoot. Isn't that something? That's the difference between the Department of Justice, cooperating in Hitler's birthday celebration, and this crazy outfit--the Army.

M: The flag that the Germans used, was that the swastika or was it a regular German flag?

N: I don't know what it was. They didn't say. He said, "They put up a
German flag." I don't know where they got it either. How they ever
had it there, I don't know. (laughter) The immigration officials weren't
so strict about things; they let things happen.

Well, anyway, I asked this lieutenant, "I'd like to know about this
man," and I gave the man's name. He said, "He died." "Why did he die?"
He said, "Well, he was from Santa Fe. They brought them from Santa Fe,
New Mexico, detention camp. And he was sick in the hospital with TB.
They came here to this station. They had to walk out here. It was a
terribly hot day. And this fellow was just out of bed, he was sick, and
he couldn't keep up with the crowd on this four mile walk. He lagged
behind and one of the soldiers thought he was trying to escape and shot
him." Well, not long ago I met a man who was there at Lordsburg, and he
said that they shot two men, not just the one. They were just too sick
to walk. Wasn't that a sight though? But this gentleman was very nice.
He said, "But don't tell the wife what happened. Just tell her he died
of TB." So I never did tell the wife.

But the very last thing I was in on was at Santa Fe, the last of the
hearings at Santa Fe. I was there several days, and that's where the
Ennises were. I had tea with them. But the next to the last hearing
I was in as a witness was for an old Methodist preacher. They always
put this thing to them: "If the Japanese were landing on the California
coast, and the Americans were up in the mountains and you were standing
between with a gun, which way would you fire?" They always asked that
crazy question. This good old Methodist preacher said, "I'd fire at the
Japanese." I was disgusted with him. I didn't give him a good report,
although he was a good friend of mine. Well, the next man was a pacifist, a younger man, and a very dear friend of mine. They asked him
this thing and he said, "I wouldn't fire either way. I'm a Christian.
I don't believe in killing anybody." They kept pestering him to say
one way, but he wouldn't do it. He stuck by his guns. Then when it
came my time to talk--this was the last hearing--I really let off what
I thought about the whole situation. I told a lot of things that I had
heard from FBI men and from Ennis. I finally said, "You've had four
thousand five hundred hearings, and you haven't found a single case of
espionage or sabotage, and still you're keeping these people here. It
just doesn't make sense." The FBI man present said, "That's a lie!"
I said, "If it's a lie, I'm through!" and I got up and walked out. Well,
the FBI man followed me out and he said, "Say, Nicholson, where did you
get all this information you're giving here." I said, "I got it from
you fellows." He said, "But we're not supposed to talk." I was always
getting in contact with these FBI men. I said, "Well, I know, but you
let out a lot to me." I didn't tell him about Ennis--he gave me most of
it. But anyway, he never apologized but he did admit it. He said, "What
you said is true." I said, "Why did you call me a liar then?" And he
walked off in a huff.

M: He did it for the record, no doubt.

N: Yes. But wasn't that something?

M: Do you know if the records of those trials . . . . While you were giving testimony, was that all being taken down?

N: Oh, everything I said was down in black and white.

M: So supposedly that's on record somewhere.

N: I wonder if I could get a hold of it. I never thought of it. It must be somewhere.

M: It must be in some archive somewhere, I suppose.

N: It must be. I would like to go and hear what I said. (laughter) Wouldn't that be fun?

. . . . .

Nicholson continued to visit the people in the detention camps and report to their wives and families in the relocation centers on their welfare. An Issei in Manzanar turned over the pink slip to his stake truck and with that Nicholson made regular trips to the centers, particularly Manzanar, Poston, and Gila River, bringing whatever the internees wanted: organs for churches, books, furniture, personal belongings, etc. On one occasion he brought in what was purported to be vinegar, but which turned out to be sake, contributing to his exclusion from Manzanar for six months. Each trip was dual in purpose, for he came to bring spiritual uplift as well--often bringing along another evangelist. Former resident of Manzanar Togo Tanaka remembers that Nicholson brought "warmth" to places that were largely devoid of such emotion.

N: I'd like to go on now and tell another story about the 442nd. This was really important. I visited the 442nd Regiment very early, before the soldiers had really gotten there. The cadremen were there, and one of my very close friends, James Kitsuse, was one of the cadremen, a sergeant who trained the recruits. They were mostly stateside people, but the day that I got there . . . .

M: Where?

N: In Camp Shelby, out at Hattiesburg, Mississippi. The day that I got there a freight train load of men from Hawaii had arrived, volunteers. They had taken a week in coming across and were just all fagged out and homesick. They were sitting around that evening playing their ukeleles and singing their Hawaiian songs. It was really pathetic. There was a chaplain there. I think his name was Chaplain South. He was a Southern Baptist, a lovely man. They really had no officers among the Nisei at the time. So the officers, the lieutenants and the colonel in charge, were all white people. But the sergeants and the people from there down were Japanese, Nisei. The next morning Chaplain South took me through all the companies and had each company out, line up at attention, and salute, and he saluted. He was a captain, I think. He introduced me, and I gave them a little pep talk. It was really good. I remember asking them if they went to McKinley High School. When McKinley High School and Miles Carey was mentioned, they said, "Oh, we know Miles Carey; he's our principal." I said, "Well, he's at Poston camp now, the head of the schools there, and he sends his 'aloha' to you." They said, "Tell him to come and see us." They were so enthusiastic about Miles Carey. Dr. Carey had given up his job as a principal to go to Poston to take charge of the schools because he felt this whole evacuation was caused by the lies that had been told about the Nisei in Hawaii.

I remember one evening Miles Carey was talking to me outside the camp at Poston, and he said, "This whole business"--and he waved his hands toward the barracks--"was caused because people were emotionally upset by what happened at Pearl Harbor and by the lies that were told about our Nisei from Hawaii. Those Nisei are the most patriotic, loyal Americans that we have." He was all for them. He said, "That's why I gave up my job." And Nell Finley was a YWCA secretary in Honolulu who did the same thing. She was head of the social service work at Poston. Two wonderful people! You know, the WRA had many wonderful people like that. They had some "roughnecks," but they had a lot of good folks, too, and they did a great deal of good. I was really proud of the way they acted. I just happened to have a different kind of conscience. I just couldn't work with the outfit because I didn't believe in it. But those people went there, and every camp had people like that. They were really worthwhile.

M: By the way, while we're talking about that, we have a dean at Cal State Fullerton who was a teacher at Manzanar by the name of Dean Hazel Jones. Does that name ring a bell with you?

N: No, I wouldn't remember. Did you get any information from her?

M: We're planning to do an interview with her. We haven't done it yet. But I know she was a very dedicated teacher and went there because she . . . .

N: Oh, some of the teachers were wonderful! Quite a few missionaries in the camps, Japanese missionaries as well as others, did a good job. I can't run down the WRA entirely. They did much good besides evil.

On Sunday morning I preached in the chapel to these volunteers, and their chaplain said, "Nicholson, you can preach anything you want." I said, "I'm a Quaker and a pacifist. Is it alright for me to preach that?" "Absolutely," he said. "You can preach anything you want, and you won't be criticized." I preached on the love of God, and the fellows came to me afterward saying, "That's wonderful. God is love, but since the war broke out nobody talks about loving anybody anymore." (laughter)

But I must get to my second visit to the 442nd, which was really more important than the first one, because they were really underway at that time. In February 1944, Dillon Myer, head of the WRA, who was a very fine man, a Methodist minister's son, a man of high integrity and a Christian, was in Pasadena, and we had a small meeting with him--I think it was the Friends of the American Way and the Friends Service Committee. We met in a Quaker meetinghouse on Orange Grove Avenue. I think there were only seventeen altogether. I remember I asked Myer if it was right to draft people out of these camps with barbed wire around them and not allowed to leave. Was it right to draft them into the Army? I don't know whether I said it before or not, but when the war broke out they had at once put a lot of the Nisei who were already in the Army onto KP duty and took their guns away from them. And they put a lot of the Kibei out of the Army; they were afraid of them.

M: I have heard that some were discharged. Then it was just Kibei who were in the Army that were discharged?

N: Yes, the ones that had been drafted, they were put out, or some were kept in and put on KP, but they weren't given guns. From that time on the Nisei were put down as "enemy aliens," and that made them feel terrible. Well, because the 442nd had already made such a good record, the policy had changed in 1944. They were drafting them again.

M: Do you know whose idea it was to draft them?

N: Well, I think that the 442nd did it. See, the 442nd was already overseas being killed.

M: They were volunteers?

N: They were volunteers. They were over in Italy making a wonderful record. Of course, there were more here. Replacement troops were still in Camp Shelby getting trained to take the place of those who were killed and wounded. So many of them! Terrible! The death list was awful.

M: Do you think the fact that they were making such a good record inspired the authorities to begin drafting them?

N: That's why it was. So they decided to make them regular soldiers and draft them. There was some pressure from the JACL and these very ultra-patriotic Nisei to have them put back in their status of 1-A, that is, the regular service again. But anyway, Dillon Meyer said, "That's right. You're right." I said, "I wish you would go back to Washington and get the Army to open those camps at once." He said, "I can't do that. One branch of the government can't tell another branch what to do." I said, "Who can do it?" He said, "You can." I said, "What should I do?" He said, "You go to Washington to see John J. McCloy, the Undersecretary of War under Marshall, in charge of the war in the Pacific area; he's the one that is responsible for those camps. You will have to have a talk with him, and he'll tell you what to do." I said, "Alright, I'm on my way." The Friends of the American Way backed me up. But they didn't give me any **money**; I went on my own. I don't think I had enough money to pay for transportation all the way there when I started, but I started out anyway.

I first went to Parker and hitchhiked out to Poston which was about eighteen miles out in the desert from Parker. It was toward evening when I got there, and I went out to the Terminal Island section of the camp to see Mrs. Ishii who formerly had a drugstore in Terminal Island. I'd had a lot of contact with Mrs. Ishii. I dropped into her barrack to see her, and her son-in-law Shigekawa was there at the time.

M: Kiyoshi Shigekawa?

N: Yes. He was a fisherman at Terminal Island, and he was there at the time, so he heard me telling what I was doing. I was going to Washington to see McCloy. He said, "Say, Nicholson, that's interesting. Will you come with me?" So I went with him. He went into another barrack, and there were a bunch of these rough fellows from Terminal Island who were having a conference. I found out they were deciding to have a demonstration. They were going to set fire to buildings; they were going to just tear things up because they didn't approve of being drafted into the American Army when they were locked up in this place. They had a just cause. But I told them, "That's not the way to do it. I'm on my way now to see McCloy to try to get these camps open, and I'll do my best for you. I advise you to send a telegram to Eleanor." Eleanor Roosevelt had been to Poston and had made a great impression, and they all felt that Eleanor was alright. I said, "You send a telegram to Eleanor, to McCloy, and to Dillon Myer." They said, "That's a good idea. Let's try it." So two or three of them went with me to Mr. Head's office, who was the camp director. He was a very good man, a good administrator, and an Indian Bureau man.

M: Oh, he was a Caucasian man who had worked for the Bureau of Indian Affairs?

N: Caucasian. The heads of these camps were all Caucasian. There were no Japanese in any of them. I went to Head's office, and told him what we wanted to do, and he sent for a lawyer to help word a telegram. It was sent off right away; I believe it told that Nicholson was coming to see McCloy. Then the men left, and Head came to me and said, "Nicholson, I'm so glad you came! We knew something was going to happen. We knew there was going to be a demonstration of some kind. We could do nothing to stop it. You came here at just the right time. We thank you for it." The men agreed to do nothing until they heard from me again. Then I went to the Rivers camp, and there was no demonstration planned there, but it was the same thing; the Nisei were feeling very badly about the draft. I talked with them also. I think I also got them to send a telegram to McCloy.

Then I got on the train and went to Hattiesburg. I got there in the middle of the night on a coach and phoned out to the camp. Mike Masaoka answered the phone. Mike was a very capable fellow and sort of stuck-up; he thought he knew everything, and he did. But he was hated by the fellows from Hawaii, and they said they were going to kill him. So the Caucasian officer in charge gave Mike the job of being on night duty at the office, so he wouldn't be out in his bed to be murdered by the Hawaiians. (laughter)

M: Do you think it was jealousy over leadership? Was that the trouble?

N: Well, partly. You see, the Hawaiians had really started the whole thing, and they didn't like these California fellows to be officers over them. They resented it; there was quite a lot of hard feelings there. Mike said he would send a jeep for me right away, so I got out to the place around one or two o'clock in the morning. He said, "My bunk's empty in this barrack. You can sleep in my bunk." I went in quietly, didn't waken anybody up, and got in his bunk. I think they were three high, and I got into the middle one. I climbed in and went sound asleep. The next morning when the bugle blew, they all got up and said, "Hakajin!"-- a Caucasian was in Mike's bunk. (laughter) Well, I had a very happy weekend with the boys.

M: By the way, was Joe Masaoka there too?

N: Joe wasn't there at that time. He went later. I think three of the Masaoka boys joined and one was killed.

That Saturday night they had a dance in the gymnasium, and three or four busloads of Nisei girls had been brought from the Arkansas camps, Jerome and Rohwer. They came down with some chaperones to have a dance with the boys. I went into the gallery to watch the dance, and I sat with a dear lady who was a chaperone. She was a daughter in the famous Kawai family of Pasadena who was married to a man in the Hillcrest Sanitarium. Her father, Mr. Kawai, was the one who had built the Japanese Tea Garden at the Huntington Library in San Marino. She heard my name Nicholson and she said, "Are you the Mr. Nicholson?" I said, "Well, I'm the one who buried your father's ashes up in the Mountain View Cemetary." "Oh!" and she shook my hand; she nearly threw her arms around around me. She was a beautiful lady. I'd never met her before. On my other side sat a colonel who was going around to all the different military outfits grading them. He showed me his book and what he had found out. He said, "You know, this 442nd is number one in so many things. They're number one in discipline. They behave themselves, and they're really disciplined. And they have more money than anybody else. They buy more Liberty Bonds, and they're best in baseball, in wrestling, in swimming, and boxing. They're number one in so many things."

M: Would you explain why they had more money than anyone else?

N: Well, they had more money because when the Japanese were taken into the army in Japan, they were paid hardly anything. They were given their uniforms, their shoes, their guns, and their food, very poor food, but they were given very little money. However, in the American Army they got good pay. But because of that in Japan, the men who went into the American Army were always given money by their folks when they went away. So these people had lots of money in their hands when they went in.

M: Their parents thought they wouldn't have much money, I guess.

N: The next morning I spoke in the chapel again, and in the afternoon I went back to Hattiesburg to see Earl Finch. Earl Finch was a very influential businessman there, a young fellow that was so kind to the Nisei. He did everything for them. He had a USO service place for the outfit with billiards and other games and reading materials and drinks. They could have all they wanted. He gave them cigars and everything else they needed, and was very friendly with them. So I wanted to see him, but he wasn't at the USO, and he wasn't at his home. They said he was over at his bowling alley. He owned a lot of the town. I went to the bowling alley and there was Earl Finch, this wealthy man, taking in money at the bowling alley. Somebody hadn't turned up for the job. I said that I would like to have a talk with him. So he got somebody to take over the job, and he went back to his home, and we had a lovely visit and it was really fine to know Earl Finch. About eleven o'clock at night he took me to the station and put me on a train.

I rode coach to Washington and got in between eight or nine o'clock in the morning. As I got off at the station, I saw a newspaper headline: "American Council of Churches Advises Bombing the Emperor's Palace." I was amazed at that. I couldn't understand it, but I didn't buy a paper. I got in a taxi and went to the Pentagon building. I got over there about nine o'clock, and went to the office and said, "I'd like to see Colonel Lee." They said, "Alright." They gave me a badge that had a number on it, and it had on it "Escort required." They took me to a waiting room. Colonel Lee was heading G-2, the military intelligence. I'd known him in Japan in the summertime at Karuizawa in the mountains. He was a language officer at the embassy studying Japanese, and I'd had contact with him and knew him, so he knew who I was, too, so that made a good contact. Instead of asking for McCloy, I asked for Lee. After sitting for a short time, in came a little major with greying hair and bald on top. He came in with a grin on his face and put out his hand, "Hello, Nick!" I said, "Who are you?" "Don't you remember me? I'm Stier of the Tokyo YMCA." Stier's wife was a pacifist and, during World War I, once a week we got pacifists together in the Fellowship of Reconciliation of which I was secretary. Stier always came with his wife, but he was not a pacifist, and he would argue with us. Here was Stier as my escort! So that was pretty good; I was in the hands of friends. He took me right up to the G-2 section. The hall was full of missionaries' children whom I knew. I shook hands. Many of them were working there because they knew Japanese. As I mentioned, I had been offered a job but I'd refused, and my son had been offered a Naval job and he'd refused. Anyway, we went into Colonel Lee's office, and I told him what I was there for. He said, "That's a good job. I'll get an appointment with McCloy right away." So he phoned McCloy, and I had

forty-five minutes to wait. So I said, "Now while I'm waiting, Stier,
I'd like you to take me to see the man that has charge of drafting these
Nisei." He said, "Alright, that's Captain So-an-so," an Irish name. So
I went into his office and began talking with him. He said, "Oh, they
are a lot of roughnecks. Look at this letter." I read this letter. It
was a terrible thing! Swear words and poor language, not very well written, but very dramatically written. "We don't want to get in your blank
old Army." It had a lot of threats. It was terrific! I looked at the
captain and said, "Captain, you're Irish, aren't you?" He said, "Sure I
am." I said, "My father grew up in Ireland and almost married an Irish
girl. I'm pretty nearly Irish too." If they put us Irish behind barbed
wire with towers around it and men up there day and night with guns to
shoot us if we tried to get out, concentration camps like that, and then
they tried to draft us in their old Army, do you think we Irish would go?"
He said, "Of course, we wouldn't. We'd kick over the traces." I said,
"Now put yourself in their shoes and you read this letter." He read the
letter again, and he kind of smiled and said, "These fellows have guts,
haven't they?" (laughter) So after the talk with him, he shook his head
and said, "Say, Nicholson, I'm so glad you came in here and talked with
me about these fellows. I'm glad to see their point of view. And good
luck with McCloy. I hope you get those camps opened."

Well, I went to McCloy's office and Colonel Gearhart and Colonel Scoby
were there with him. Colonel Gearhart was middle-aged, about in his
forties perhaps, a gentleman, and Scoby was a white-haired tough militar-
ist. Scoby was the one who had gone around to all the camps recruiting
the 442nd volunteers, and he was the one that had helped make the 442nd
under McCloy. It was called "McCloy's baby." McCloy was quite proud of
what they were doing in Italy. Gearhart said, "Shall we leave the room?"
And McCloy said, "Oh, no, you can stay." First, I told about my visit to
Shelby, and they were thrilled. Scoby was happy and McCloy was delighted;
his baby was such a wonderful thing! I told him about the colonel. So I
got off on the right foot with all of them; they thought I was okay, although I was a Quaker pacifist. Then I got to the question of the war in
Japan. I said, "When you get to Japan and get within striking distance"--
they weren't there yet; they'd had one attack over Tokyo, the Doolittle attack when they came from a carrier, but that didn't amount to much--"are
you going to begin bombing like you're doing in Germany now, with these
blockbusters killing thousands of civilians every night?" He said, "No,
we're not. The Royal Air Force is doing that. When we get to Japan we're
going to have only daytime precision bombing; no bomb more than a thousand
pounds." I thought that was big enough! "And no nighttime bombing of civilian populations." I said, "That's wonderful. Are you going to bomb the
Emperor's palace? I saw in the paper today that this Council of Churches
says that you're going to bomb the Emperor's palace." He said, "No. That's
not the National Council, that's just the American Council of Churches which
is run from New Jersey by a fellow named Carl McIntyre." "Oh," I said,
"that relieves me. I thought the Council of Churches had more sense than
that." He said, "No, we're taking Ambassador Grew's advice. He says,

'Don't bomb Kyoto with all its history and so forth.' And we're not going to do that at all." I said, "Are you going to bomb my town of Mito in Ibaraki Ken?" He said, "I don't know where that is." He got out a map and put it on his big flattopped desk. It had red crosses on the places they were going to bomb. He showed me that map with its plans for the future. Ibaraki Ken had two crosses on it. One was the Hitachi factories. I said, "That's natural. That's where they're making all the war stuff, and that's definitely a military objective." The other was a naval airbase outside of Tsuchiuru. I said, "That's a military objective." There were other places on the map, but I didn't look down at Kyoto and so forth. But anyway, I got up and shook McCloy's hand and thanked him. "You're not going to bomb my town of Mito. It's just a provincial capital; there's nothing military there. There is a barracks there where the Second Regiment was stationed, but they're practically empty now, gone out." I was quite happy about that. Then I got on to this thing about the camps. And he agreed with me; all of them agreed with me. The other men did, too, that these camps should certainly be opened.

M: They agreed that it wasn't right to draft men while they were in the camps?

N: Not to draft while they were in these concentration camps. He said, "But I can't do anything about it because of public opinion." That's what everybody told me. Public opinion; it was not military at all, it was public opinion. And here was a man high up in the Army who said the same thing. "It's just because of public opinion we have them there, and because of public opinion we can't send them back to the West Coast. We get letters every day. They're just mimeographed copies. Sometimes they're not well written. We get these letters every day saying, 'Don't let those Japs back again.' We get very few letters on the other side. It's just disgusting." He said, "If you can fill this other basket on my desk with letters saying, 'We want our Japanese friends back again,' letters from California, Oregon, and Washington wanting them back again, we'll open the camps as soon as we're sure that public opinion is not one hundred percent against it." According to the letters, it was, say, about ninety percent against them coming back.

M: When you say "mimeographed copies," do you think, then, that there was sort of a group effort to send letters?

N: Yes, sure. Yes, these different people, the Sons of the Golden West, the nurserymen and gardeners associations, these associations were getting these things out and just having people sign and mail them in. That's all there was to it. "But," he said, "we have to count every one of them, and we don't count enough on the other side, and so we can't do it." I said, "Alright." And I said goodbye to them and thanked them very much for their giving me the time. I had about an hour with McCloy, I think. I went outside, and Scoby followed me out. He grabbed my arm and squeezed it viciously. He said, "Nicholson, those men don't know what they're talking about. When we get to Japan we're going to send them all to hell!" Then he turned around and went back into the office. Wasn't that awful, though?

I went right out and sent telegrams at once to Poston and back to the Friends of the American Way, to William Carr in Pasadena. And I went to Philadelphia right away and got in touch with the American Friends Service Committee headquarters, and they said they would contact all their offices in Seattle and San Francisco and Pasadena. I didn't go to New York, but I got in touch with the man on the Council of Churches. He was a Quaker who was in charge of this Japanese problem, Rustadt, or something like that, I think his name was. He went down to Washington and spent three days and never saw McCloy. He wanted to see him and get it for himself firsthand.

M: Did he do anything about the letter writing campaign?

N: I think he did. I think they sent letters to churches back on the West Coast to send letters in. But then I went to the Amache camp, and the camp director was a very fine Christian man. I told him what I wanted to do. I'd like to meet the camp council. The camp council came together, and I told them about my visit with McCloy, and I suggested they get a mimeographed letter, which they would send back to their friends, and enclosed three air mail stamped addressed envelopes to the President, to John J. McCloy and to Dillon Myer. "Get them all stamped and addressed and write back to **your** Caucasian friends and tell **them** to send letters in." Then I went up to Manzanar, to Poston, and to Rivers and wrote letters to all the other camps telling them to do this. That was March. I was at McCloy's office on March 20, 1944. By July, one hundred and fifty thousand letters had reached McCloy's desk, way out-numbering the ones on the other side. And most of them were good letters. They were personal letters which really made a great impression on the office. So they wrote at once to us, to William Carr in Pasadena. I wish I had a copy of their letter, but I don't.

M: They wrote to the Friends Committee?

N: No, not the Friends. To the Friends of the American Way, this little group who were writing letters. We believed in writing letters, you see.

M: Do you happen to remember some of the names of the people who belonged to the Friends of the American Way?

N: They were mostly Quakers.

M: Do you have a list anywhere?

N: No, I don't. William C. Carr was the one that ran it, he and his wife; we usually met at his home. And this Catherine Fanning I mentioned, she was always there. Alice Lewis Pierson was a Quaker lady missionary from Japan. When Esther B. Rhoads was here, she was always there. Dr. Douglas of the University of Southern California and his wife, Mr. and Mrs. Hugh Anderson of Pasadena, and my wife and I always went if I was around. I've forgotten the names of the Secretary and other people, whose faces I can see, but I can't remember names. About fifteen of us met two or three times a month or when a need arose. We were always active at Christmas time, arranging for presents for the people in the camps. We wrote a lot of letters and were generally being friendly. The American way is to be friendly with those within your midst, and we were being friendly with them. The American way was to tell your government what you thought of them. It's our government and our Army, and we should do it, see.

M: So he wrote a letter to the Friends of the American Way?

N: He wrote a letter saying that more letters came from Pasadena than from any other place. They'd been wonderful to send letters. The school here, Pasadena City College, sent lots of them. Harbison got under it and got the children to do it, you know. Oh, they just got stacks from Pasadena! It was wonderful!

M: So who was it that wrote the letter from Washington?

N: McCloy wrote a letter back saying that so many of the letters had come from there that "we'd like to send a girl to Pasadena Junior College in September 1944 and see what will happen, if she will be killed or what." So they picked a very attractive girl, very bright, from the Amache camp, whose brother had been killed in the 442nd in Italy. They asked her if she would go, and they made arrangements for her to come. We welcomed her and she went into the home of one of the Friends of the American Way, Hugh Anderson. For a month they had a lot of blackmail letters, threatening letters, telephone calls, and it was kind of nerve-racking. But out of a hundred letters that came, ninety-nine of them told her not to get frightened and stay by her guns, and only one out of a hundred took the other side--which was rather remarkable.

M: Did you tell me they took a poll at Pasadena College?

N: At Pasadena Junior College, Dr. Harbison took a poll and one hundred percent of the students wanted her to come, and ninety-eight percent of the professors. Two percent were a little scared that something might happen to the girl. So she came and was very successful after the first month. So in October--now this is a thing I'd really like to check on; I don't know how to do it, but I remember that it was about that time that the WRA sent word around to all the camps to make preparations to get out on January 2, 1945. But nobody else has said that in any book, and it's just memory. But I know that way before December the camps were working on clearing out and I was around, active, talking with folks and trying to make plans. I know that for a fact. I hate to be the only one that says it when others say that other things did it.

M: So in other words, it was the letter writing campaign and the good experience with this young lady that resulted then in the opening of the the camps? Is that right?

N: That's right. In Bill Hosokawa's book, Nisei: The Quiet Americans, which is very good, he gives dates for things that happened. I was very glad to see those dates. He put in this date that it was December, just before Christmas, I think, December 18, that the Army said the camps could be opened. And the Supreme Court gave its decision after Christmas, so the Supreme Court had nothing to do with it. It had all been decided way before that. The WRA made up its mind that it was going to happen before that. It was just public opinion, not a military necessity. Everybody still doesn't know it. There are still a lot of people that think it was the other way around. But I'd like to find out from the WRA records somewhere back there just when they did begin telling the camps. They sent out letters to them. Those letters must be in the files somewhere.

M: But you think it must be about October that they decided they were going to open the camps?

N: Oh, I think it was as early as October.

M: Do you know if this young lady still lives in the area?

N: She lives here in Pasadena and she's married. We see her. That was quite an experience.

ANNA T. KELLEY

THEY DON'T LEARN FROM HISTORY

AN INTERVIEW WITH ANNA T. KELLEY

INTRODUCTION

In studying the Japanese-American evacuation period, scholars tend to forget that thousands of other Americans also had their lives altered by that reality, not in the same way as for the internees, but changed nonetheless. Many administrators and teachers worked for the War Relocation Authority, never to return to former homes to live.

For example, Ed. H. Runcorn came from New Mexico to organize the cooperative stores in Amache camp. In the postwar period, he settled in the Quaker town of Whittier, California and converted to the Society of Friends, largely because he admired their dedicated work in the relocation centers.

Then there were those who were left behind--those who may have had emotional or economic ties with Japanese Americans. Sue Kunitomi Embrey recalls an old bachelor, veteran of the Spanish-American War, who lived in Little Tokyo and relied on that community for his total life sustenance: friendships, shops, restaurants, etc. When the community left, he withered away from loneliness and neglect.

Communities located in close proximity to relocation centers are untapped repositories of vast amounts of potential oral history documentation. Some communities turned inward and chose to pretend that the nearby "Jap camp" didn't exist. Others established something of a liaison with the interned people, encouraging them to come into town to shop. Still others seem to have taken a mixed course, excluding internees from town while, at the same time, selling supplies to the local camp and furnishing employees to work in some phase of administration.

Anna T. Kelley, in the early days of Manzanar camp, was the first-aid operator for the crews constructing the buildings. At her post she was in a unique position, as a disinterested party, to observe the scene inside the camp in its beginnings. As a town resident and an operator, with her husband, of a gas station, she was, during the same period, able to observe the reactions of townsfolk to the camp.

Arthur A. Hansen and David J. Bertagnoli interviewed Anna T. Kelley at her home in Independence, California on December 6, 1973. The interview is reproduced in its entirety and, while it deals mainly with the internment period, of particular note are Mrs. Kelley's remarks on the historical marker placed at the Manzanar site and her comments on the possibility of such a thing as mass internment of a people ever happening again.

H: Anna, when was it that you had some information that there would be a relocation center in the nearby area, close to Lone Pine and Independence?

K: Well, probably about six months prior to the beginning of actual construction.

H: Were you involved in any way in the construction process?

K: I ran a first-aid shack. I was the first-aid operator for Pacific Indemnity Company, the insurance company that carried the insurance for all five construction companies that built the camp.

H: Did any of the internees have anything to do with the construction of the camp?

K: No, not at that time. The only construction they did came later, when they built such buildings as the auditorium on their own. But they did not participate in the actual building of the camp.

H: Do you know where the construction companies came from? Were they based in Los Angeles?

K: I believe the main construction company was Griffith and Company. I'm not sure, it has been so long. And then there would have been the plumbers, the roofers, and the electricians that were subcontracted. But I think the main construction company was Griffith out of Los Angeles.

H: Were the subcontractors local people?

K: No. All of these people, all of the companies, came from Southern California.

H: To what extent were people from the nearby area hired to work as carpenters, plumbers, or whatever?

K: See, it was such a crash program, and they had to get this thing built in such a hurry that anyone that was interested could apply for a job. But I believe the biggest percentage of the workers came from outside the county.

H: Do you think there was any impact at all on the economy of the neighboring towns of Lone Pine and Independence?

K: There couldn't help but be, because of the need for supplies.

H: In what ways did you see this reflected? Did you see some people having their standard of living raised as a result of the camp?

K: Oh, no. I think the materials to build the camp were all brought in. I mean, they wouldn't have been purchased locally because there was nothing big enough in the area at that time to supply the needed quantity. Everything was brought in. The only impact at the time of construction would have been from the purchasing and the buying in the towns on the part of the people that worked at the camp.

H: How about employment as security officers, and so forth. I believe some local people were involved in that, weren't they?

K: Yes, that's true, but I think the security business came later.

H: You are talking just about the early stages and early construction.

K: Early construction period, yes.

H: The reason I'm trying to find out about whether there was any profit, etc., is because it has often been said that certain areas actually vied to have relocation centers placed in their areas, since these camps entailed, you know, sometimes upward of four or five millions of dollars in terms of total investment. But you say most of this was really going back to construction companies in Los Angeles and not really going locally at all?

K: That's right. I think the greatest benefit, as far as the economic impact on this area, would have been after the camp was established. Then local people worked there in various capacities. But at the time of construction, no.

H: Can you remember the attitude when the people in the area found out a camp was going to be built there at Manzanar?

K: They were very much against it.

H: Can you recall any specific instances or demonstrations?

K: No. Well, we wouldn't have had any demonstration or anything like that. It would have been just opinion.

H: What kind of opinion circulated around the markets, for instance? Can you recall any general feelings that you observed when you went to the store or talked to people?

K: Well, it was just like, you know, "The damn Japs. Why do we have to have them here?" Up here, I think, it was mostly fear because, well, it was wartime and they were panicky. The fear was no different up here than it was in Southern California, otherwise this thing would never have happened, you know, because these people [Japanese Americans] were American citizens.

H: What about when you went out to the camp yourself, when you were working out there? You had a chance to not just hear about the camp and hear about ten thousand people being kept up there, but you had a chance to experience some of the early arrivals, didn't you?

K: I was there when the first group was brought in. The opinion . . . . We're discussing opinion, and I must say this: the people that worked to build the camp were nothing but sympathetic. They had the greatest sympathy for the people that were being brought into the camp, particularly under such horrible conditions, because they weren't ready for them at all when the first group was brought in.

H: Were the barracks still not built?

K: Oh, no, there were some barracks built, but they didn't have doors or windows in them. The construction people worked far into the night to get some of the barracks closed in and to get some of those people in out of the weather. There were women, children, and old people-- just everybody, you know. It was a cross-section of humanity.

H: This was in the spring?

K: Yes, it was early.

H: In March, or something?

K: Yes, early spring, and it was very cold and very windy. It was very disagreeable.

H: What was the response of the Japanese Americans to the Caucasians who were working there, like yourself? Did they exhibit hostility toward you?

K: No, no. I never felt any hostility. I didn't come very much in contact with them because, you see, the first-aid shack was out in front where all of the saw tables and stacks of lumber and everything else was, out in front--well, it would be to the east, and all of the buildings lay farther on to the west. I wouldn't have seen very much of the Japanese, hardly at all.

H: How long were you at Manzanar?

K: Two and a half months.

H: What did you do after that?

K: Oh, I didn't work out there anymore. I could have, but I turned it down.

H: I expect you remember that at the end of the first year, December 1942, almost on the eve of Pearl Harbor day, there was a riot of some proportions out at Manzanar where two people, two Japanese Americans, were killed, and ten others were wounded. Do you recall any sort of response to that in Independence? Were people aware of it?

K: Oh, yes, they were aware of it because, you see, part of the Japanese were taken out of the camp and taken over into the Death Valley area for security purposes, until the troublemakers were weeded out and the situation was taken care of. But that's the only trouble that Manzanar ever had.

H: Did that cause a lot of anxiety on the part of the people in the town? There was a lot of publicity about it in the newspapers all over the country.

K: Well, there couldn't help but be, you know. I think it didn't bother a few people, but most were again afraid.

H: Did you ever go back to the camp after you left your job?

K: No. Well, now that's not quite true. After everything settled down, there used to be baseball games on Sundays between the Japanese and the construction people that were still there. I went to a couple of those.

H: I've heard from some people that when teachers who were employed out there, Caucasians, would come into Independence and into Lone Pine, they met with a good deal of hostility and were called "Jap lovers," and so forth, and some restaurants refused to serve them. Is this factual?

K: It is to a certain extent, but I don't think a great deal of it was. Well, it's a small town and people never change, even though . . . . I mean, they were opinionated, and they don't dig very far to get facts and all this sort of thing. Ignorance makes for criticism.

H: Can you recall any specific criticism? Was there some vigilante activity?

K: Oh, not that I know of. I don't recall any vigilante activity. There was one thing that I never will forget, and it made me feel the saddest of all. There was a young man who was home on furlough, a Japanese who wore the United States uniform--he was in the Army--and all of his people were in Manzanar. Of course, he was going to be shipped overseas. He came to Manzanar to see his people. People were so stupid, particularly the people of Lone Pine, that they wouldn't allow that young man to come out of camp and go into the town as long as he was on furlough because his folks were in camp. Yet he was an American soldier. This was the type of feeling that I'm trying to tell you about. It's hard to explain.

H: Yes, there was a sort of tension.

K: That's right.

H: And there was this fear we were talking about.

K: There was a lot of gossip, too, about how much the people in the camp made that got paid, such great amounts of money, and they lived like kings and all the rest of the things. It wasn't true.

H: Can you remember a bit more about the gossip because I think this kind of stuff is an important indicator of the sort of feelings people had. Did they feel the Japanese were eating rationed goods--sugar, meat, and so forth?

K: Well, there was one person that I know criticized the camp and made a lot of misstatements about how they lived, the things that they had, the food that they ate, and all of this sort of stuff. And he himself was a hoarder.

H: Really?

K: Yes.

H: So it was somewhat hypocritical.

K: He was a definite hypocrite. I mean, this is the type of thing, and there were many of them.

H: Do you think the rumors were widely believed among most of the people in town?

K: Unfortunately, I think it is true that the rumors were believed. You know, we were pretty busy right at first trying to get this thing under control, but after the work slacked up a little bit, I had a chance to do a little digging for information on my own. All of the information that these people were yaking about and all of the things they were saying were all wrong. They had professional people down there, such as Dr. Moto who had been a physician and surgeon at the Los Angeles General Hospital. That man worked in the hospital at Manzanar. I think he was paid eighteen dollars a month, barely enough to keep him in shaving cream and face soap and this type of thing.

H: This is Dr. Goto, though, rather, isn't it?

K: No, it was Moto. I'm pretty sure it was Moto.

H: Because there was a Dr. James Goto. I was just wondering if it might have been him.

K: Well, I might be mistaken; it could be. But anyway, he was quite a famous physician doing work at, well, it was Los Angeles County General then. The name is changed now. But for the other professional people, professional nurses, lawyers, teachers, and all of them, I think the top pay was twelve dollars a month. And they were glad to get it because everything that they had had been impounded.

H: I expect your situation was a little bit different, in that you had some firsthand exposure to the camp, whereas a lot of people had no personal contact with the situation.

K: Yes, this is true but, if I started talking to the outside people, they wouldn't believe me; they wouldn't believe you. Such crazy things happened, for instance: this was wartime, an emergency situation. Good or bad, whichever way you want to look at it, it was still something that had to be done because the powers-that-be said that we must build camps and put these people in them. Okay. There was a union representative out of Bakersfield, and I can't say that he was a type that would do credit to the human race. Anyway, this character . . . . See, my first-aid shack was about right here, and right over here was the main office of Griffith Company, the main construction company I told you about awhile ago. Their pay window was at the end of this barrack-type thing, and the people were paid every week. This character would stand right there by that pay window. These people were working like dogs to get this meager pay, and the vast majority of the construction people really felt so sorry for the people. They were sympathizing with these Japanese. But this character would stand by the pay window and, as the men would come up to get their paycheck, if they didn't have on a union button, he'd say, "Okay, friend, I'll cash your check. And if I don't cash your check and take your dues, you don't work tomorrow."

H: Very hardheaded.

K: Oh, horrible. And everybody hated him, you know, wished that something would drop on his head or something. But I think the worst was when the union organizers got into camp. I can't remember the man's name who was the head of Griffith Company; it has been too long and you don't think about it. But anyway, he came into the first-aid shack one day and said, "Anna, you'll never guess what I just found out." And I said, "What?" He said, "You know the camouflage work?" The Japanese were making camouflage nets, and they didn't get paid [much] for it. They were glad to have something to do. They were making camouflage nets for the government. Somehow or other, two union organizers got into the camp, and they never did find out how they got in, because there was a main gate, you know, with guards and all. You had to have passes and all this kind of thing. Anyway, there were two union organizers, and they went up to this area where they were making the nets and proceeded to try to organize the Japanese who were doing the work. (laughter) This was stupid! This is the type of thing that you would run into, you know.

H: It's a wonder how they got access into the camp.

K: We never did find out. They went through the fence, I guess.

H: They started to organize the Japanese in the camouflage net factory?

K: Yes, these Japanese who were working for [practically] nothing. The camp was pretty much self-sufficient and self-supporting because there was water that came down from Bear's Creek and Shepherd's Creek, and they had built quite a reservoir which they needed to store the water in to supply the needs of the camp. It was built for ten thousand people. I think they had about eight thousand there. They built a large-sized reservoir and used part of this water, and then part of the water was diverted from the creek for irrigation purposes. They had huge gardens.

H: Already, in the first couple of months?

K: Well, they started as soon as they were able to. And they had poultry and pigs and that type of thing. In fact, quite a bit of the food that was produced there was shipped out to other camps.

H: Was any of it shipped out to the towns?

K: No. Of course, people stole it. (laughter)

H: They did?

K: Oh, it was just like any government project. The people that worked there . . . .

H: Oh, the people at the project?

K: Yes, the Caucasians that worked there would come home with stuff.

H: Anna, what were you doing after you left the camp? Did you have employment in the town of Independence?

K: Well, we've been on this corner for forty-three years. My husband and and I started here in 1931.

H: Started a gas station here?

K: Yes. Well, my husband was here a year before we were married. The gas station is much older than that by ten years. As I said, I was drafted into this job at Manzanar. You know, everybody was gone, there was no help, and they needed people, so I took that job. Then shortly after that, I was drafted into another one, and became Welfare Director for Inyo County. I took that job until I figured I had a husband who could support me, and I expected them to accept my resignation when the men came home from war.

H: So you were working, then, as an Inyo County employee after you left Manzanar?

K: After Manzanar, yes.

H: Do you recall any public pressure put on people in the towns of Lone Pine and Independence who might have reacted favorably toward the Japanese? Was there a sort of silent agreement that you weren't supposed to speak on their behalf or to criticize the government for placing them in relocation centers? Do you recall that kind of conspiracy of silence or anything like that?

K: I didn't witness anything like that but, like I said awhile ago, I have a sharp tongue, and people would be hesitant to criticize me because I'd stand up to them. On top of that, I had information, so they knew that I knew what was the truth concerning the camp and the people at Manzanar.

H: Were you at least partially associated with the gas station during World War II?

K: Oh, yes.

H: You had travelers coming through. What kind of curiosity about the camp was aroused on the part of people who journeyed through here?

K: You know, people seem to get hypnotized when they're in an automobile. A lot of people that passed by the camp didn't even seem to realize it was there. Of course, there was no big thing at Manzanar, no big sign or anything like that.

H: There were some guard towers there.

K: Yes, there were guard towers but, if they were going at a pretty fast clip, they wouldn't even have noticed them.

H: Was there a lot of fear in either Independence or Lone Pine--maybe you can't speak for Lone Pine, but in the surrounding area--some fear that the Japanese might stay in this area after the camps were disbanded?

K: Probably, but I don't know of a great deal. Like I say, I had this other job, and it took all of my time. I worked about seven days a week on it, and other than just the people that I worked with and knew, we were too busy trying to keep things going in a wartime situation. You see, we had gas rationing and everything else, so it took . . . . If I had to go to Death Valley, it took a long time to get there. You know, this type of thing.

H: Do you recall any kind of programs that were held out at the camp to which people from the local communities were invited?

K: Oh, yes, there were a great many, and a lot of people did go. This was later, after things started settling down.

H: Did they reciprocate by allowing Japanese to come into the towns once in awhile?

K: I can't recall that they did. I think the Japanese had to stay there. I can't recall that the Japanese were allowed to come into town. But some of them may have had passes. I don't know; I can't say for sure.

H: Do you think that very many of the people around here, prior to the installation of the camp, had seen Japanese Americans before, or any other Asians, such as Chinese or Filipinos?

K: Well, we had a few Chinese throughout the area, and we had a few Japanese. We had a Chinese cook here at the Independence Hotel for a number of years, and we had a Japanese section foreman at the railroad station. You know, there used to be a narrow-gauge railway that ran through the area. And we had a Japanese section foreman over there and a Chinese section hand. So local people weren't completely ignorant of Asian people, but we didn't have very many. It was just like with blacks; we had maybe one or two. Of course, this goes back thirty years, you know that?

H: You don't remember that there was a strong anti-Japanese feeling in the area prior to the war?

K: Oh, no, I don't think there was any prior to the war. I don't recall any definite anti-Asian feeling or anything like that.

H: There is sort of a paradox here, in the sense that the area had actually depended to a large extent on tourist travel.

K: That's right.

H: And during the war, the tourist travel considerably dried up.

K: Yes, it practically did.

H: And one of the things which kept the economy of the area functioning somewhat was the fact that jobs were supplied by the camp. They got something out of it, and yet they were against the Japanese being here.

K: That's right.

H: It was an irony of sorts, wasn't it?

K: That's right.

H: We're going to move beyond the camp experience now. Do you recall that last year in the spring of 1973 there was a monument installed, a commemorative plaque installed, out at the camp which indicated that the camp had had to exist because of certain factors in American society. "Racism, hysteria, and economic exploitation" were things that were mentioned. Do you recall any reaction around here to the installation of the plaque?

K: You mean against it?

H: Yes, against it.

K: I don't know of anything against it. There might have been, but I don't know of anything against it because of the dedication of that plaque. A great many people came, you know, busloads of people came, Japanese, whites, and just everybody, and a lot of local people from the county around.

H: You didn't see anything in the local newspaper which brought it up?

K: I don't recall anything. I doubt whether anything adverse would be put in the local paper, anyway.

H: You get the Chalfant Press newspaper, is that it?

K: Yes. The Chalfant Press prints all of the papers for the towns of Lone Pine, Independence, Bishop, and Bridgeport.

H: They have separate editions, but they essentially just change the first pages for the various towns?

K: Yes, the front page. (laughter)

H: Do you recall the Chalfant Press's attitude back in the 1940s toward the existence of the camp?

K: I can't recall. I don't know, and I doubt whether there would have been anything in the papers then, because the paper is noted for not taking stands, if you know what I mean.

H: A rather wishy-washy editorial policy?

K: It always has been in the past, that's right. In fact, they're taking more of a definite stand just recently than they ever did in the past. They didn't deal in anything controversial.

H: I probably haven't covered all the kinds of things we should cover, so I would like you to just think back over the whole experience, your work experience at the camp, the community response to it, etc., and discuss anything that you think needs to be recalled at this time.

K: I am positive that, perhaps excepting for Mexican people who are easy-going, I don't think any other nationality would ever have been contained in a barbed wire encampment by a small company of soldiers. To me, this is an indication of the type of people that these Japanese were. When they first started coming to the camp, you watched their faces, and they were afraid, you know. There was fear and there was uncertainty, yes; a lot of them had almost given up. What was ahead of them? They'd had everything that they owned confiscated, and they didn't know whether they would even have a place to live. But these people overcame all of this. Working with nothing but their ingenuity, the native plants, the scraps of lumber and bits of metal that the construction company was glad to let them have, they built furniture for their barrack apartments. They built a little park with a little stream and put a little Japanese bridge over it. They grew all of the native plants because, you see, there was nothing else available for them at first. They would go out on the desert where they could go, toward the mountains, and bring in cactus and wildflowers and things like that and plant them around the doors of their barracks to make it pleasant. I have one chair; I had four of them. When they broke the camp up, the Japanese were all gone, and they were selling what was there. I bought four of the chairs for a dollar apiece that were made by the Japanese out of scrap lumber. In fact, I used those four chairs around this table for a long time.

H: Did the government auction this material off?

K: Well, it wasn't particularly an auction. The stuff was there for sale. I guess it should have been an auction, because it was public property, but I can't recall whether they actually had an auction there.

H: The government sold it?

K: Yes.

H: I've seen several buildings in Lone Pine which were previously barracks out at Manzanar. Are those dotting the area all around here? Do you know of any in Independence?

K: I don't know of any in Independence, but you wouldn't recognize them.

H: The facing has been changed considerably.

K: Well, the whole thing has been changed. There might be one down there that is an apartment house now. Perhaps that building might have been; I'm not sure about that one.

H: Do you remember seeing a lot of townspeople out at Manzanar after the Japanese left, similarly buying furniture and things like you were talking about?

K: Oh, yes. Yes. I gave three of my chairs to the Eastern California Museum here in Independence, because I thought they would preserve them.

H: I think I've seen one of your chairs down at the museum. It had a
    little note on it that this was built by an internee at the Manzanar
    War Relocation Center.

K: I'm glad. How those people managed to put up with everything!
    Because, you see, the lumber that was used in the barracks was green,
    and this is arid country. This is dry, so you know what happened.
    It dried out immediately, and big cracks appeared. They were covered
    with tar paper. Well, it was building paper; it wasn't even roofing
    paper, but heavy black paper, tar paper. We used it all the time at
    the camp. When the boards would crack, the paper would split too and
    let the weather in. Yet they managed to live.

H: Did this whole business of incarcerating out at Manzanar a population
    that amounted to perhaps two-thirds or more American citizens lessen
    your faith somewhat in democratic institutions in the United States?

K: I don't think it lessened my feeling toward the democratic form of
    government, but I think it's one of the worst blotches that we've ever
    had in our history. But people being such as they are, when they
    push the panic button, anything can come out. It could happen again.

H: What about people here in town whose sons were killed in the war?

K: Some were pretty bitter and others not. I mean, you know, forgiving,
    realizing . . . .

H: Would it be possible for a Japanese American to live very happily in
    Independence now, or do you think some feelings against them remain?

K: Oh, I should think, yes, they would be able to live here if they
    wished because, you see, a great many of the people are gone--they're
    dead because they were older people--that worked down there or were so
    opinionated at the time. A lot of the younger ones have moved away;
    they're not here anymore. The population of our town has had a pretty
    good-sized turnover. There aren't that many of us left around now.

H: Was the town bigger before the war?

K: No, our population stays pretty much the same.

H: About a thousand?

K: I think we have, maybe, twelve to fifteen hundred now, counting every-
    body. But what we're getting now is an influx of retired people from
    Southern California. It changes the picture.

H: It seems to be a different sort of town from Lone Pine. Are these
    retirees from Los Angeles welcome?

K: Well, I don't know whether you could say they welcome them or not. I

think one thing that is resented is that they take the available property and/or the available housing, and there isn't much left for
people that make a living here. There is this feeling. However, at
the same time these people have bolstered the economy of this little
town for the simple reason that they spend money here. So there is a
balance.

H: So it's the same sort of irony that we noted before.

K: Yes, it's the same thing we had before, only . . . .

H: I want to go back to the prewar situation again. We've talked a little
bit about Independence. Was there a small circle of important people
that pretty much ran the town of Independence?

K: Oh, yes there was. There always is a certain amount.

H: First family types, or businessmen?

K: Let's see. Well, as far as Independence is concerned, it would probably be a sort of cross-section. We had the main headquarters of the
Department of Water and Power for the City of Los Angeles here. Their
main offices are here, and it's the county seat. We don't have much
ranching area or anything around like we used to a long time ago, so
those people would have left or moved into town and changed their
occupation. But as far as running the town affairs are concerned,
it's called the Civic Club. It started out as the old Commercial Club
and then it changed its name. And to this Civic Club, everyone can go.
The Commercial Club was business people, and they looked out for the
town pretty well in those days. I was a kid then, you know; it was a
long time ago. And the business and professional men's organization
kind of deteriorated a little bit, because they let in people who were
not really professional or business, either one.

H: Into the club?

K: Into the club, which changed the picture, you know. Now, I think, once
in awhile a businessman is president of the Civic Club.

H: What was the attitude back then toward the Indians? Did they fit in
the town or not?

K: I don't think that one could say that the Indian was ever excluded in
this area. This is my own thinking; I went to school with Indian kids.
The people that are the same age as me work for the Department of Water
and Power, or they work for the county, or they work for the state, the
same as all the rest of us do. Many of them have good educations.

H: Would you say their social status is high in the town relative to
Caucasians, or not?

K: Now?

H: Then.

K: Then? Maybe social status was not so high then, but it certainly has changed as far as now is concerned. I mean, a long time ago, in the early days, of course, you have to remember that the old people, the old Indians, such as the ones who wove my baskets, stuck to their way of living because they preferred to. Some of them that I know even lived in little wikiups over in Death Valley. The rest of them lived in rehab [rehabilitation] houses that the government had built after the [Death Valley] Monument was established. Here there were areas outside of each town where the Indians lived on reservations--not a true reservation, it's different. They had little frame houses, some kept in pretty good shape and others not, just like us, you know, the same thing. At one time they had an Indian school at the fort, but this was before my time. There was an elementary school out there at the fort and one in here. Afterward they went to the elementary school. They consolidated the schools and brought everybody into the elementary here, so the Indians came in here, the same as they came to our high school. And in my days of going to school, some of our greatest athletes were Indians. We had track teams and basketball teams--not football in those years--baseball, and this type of thing. And they were good students.

H: Do you remember any athletic competition, during the time of the camp, between Independence High School and the Manzanar young people?

K: Manzanar, you mean?

H: Yes.

K: They had baseball games.

H: But did they have games with Independence teams; did the high school teams play competitively?

K: No, I don't know. I can't recall whether that school down there and the one in town entered into competition. I don't think so.

H: One further question, Anna. Was there a great amount of fear? I mean, here you have a town of roughly a thousand, and you have in Lone Pine a town not much larger . . . .

K: It's about the same.

H: And then you've got a town with ten thousand people located right in between, in a wartime situation. Was there an underlying fear that something would happen? Was it a tense period for people living in Independence?

K: I think for some people it was tense. They were afraid, but others weren't. I don't know how widespread the fear would have been because, like I say, I was pretty busy at the time and didn't have a chance to talk to very many people.

H: Okay, Anna. David Bertagnoli, do you have any questions you would like to ask?

B: I'd like to talk about the Manzanar plaque for a minute. You talked about the general feeling of the town toward the plaque, but you didn't say anything about your own personal opinion.

K: I think it's fine that they've put a plaque there. I only hope somebody doesn't steal it like they've done at so many other places. I think the camp should be a registered historical site.

B: Do you agree with the wording on the plaque?

K: I don't know what the wording says. I didn't get to the placement ceremony, and I don't know. I haven't had a chance to stop and read it. It sounds stupid for me to say that, but it's the truth.

B: I have a copy of the wording here, if you'd like to look it over.

H: Anna, let me read that aloud for the tape, then we'll have it on there, and you can comment on it.

K: Alright.

H: "In the early part of World War II, 110,000 persons of Japanese ancestry were interned in relocation centers by Executive Order No. 9066, issued on February 19, 1942. Manzanar, the first of ten such concentration camps, was bounded by barbed wire and guard towers, confining 10,000 persons, the majority being American citizens. May the injustices and humiliation suffered here as a result of hysteria, racism and economic exploitation never emerge again."

K: It shouldn't say "concentration camp." It wasn't one.

B: Why do you say that?

K: Well, it was a . . . . In a concentration camp the people are in horrible straits. I mean, in Europe, you know, just terrible and all jammed together and no privileges, no means of keeping themselves clean or anything else. And this is not true of Manzanar. Manzanar was a war relocation center. The living conditions were pretty adverse at first, but after the camp was built and the people had a chance to, like I say, make themselves comfortable, it was pretty good. It wasn't bad at all.

B: Do you feel they were given a limited amount of freedom?

K: Well, they couldn't come in and out of the camp. They couldn't come in and out, except to go fishing. They were allowed to go into the mountains to fish.

B: Could you elaborate on that a little bit?

K: Well, I don't know what else to say. You see, the streams have trout in them, and the lakes in back of the camp up in the high country have trout.

B: Did they go up there quite frequently?

K: Well, probably whenever they could.

B: I've heard from others that many of the Japanese Americans were happy to be in the camps because they felt that they were being protected from the American citizenry.

K: That's right.

B: Did you ever get this feeling from the Japanese Americans?

K: Well, I can't say that I got it directly from them, but only from people that were friends of mine who took positions in the camp after it was established.

B: Do you remember any instance they told you about or any conversation that they had with the Japanese Americans?

K: Well, not particular conversations or anything like that, except that I know that a great many of the people, particularly the older people, were happy to be in the camp after it was established, you know, when they got over the fear of not knowing what was going to happen to them. It's just awful to think about being uprooted out of everything and not knowing what's going to happen. Then when it turned out to be not as bad as it could have been . . . . Of course, it wasn't like living in your own home, but they made it pretty comfortable, and they had good food and good care. Of course, they brought all of their professional people with them. They had schools, they had good teachers. They made furniture and clothing and all sorts of things.

B: You indicated that you think that, under some circumstances, a situation like this could arise in the United States again?

K: It probably could. Sometimes people don't learn by experience, and they don't learn from history. People being what they are, they push the panic button.

B: In view of the civil rights movement and everything, do you think the

Caucasian people would stand for such a thing again?

K: I should hope not, but I wouldn't guarantee it. (laughter) Maybe that is a harsh statement, but . . . . I don't know.

B: I have no further questions, if you don't, Arthur.

H: Well, Anna, I'd just like to thank you very much for the Japanese American Oral History Project at Cal State Fullerton, and myself and David. Thank you very, very much for your cooperation and for your frank responses.

K: You're entirely welcome. Quite a few of the Japanese stop here when they come to see where their parents or their grandparents were during the war. We're close, and I'm able to give them information on how to get there. A niece of mine worked with a Japanese in Southern California. He's a younger generation, and his parents were at Manzanar. He came up here several years ago. One of the women of Independence, Helen Gunn, worked at the camp and she did as much as she could. She was one of these people that would cook a turkey and go out to the desert and call in all of the old desert rats to have Thanksgiving dinner. Well, she did what she could for the Japanese and they respected her for it. In fact, they loved her. So anyway, she was married here, and they went to San Francisco, and somehow or other the Japanese found out about it. She and her husband were going to Mexico on a trip, so this young man got in touch with as many of the Japanese who had been at Manzanar as he could possibly reach. And when Helen and her husband got to Los Angeles, they had a bang-up party for them and gave them a beautiful set of dishes as a wedding present. I thought that was pretty nice. She was the type of person--there were some, you know--who felt very sorry and very sad about this and did what they could to help them.

H: Is she still living?

K: No, she has passed away.

Courtesy of
David Payne

MANZANAR—THE CONTINUING STRUGGLE

An Interview with Sue Kunitomi Embrey

INTRODUCTION

On the morning of April 14, 1973, a plaque, sponsored by the California State Department of Parks and Recreation in cooperation with the Manzanar Committee and the Japanese American Citizens League, was cemented into the facade of the sentry house at the entrance of the Manzanar War Relocation Center in Owens Valley, California. More than one thousand "pilgrims"--former internees and their offspring, governmental representatives, and a sprinkling of interested spectators-- listened while the Co-chairperson of the Manzanar Committee, Sue Kunitomi Embrey, presided over a short dedication ceremony. The assembled gathering, which had grouped itself into clusters under raised placards signifying the various internment camps, were asked to ponder the meaning of the words inscribed upon the plaque.

These words (see opposite page) had a dual significance for Sue Embrey. As a young woman she, along with her family, had been uprooted from her Los Angeles home and incarcerated at the Manzanar Center. There she took an active part in camp life for two years, serving as managing editor of the Manzanar Free Press before resettling in Madison, Wisconsin. She did not forget Manzanar and the evacuation experience, however. After a postwar respite from involvement in the affairs of the Los Angeles Japanese American community, she increasingly became committed to community causes. The most recent and celebrated was her participation in the Manzanar Committee and its successful struggle to place the historical marker at Manzanar to remind Americans that freedom denied to some is freedom denied to all.

The portion of the interview which follows was conducted by Arthur A. Hansen and David J. Bertagnoli at Ms. Embrey's office in the Asian American Studies Center at the University of California, Los Angeles on November 15, 1973. Although it contains her reflections on her earlier internment at Manzanar, it emphasizes her later activities with the Manzanar Committee.

H: When did you, in the postwar period, start to work more in the Japanese American community?

E: After I was married in 1950 I didn't have too much to do with community groups; there weren't too many political activities going on. I joined the neighborhood Democratic Club, and I did see some of my friends, but we never had any kind of a group that was organized. There was a West Jefferson Democratic Club, which was considered kind of a liberal Democratic club, and it was all Japanese. There were a few Chinese in it, but that sort of disbanded in the 1950s, and my husband and I got more involved in our local Democratic Club in the neighborhood. So I sort of drifted away from the Japanese community during the 1950s, and I didn't get back to it until I was at Cal State Los Angeles in 1968-- let's see, I started there in 1966, but it was around 1967 or 1968 when the San Francisco State strike and all of these things were happening, and by the end of 1968 people were talking at the Cal State campus about forming an Ethnic Studies group. Black Studies and Chicano Studies got started there and some of the Asian students thought we should get a couple of Asian History classes going, or Asian American History. So I was involved in a study group there most of 1969, but I was about ready to graduate so I wasn't really that involved until toward the end, maybe the summer and the last quarter, last two quarters of 1969. We did get an instructor, we did get a class going, and it was so full that they had to divide the class in two and get two instructors. They did get some money and an office on campus, but there wasn't much more than that. Then I went over to the University of Southern California to work on my Master's, so I kind of dropped out of that group and started doing my intern and student teaching. That was in Culver City. I was going to a few meetings. Then around 1970 I saw a notice in the paper that there was a task force trying to form an Asian American Education Commission to advise the Los Angeles City Board of Education. They had organized the Black Education Commission and the Mexican American Commission after some high school students had walked out and caused a student strike. One was in East Los Angeles with the Chicano students and one was in a predominantly black high school. So they thought that in order to avoid any other kind of confrontations, possibly, which might come from the Asian community, it might be a good idea to form a task force and start a commission before the problem started, and try to identify problems, if they existed in the Asian community. So I got involved in 1970 and 1971 with helping to write the proposal for a commision, holding meetings in different parts of the city--we had a couple in Chinatown, one in Gardena, a couple in the Japanese community, and we got the commission formed. I was asked to put my name up for nomination as one of the commissioners, to be elected by ballot. We had something like forty-five names on the ballot and we were supposed to pick a total of twenty-seven, and then three would be appointed to kind of balance geographically, ethnically, and occupationally, because we had decided on five ethnic groups in the twelve geographic areas of the city school district, plus grass-roots community people, teachers, and students, and they didn't want one ethnic group or one occupational group predominating. I was elected for the first year and helped get the commission going, and I served as its secretary. From then on I got involved in other things. A group of young girls wanted to help other girls who had been on drugs and formed a group called Asian Sisters, so I would go to their meetings and help them a little bit. By that time we were talking about starting the Manzanar Committee, so I didn't want to get involved in too many other things.

H: Who is <u>we</u> that were starting to talk about forming the Manzanar Committee?

E: After the San Francisco State College strike, a group of college students became involved in setting up Asian American Studies programs on different campuses, and one of the things they wanted to talk about was the evacuation and internment period. Most of them complained, to me and to others, that their parents didn't want to talk about it, that the information was not coming from their parents, and they wanted personal interviews, personal experiences. So around 1969 they decided to have a pilgrimage to Manzanar, and they picked December 27. When they told me about it and asked if I would be interested in going, I said, "You picked a terrible time of year. It's going to be cold up there." And their answer was, "That's why we picked it; we want these young people to know what it was like physically, and then from there on we can talk about camp experiences." I don't know if you have anything in your Oral History collection of that first pilgrimage from anybody else. Do you?

H: No, we don't.

E: You don't. Okay, there were two television networks that covered that event; one was NBC, the other was CBS. I think ABC also had some coverage.

H: There wasn't a committee that was . . .

E: There was no real committee. There was a group that called themselves an organization, an umbrella organization supposedly, which had just been formed, but it wasn't really a permanent group. Most of the coordinating was being done by college students on the campuses, and the whole idea had come from Reverend Mayeda, who had been a Buddhist minister in Manzanar, who since the close of the camp had been going every year by himself or with his family and who conducted a Buddhist service once a year for the people who had been buried in Manzanar. He had a son going to UCLA, and he suggested to these young students, "If you really want to start getting action and getting your parents to talk about the camps, why don't you have a pilgrimage up there?" So they decided to have one, and they didn't really expect a lot of people, just a few college people who were willing to drive up there, maybe go up to Mammoth (a ski resort north of the Manzanar site) for the weekend and come back, but they started getting a lot of phone calls from people who wanted rides, that didn't want to drive up there. So they got a bus, a small school bus type, and they didn't want to really bother with those things because it meant, you know, you had to get money in advance and figure out how many people were going to make reservations. I don't think the bus held more than thirty-eight or so. Then they decided that they would charge and would furnish lunches for the people who were going up there. But they also told people to bring tools, for they were going to have a work day cleaning up the camp area.

I told my husband that I had not been back to Manzanar since I left, and that I wanted to go back with this group. It being very cold, I said, "I don't think we should take our kids with us." My younger son was, at that time, having a whole series of ear infections, and we decided it really wouldn't be a good idea, so we left the kids with my sister and my mother, and we went with our car to get on the bus. And when we got there and saw the bus, my husband said, "It's going to be an uncomfortable five hour ride if we get on there. Let's take our car." So we gave up our seats to two other people; there were quite a few who had come without reservations, hoping they could get on. There were two guys standing there by the sidewalk and the people in charge were saying, "Does anybody have room in their car?" So we picked two of them up and took them with us, and drove all the way up there. We have a small Volkswagon squareback, and by the time we hit the town of Mojave the wind was blowing so hard it was really hard to drive that car. We got some gas in Mojave and my husband said, "Okay, you drive, Sue, you know the way from here." I said, "I don't know the way from here, but I'll drive," because he'd been driving for two hours. So from Mojave we got on Highway 395 and after we passed the town of Lone Pine (five miles south of Manzanar) no one really knew how far Manzanar was at the time. You know, we weren't really quite sure how many miles out of Lone Pine it would be, so I kept looking at the mountains and I kept thinking, "It must be around here somewhere." I remembered a grove of trees, and I remembered an alluvial fan--a term I acquired in a college geography course years later -- and a little creek that ran down from the mountains. So I kept looking for these landmarks, and pretty soon my husband said, "It says Manzanar Street on that sign." But the sign was on the right hand side of the road, so I said, "Oh, that must go to the airport," because I remembered that there was an airport situated across from Manzanar. "Well, we're getting close then," he said. "Don't you recognize anything?" And I said, "Oh, there's that thing by the mountain, an alluvial fan." So we were getting close. I said, "I remember seeing it every morning from my doorway." And then we saw the guys with their flags, waving us into Manzanar.

We didn't stop at the stone entrance at that time for any ceremonial affair; the students were more concerned about cleaning the cemetary [situated behind the camp site], because they were going to have a religious service. When we pulled up I was really surprised at the number of cars; the bus hadn't shown up yet. Here were the NBC and CBS camera crews all set up, and they were really in the way. Our guys were getting a little bit annoyed. Finally Warren Furutani, who was one of the coordinators, turned to me and said, "Sue, take care of the media people for us, get them out of our way." So I said, "Alright." Everytime one of them would start interviewing anybody else, they would be told, "Go see Sue Embrey over there." I got involved in this thing, with interviews with NBC and CBS, and Karl Yoneda and his wife Elaine joined the group, so actually we didn't do any work; we did very little work. We were constantly being bombarded with questions from these guys. It was icy and cold and the wind was whistling. And NBC was asking, "Was it really this cold? We had to stop in Lone Pine and buy gloves and ski caps and mufflers because it was so cold." They had flown in from Los Angeles. I said, "Yes, it was this cold, but at least we had barracks to get into. They weren't much warmer, but it kept us from the wind." They wanted to know how many people lived there; they asked all kinds of questions.

By six o'clock that night they had taken off and it was on national television. And it really had tremendous influence in the Japanese communities, because it was the talk of all the Little Tokyos for months and months--how these young people had gone up to Manzanar. And the television showed them painting and fixing the monument--the chain was still around that area--it showed them with their tools raking away all the sagebrush and the tumbleweed, and then it showed people sitting there, cold and shivering, huddled around a fire, and eating lunch together. A friend of mine down in Santa Ana saw it and said that he flipped on all three stations and it was on all three of them for at least five minutes. So he said, "You got a lot of publicity on that thing."

H: How many people were there for the pilgrimage?

E: There were close to two hundred and fifty, and that was really much more than they expected. One of the people who came was a man who during the war was part of the military police group guarding the Manzanar camp. He recalled that it was one of the happiest times of his career as a soldier, as a draftee. There were some blacks there who were trying to sort of connect it to their movement. Mostly young people. I was disappointed that there weren't more Nisei. There were quite a number of Issei. There was a woman who was something like eighty-two years old who came back, who said she had relocated to Chicago. There was a woman there who had been with the first contingent of evacuees [who came to Manzanar in March 1942], the volunteers. I guess there were only like five women who had come at that time. She was single and in her early twenties when she arrived at Manzanar and left immediately afterward to work for the

United Methodist Church back East, so she didn't stay very long. But she was there, and she said that she came because she was very annoyed that the Nisei weren't doing anything in politics or with problems of the community, and she said, "I've been talking about these things, and I thought I'd better follow it up with some action, so I came." The Los Angeles *Times* interviewed us, and we really got a lot of coverage.

All through 1970 we were trying to organize the Manzanar Committee, and we would get a few nibbles but nobody really came to any of our meetings. We used to have about four or five people, and we'd talk about, well, should we organize? And what could we do with the place up there? One day the Los Angeles Water and Power Department [who own the land encompassing the Manzanar site] sent the Japanese American Citizens League, through the mail, a lease to the cemetary area of Manzanar and said, "You can have it." The JACL really didn't want it at the time, but it happened that Warren Furutani was working as National Youth Coordinator out of Los Angeles.

H: For the JACL?

E: For the JACL. They'd hired some young fellows . . . decided they ought to incorporate some of the young activists into JACL, so they hired Warren and he was working as National Coordinator. He called me on the phone and he said, "You know, there's a lot of interest among the young people; I'm getting a lot of calls; would it be alright if I used you as a resource person for them to come to? Because they're writing papers, and they keep telling me that their parents don't want to talk about it." So I said, "Okay." Kids started to come to me, and I would show them what I had in terms of photographs of Manzanar and talk about my own experiences. Toward the end of 1970 we formed a small committee and we kept sending notices out saying we were having these meetings. Very few people would show up.

H: Were you calling yourself the Manzanar Committee?

E: At the time we were calling ourselves the Manzanar Project Committee. Warren had a column in the *Pacific Citizen*, the weekly newspaper of JACL, and a couple of times he had mentioned that we were trying to form this committee, asking, "What would you like Manzanar to be? Would you like it to be a historical landmark? What kind of input can I get from you?" He wasn't getting very much response. Finally, Warren and I decided we would go ahead and form the committee anyway and see what happened. By 1971 we had maybe eight or ten people who decided to stay with the group and really work on it. We did a lot of research and got an application from the state. The word was that the state was willing to do away with several things that really were required and make it a landmark. One of the things was that it had to be a place or an incident which was not within the living memory of man.

H: What do they usually mean when they say that?

E: Fifty years. They said they would be willing to set that aside and let us have Manzanar as a landmark. We started to do research, and the things they wanted to know were: What significance does Manzanar have today? Why was it of particular interest when there were ten camps altogether? The justifications we used were: one, it was the first camp that was built; secondly, it was the nearest camp to Los Angeles, where there is the biggest number of Japanese Americans living and where most of the internees at Manzanar had come from; and thirdly, that there was a cemetery at Manzanar, and we wanted it preserved as a landmark. We sent a lot of photographs up to Sacramento with the application, and we turned in our proposed wording for the plaque, which most of us felt was too strong a wording from the very beginning. It was, first of all, too long. We knew there was a sixty word limit, but we decided that we would go all out and that we could always back down.

H: Who composed the wording?

E: The words were written by three people on the committee. We broke ourselves up into groups: a group of three of us worked on the history of Manzanar and its significance to California history, three others worked on the plaque wording, and then another group selected photographs to accompany our application to the state.

H: Do you remember the three who worked on the wording?

E: One actually had a kind of a wording he wanted himself, already written when he came to the meeting. That was Rex Takahashi, a Sansei whose parents had lived in Manzanar--he was their only son--and one of the original members of the committee. After we turned in the application he got a scholarship to work on his Master's degree at Roosevelt University in Chicago, so he went there to study political science. Rex and, let's see, who else? I think there was a woman who worked with him, Faye Matsuoka, whose husband Jim had spoken at the 1969 pilgrimage. His one quote got some very negative responses from the Nisei. An NBC reporter asked him, "How many people are buried here in the cemetery?" and he said, "A whole generation. A whole generation of Japanese who are now so frightened that they will not talk. They're quiet Americans. They're all buried here." And they took that one quote and it was broadcast all over, so the reaction from the second generation was really very negative. Jim was only about seven when he went to camp--he stayed there all three years--and he said it took him a long time to really look back and think about the consequences of the evacuation, in his own life and in the lives of other people. He was on our committee. I think he worked on the history of Manzanar, but his wife helped on the wording. There was one more person. I think Warren Furutani helped on the wording. I helped on the research of the history of Manzanar and its significance as a landmark. We had the Rundström brothers, who are twins, Ron and Don Rundström, who are both working on their doctoral dissertations here [at UCLA].

H: They're both Caucasians?

E: Yes, they're both Swedish Americans. Don is married to a young Sansei girl whose father was in Manzanar. They were also on the original committee. Ron and his girlfriend Pat Rosa, who is also non-Japanese, have been on the committee from the very beginning. After Rex left we got Ken Honji interested, we had Amy Ishii, who came in after the 9066 exhibit in Pasadena. I invited her to be on the committee. She was invited to come to the working meeting when we did all this, but she was unable to come. We had two other women who occasionally helped us and who were there at the original meeting: Kiku Uno, who is Amy's sister-in-law, and Toshi Yoshida, who is quite active in Democratic clubs and politics. Toshi was just recently elected as a commissioner to the City Human Relations Council by Mayor Tom Bradley. She doesn't remember being at the working meeting, but I do because she said, "Those are awfully strong words." And we said, "Well, should we re-write the whole thing?" And she said, "Well, I don't think they're going to take that; they're not going to like those words." But then we talked about it, we passed it around, we changed a few words, and my husband looked at it and said that it was pretty strong--everybody thought it was pretty strong--but we decided, "Well, at least we could back up if they don't want it; at least let's have a starting point." It was ninety words long.

They okayed our application in January of 1972; it was sent in November of 1971. We got word through Warren Furutani of the JACL that it was now a historic landmark. We sort of thought it would be the cemetery area. But because we put the plaque by the stone house at the camp entrance, I guess that is really going to be the central landmark, although we probably will negotiate for a new lease for the whole area, and Water and Power is very cooperative.

In 1972 we sent out a news release that Manzanar was now part of a state historical landmark and that we would probably have a pilgrimage there the weekend before Easter vacation started, when most of the college students would be free. So we made plans for it and the Pioneer Project came in and helped--they got busses for the Issei. Let's see, I think I drove up Saturday, yes, early Saturday morning. We got there early and my husband insisted on stopping at Joseph's Menswear to buy a pair of pants, and he disappeared! We had stopped for gas, and I was going into the market to get some soda pop, and the . . .

H: This was in Lone Pine?

E: Yes, this was in Lone Pine. And the Manzanar Committee people up there at Manzanar were having stiches because I hadn't shown up. They said, "Gee, maybe we'd better send the car out, maybe they had an accident." So anyway, we came driving in at eleven o'clock, when everybody had already just about finished their job of cleaning the cemetery area. Some of the media again grabbed me, and we took a few shots around there. I stood and watched, because I really had nothing to do until the program was going to begin. And I saw all these people coming across the field from the M.P. sentry house, which they had cleaned up. They

Courtesy of
Visual Communications

SUE KUNITOMI EMBREY

Manzanar Pilgrimage, 1972

were coming back to the cemetery area, which is about a mile, I think, with all their tools, and I stood there and I couldn't believe it. I just didn't realize that so many people had come. I had seen all the cars in the lot, and I thought, "Gee, there are a lot of people," but the group had divided in half, and half had stayed at the cemetery area cleaning, while the other half had walked over to the entrance. I asked how many people had shown up, and Warren said that he thought that someone had estimated seven hundred and fifty. I couldn't believe it.

H: Excuse me, Sue, but you mentioned the first pilgrimage in 1969 and now we're talking about the one in 1972. Were there pilgrimages in the intervening two years?

E: There was none in 1970, and in 1971 we tried to get, I think it was 1971, a group to go up to Manzanar over Memorial Day weekend. I think only about twenty-five or so showed up. I think the core of the group that had helped with the pilgrimage went up in 1971. There was a group going from a Pioneer Project in a bus, who had not been interned in camp, Issei mostly, and they wanted to see what the camp was like. Because they were mostly Buddhist they wanted to have a service there. The young people felt that they didn't want to let them go up by themselves, so they asked for a few people to come. So we spent the weekend in Lone Pine, and I remember it was Memorial Day weekend. There were about maybe twenty-five young people there. After they had their service then they went on up to Reno, I think, and they were going to kind of make a round trip, sort of a sight-seeing tour for the weekend. The other young people decided to camp out in Gray's Meadow [north of the Manzanar camp]. We had lunch there and then we came on back to Los Angeles. So actually there was no real big pilgrimage until 1972, and then the last one was in 1973. Some people say that there were only a thousand at the 1973 pilgrimage in April, but the Lone Pine newspaper estimated 1500. So it almost doubled. Again, there were very few Nisei, the second generation that Jim said had died there. There were a few more, but not that many.

H: Coming back to the 1972 pilgrimage, you have mentioned that Manzanar was accepted by the state as a historical site, but you still have not straightened out what wording the state accepted to appear on the plaque.

E: Right. In 1972, after the committee had okayed Manzanar as a landmark, we heard nothing about the wording. Then Warren called me one day and said that he had word from the JACL officer near Sacramento that the Parks and Recreation committee thought our wording was too strong, and could we possibly not only shorten it, but also compromise with the state and make it a little less explosive. We shortened the wording to the maximum of sixty, but we, after reading it over, felt that it was even stronger because of our having to shorten it. We weren't so sure that the State Advisory Committee would accept it. We heard nothing from them until around August, when Warren and I were going to fly to Catalina Island and meet with the Advisory Committee. But Warren got very involved in JACL activities and he said he really didn't have time to take off, so could we just skip it. So the Manzanar wording didn't get on the agenda. That was August of 1972. In August I was away on a trip to Japan with my family when Mr. John Michael from the Advisory Committee evidently flew down to Los Angeles to meet with the JACL people. They couldn't get hold of Warren--it was a Saturday morning meeting--and by this time Warren had resigned from the JACL because of the differences in policy and things. The whole group of Los Angeles staff people had resigned. He said he thought it was just a JACL meeting, so he hadn't even thought of going to it. They couldn't reach me, so they had some people in the office, who were working there, sit in as part of the Manzanar Committee, which we said was okay, and they had discussed the wording at that time. The people who sat in on the meeting backed our wording against the State. The State was working on a different version of the wording, but they were taking out the words which we felt were the most important. Anyway, they went back to Sacramento. I got a call in early October that two of the JACL people were going to meet up in a small town near Fresno--one was the legal counsel; the other one was the vice president of the JACL--and they were going to discuss Manzanar. At the time, Warren and I couldn't figure out why they were consistently talking through JACL and giving us thirdhand information. We didn't find out until later why this was being done, but they had a meeting in October . . .

H: Who is "they"?

E: The Advisory Committee of the State Parks and Recreation Department-- which usually suggests the different landmarks--Jim Murakami, who was vice-president of JACL in charge of research, I think, and Frank Iwama, the attorney, who lives in Sacramento. Helen Kawagoe, who was then the district governor of the Pacific Southwest District of JACL, called me and said that these two fellows were going to meet with the State and that they were going to back us up on the wording that we had sent up, the shortened version, except that they thought maybe the last word we had in there, which was a Japanese word, really didn't have any meaning. So she wondered whether it would be alright to take it out? That word was tondemonai, which means "incredible," "it never happened," "I can't believe it." It's an expression that Japanese people use when they can't think of anything else. So I said, "Okay, it's alright." And Warren said, "Okay," but it never occurred to us that we should have been up there, that we were Manzanar Committee people and we should have been up there.

On October 30 I got an air mail letter from Edison Uno, Amy Ishii's brother, with a photostat copy of a UPI dispatch from Truckee, California, which said that the State Advisory Committee on Historical Landmarks had turned down, completely, the wording for the Manzanar plaque. I called Jim Murakami and we talked about the possibility of compromising. And at this point he really didn't want to get involved, because he felt that we were really pushing too hard on the State, and he didn't want to get caught in the middle. I said to him, "Why is it that the JACL is getting all the correspondence and the Manzanar Committee is not? I said, "I know Warren was working for JACL, but the application was sent in the name of the Manzanar Committee, co-sponsored by JACL plus a lot of other groups up in the Owens Valley." And he said, "Well, the State said that they had to rewrite your application because it was all wrong; it was on an old form, and in retyping it they took it upon themselves to decide that the Manzanar Committee was a subcommittee of the JACL. So your name does not appear on the application." I said, "Jim, you're going to have to explain this to the Manzanar Committee because they're not going to accept that. They did all the work and JACL is getting all the credit." So he promised to come down and talk to us. It was not until the beginning of December that he was able to take time off to come down to Los Angeles, and the Manzanar Committee was told this by Jim, and they really got mad.

H: Is Jim a Nisei?

E: He's a Nisei, yes.

H: Had he been in the camps?

E: Yes, he was in the camps.

H: In Manzanar?

E: No, he wasn't in Manzanar; I'm not sure which camp he was in. Anyway, they said to him, "We want that application changed. We want the Manzanar Committee's name to be on there. We don't want to have to work through a third party all the time." From October through December phone calls were coming to me from Jim, transmitting messages from the State, and I said, "I don't like that. It makes it very topsy-turvy. We don't know what's going on. We want to follow the guidelines set by the State so we won't be in trouble later with the community, who will say, 'Well, you didn't do what the State wanted and that's why they don't want the wording.'" I said, "The Committee really feels that they have to go through all the different steps and make sure that we follow the guidelines." So he said, "Alright, I'll make sure that the thing gets changed." I sat down and wrote letters to the State, asking them what had to be done in order to change the application so as to include the Manzanar Committee. Anyway, Jim asked us what we were going to do. We told him that we had decided that first, we were going to send out a news release saying that we thought that the State was taking a very unreasonable position, and second, we were going to ask the people in the community to either support us or not support us by sending letters to the State, and thirdly, if that didn't work, we would go out and get petitions signed. Jim's answer was, "JACL cannot support you on that. You will have to fight that fight yourself." We said, "Okay, we can always make copies of the petitions and letters and send them out to the media and get publicity on it, and I'm sure the State wouldn't like that. And we can always get the Democrats to put pressure on the Republican Governor.

So we decided that we would not write a reply to the State on their turning us down. We would play it real cool. And from Christmas until January 30, 1973, we sent out letters to all the people we could think of, all the organizations we could think of, and asked them to support our wording, and we sent them a copy of our wording and a copy of the State wording so that they could compare. The State got twelve letters, of which two opposed our wording; we had close to fifty, of which two opposed our wording. Petitions came in from Chicago, New York, and different parts of the Midwest, and when I counted I think there were something like three hundred and fifty signatures on the petition supporting our wording. By the end of January we decided, "Okay, now we can negotiate with the State. We can tell them we have the support of the community."

By this time the State was getting a little fidgety, and asked Jim Murakami to try to negotiate on the wording. So Jim called and asked if the Manzanar Committee could directly negotiate with the State Advisory Committee by coming to Sacramento and having a meeting with them. And I said, "Well, that would mean we'd have to take time off from work, and the Committee's going to have to raise money for plane fare. Unless we can really work something out, the Committee doesn't feel like sending anybody up there." I said, "Warren told us of one experience when he sat there and they screamed at him, they just really tore into him. And he said that in self-defense he finally yelled back. And if that's the kind of a meeting it's going to be, we don't want to have anything to do with it." So Jim called the State back and evidently talked about some of our feelings, and then he called me back and said, "They would still like to meet with you." So we met on February 4. Amy Ishii and I flew up there because the Committee felt that possibly people who had been interned in the camps would have a better argument for the wording. We took some books and stuff with us. Amy took Estelle Ishigo's Lone Heart Mountain and I took copies of my The Lost Years.

So this was February of 1973 already, and we had set the pilgrimage date for April 14, which was the weekend before Easter. That announcement had already gone out to the community by December, and we said that even though we are still having this controversy over the wording of the plaque we will go ahead with our pilgrimage. If necessary, we will put up some kind of plaque of our own.

On February 14 the meeting was held in the State Parks and Recreation offices in Sacramento with Jim Murakami, of JACL, Amy Ishii and myself representing the Manzanar Committee, Mr. John Michael, Executive Secretary of the Landmarks Advisory Committee, Mrs. Kathryn Kaiser, who had just been elected Chairperson of the Advisory Committee, and Mr. David Tucker, who was the State Parks and Recreation Historian. We talked, and we broke the wording down almost word by word and tried to explain to them how we felt. Mr. Michael and Mr. Tucker and Mrs. Kaiser said they had no objection to the term "concentration camp," which had been the one term that they said originally they didn't want. They also said that words like "racism" and "greed" were very explosive words, and they were also words which were editorializing a person's point of view, and that normally on State plaques this is not done. We said, "Well, nobody told us that." We had never been told not to do that, and here we'd been sending up the wording. Mr. Michael said, "We can make an exception in this case if we can make sure that you have documentation to back you up." And I said, "Well, in terms of racism I think you're aware of the history in California of the agitation against the Asian immigrant." He said, "Yes, but that had nothing to do with the war and had nothing to do with the hysteria that was going on, and the people were so frightened." And I said, "Well I think it does. I think that people can be put in a certain stereotype so that an observor is not able to really be reasonable or rational about it." He said, "What about this 'greed'? That's a pretty strong word." Mrs. Kaiser said she didn't object to the word "greed," she objected to the fact that we had another word in front of it. "Economic greed," I think we had on it originally. So we said we could take that off. So we hassled around for almost two hours, and wrote different wordings on the board and erased them, and counted the words, and came up with what we thought was a pretty comprehensive kind of thing. They said that they weren't going to go back to the membership of their advisory committee, that Mrs. Kaiser and Mr. Michaels, as representatives, could "okay" it; it was alright, and as far as they were concerned, that was it. We said we would have to take it back to the Committee and get the Committee's report on it.

So we flew back that Friday night and called everyone, and we had an emergency meeting Sunday morning, at which time the Manzanar Committee absolutely refused to accept the third paragraph, which had something about "man's inhumanity to man causing this kind of thing." They said that that was just such a cliché that they didn't want it in there. We hassled around again for awhile, and did it all by phone, made sure that we had the copies correct, and Mr. Michael said he would give it to Mr. William Penn Mott, Director of the State Parks and Recreation Department. This was the final wording as approved by the Manzanar Committee, the Advisory Committee, and the JACL.

Mr. Penn Mott was out of town for several days, and we didn't hear from him for a week. But on February 22 I got a phone call from Jim Murakami, who said, "Mr. Penn Mott turned down the wording. He refuses to accept 'racism' and 'greed.'" The word "hysteria" was the word the State wanted to use, so we sort of compromised on that. So in the final wording as you see it on the plaque, the first paragraph is the State's paragraph, the middle paragraph is our paragraph, and the third one is kind of a compromise.

Mr. Penn Mott said, "If they want the plaque, let them put their name on it, the State can't put their name on such a wording, it's just too much. There are lots of people who will object to it, and we just can't have it." Well, both Mr. Michael and Mrs. Kaiser were very upset because they thought it was all finished and over with and we could have our plaque by the time of the pilgrimage. We said to them, "We really don't care whether we have our plaque or not, we're going to go ahead with our pilgrimage; but if we're going to have a fight on our hands, we're going to continue this campaign." Jim Murakami then said to me, "I will go and confront Mr. Penn Mott in person with Frank Iwama and ask him what his real objections are."

Penn Mott said, "You have no documentation to prove that it was 'racism' and 'greed' that put these people in camps. I'm approving 'concentration camp' on your wording, but I'm not going to approve the other two words."

Jim and Frank also had an appointment with Speaker of the Assembly Bob Moretti on the same afternoon. So they went to him to talk about the JACL problems that they had originally gotten the appointment for, and before they left they said that they wanted his help on solving the controversy with the wording. So Bob Moretti got in touch with Mr. Penn Mott and asked him to write a letter, which I haven't seen, but I have seen the answer that Mr. Moretti wrote to Penn Mott in which he says that he realizes that this is a very touchy subject, but from the documentation in his office he would have to support the Manzanar Committee on their wording. Moretti went on to say that he would support us all the way through, and he hoped that Mr. Penn Mott could, in the very near future, hold a meeting with him and the Manzanar Committee people and try to resolve that.

I also called Assemblyman Alex Garcia, whose district covers Little Tokyo and Chinatown in Los Angeles. He has an aide who is a third generation Japanese American named Dennis Nishikawa. Jim Murakami said, "Get in touch with Dennis and see what you can get from Garcia." Dennis called Garcia by phone in Sacramento and told him what the problem was, at which point Garcia said he would support us.

We also wrote letters to Al Song and March Fong, who are Assemblypersons in Sacramento. We wrote to Senator Mervin Dymally and a couple of other people in the legislature. We got Dymally's support, we got Moretti's support, we got Alex Garcia's support. Then Dennis Nishikawa arranged a meeting with Mr. Penn Mott for March 19, 1973.

Warren Furutani, Amy Ishii and myself flew up to Sacramento for the meeting. Ken Honji, who was in San Francisco publicizing our pilgrimage, drove up from San Francisco to Sacramento. He also tried to get people from San Francisco to represent the community. The only person who was able to come was Professor George Kagiwada of U.C. Davis, who came in behalf of the people from the Bay Area. Karl Yoneda and Edison Uno, who were both on the Manzanar Committee of San Francisco, were unable to come.

So we had this meeting, at which time the aides from all the different legislative offices that supported us came: Senator Dymally's aide, Bob Moretti's aide, etc. Assemblyman Garcia was the Chairman, and Dennis Nishikawa was there also. Another person, Senator Ralph Dills from Gardena, sent his aide. Mr. Penn Mott was there from the State Parks and Recreation, John Michael was there, and a newly appointed Deputy Director of State Parks and Recreation named William Briner was also there. From the JACL Jim Murakami came with two staff people from the national office in San Francisco. I can't remember their names, but they were employed by the national office and they represented Dave Ushio from San Francisco.

The meeting lasted over an hour and a half. The JACL did all the documentation. They were quoting from newspapers and books and telling Mr. Penn Mott, "These are quotes which document racism, and this one documents the greed." At one point one of the JACL people suggested that instead of "greed" we use the term "economic exploitation," which Mr. Penn Mott, for some reason, decided was fine. It was one extra word, and a longer word. The Manzanar Committee said, "Okay, we would accept that." About ten minutes of three, Mr. Penn Mott said that he had a meeting with some people who were coming from Washington, and it looked like we could not solve the controversy. Warren Furutani, who up to this point had not said a word, was sitting in his swivel chair and he turned around and said, "Mr. Penn-Mott, you know, here are all these people who went to the camps telling you why we want the wording the way we want it, and you're sitting there and you're so insensitive, you're not even listening to us. In my terms, you are a racist, you are a bigot. The same kind of thing that happened in 1942 is happening right here in this room. One man signed the executive order that put a hundred and ten thousand people in camps, and you, representing the State of California, are sitting there and saying that the people who suffered are not going to put the words they want on that plaque." And Mr. Penn Mott said, "I'm not going to sit here and listen to you call me names." And he started to get up and walk away. At which point Assemblyman Garcia said, "If we don't settle it here the next stage is the Legislature." Mr. Penn Mott's answer was, "It should never have gotten here in the first place. You can have it all." And he walked out. That was it. Mr. Michael—and he really got the brunt of it from Mr. Penn Mott, I think he was on the verge of losing his job and he was really scared—and Mr. Briner came over to me—they had never answered the letters which I had written to them asking for verification of Mr. Penn Mott's refusal based on his objection to the two words; they never put it in writing, it was always over the telephone—when they came over to me they said, "We don't need to answer your two letters, do we? It's settled here." And I said, "Fine with me." And Mr. Briner said, "Mr. Michael supported you, and he got a lot of flak from Mr. Penn Mott, so I hope that the Manzanar Committee at least is not angry at Mr. Michael." I said, "We're not angry, we realize that this is a very controversial kind of thing, but we wanted to stick to our point that this is the way we want it written and this is the way the community backed us and this is why we didn't want to back down." So he said, "We will order the plaque this afternoon."

This was March 19, and they had been telling us since October that if we didn't order the plaque it wouldn't be ready by April 14, because it would take six to eight weeks. On March 19, in the afternoon, after we left that meeting, Mr. Michael wrote an order. He also sent out a press release in which he said that the plaque had been ordered and the wording had been approved. It took exactly two weeks and four days to make the plaque, and it was in Independence at the museum on April 10, and Mr. Raub accepted it for us. That was as much as the State would pay for; they would pay for the making of the plaque and the delivery of it to the closest point, and from there . . .

H: Who is Mr. Raub?

E: The Director of the Eastern California Museum in Independence. He had been working with us all along, so we asked him to accept the plaque since Independence was the closest town to Manzanar.

H: Earlier you said that on the original application the Manzanar Committee, the JACL, and various Inyo County groups were included. Do you recall offhand who those various Inyo County groups were?

E: One was the Lone Pine Chamber of Commerce. Another, I think, was the Eastern California Museum Association. The Los Angeles Department of Water and Power was also included, because they're the consenting owner of the land. There were a couple of others. I'm not exactly sure. But when we received a copy of the application, the only name that appeared was JACL. So we're going to have to try to find out what happened. I was hesitant to write to Sacramento because I didn't have enough information, but people were coming back from the museum and saying, "Mr. Raub is very upset because the Eastern California Museum name is not on the plaque, and he is sure that they were the ones who originated the application." Recently some other people have told us the same thing. Then I don't know what happened; I was cleaning out my files on the Manzanar pilgrimages and kind of sorting them out according to subject matter, and I came across the revised wording as we had sent it up to Sacramento originally, the maximum sixty words. And there listed under it were all the names of the different groups. We're going to have to write to Sacramento and find out what happened. Now I have the proof that they had been sent up and included in the application. We'll just have to trace it down because I know that probably people up in Independence and Lone Pine don't really approve of the wording either. It was all the work of the Manzanar Committee, really.

H: What support was offered by the various Inyo County groups so that their names appeared on the application?

E: Originally, Warren Furutani worked through the office of Eugene Chappie, who is the Assemblyman from the Inyo County area--the Owens Valley area. We also had some support from Howard Way, the State Senator from that area, but it was mostly through Chappie's office. Warren had several meetings with the aide from Chappie's office before we even sent the application.

H: So they collected the names of . . .

E: Of these different groups in Independence, right. So that's another thing we're going to have to find out about.

H: Sue, I'd like to introduce David Bertagnoli, who is going to ask you a few questions with particular focus upon the plaque. David's been doing some research in the Independence and Lone Pine communities with some of the people who were living there at the time that Manzanar was operating as a camp. He's also been interviewing some people in the Owens Valley area with respect to their reactions to the plaque.

B: I'd like to back up a little and talk about the origins of the Manzanar Committee? Did you have the plaque specifically in mind when you formed the Committee?

E: No, the first thing we decided upon was that the Manzanar Committee would be kind of an educational committee. People were calling us and asking us where they could get information on doing papers--where were the research materials on the college campuses--so we wanted to direct them to those source materials, and we also wanted to be able to direct them to people who had personal experiences in the camps. So we really had two purposes in forming the committee. One was educational, and it was sort of an afterthought to file a plaque application with the State.

B: Are you aware at all that the Inyo County Landmarks Committee had already gone ahead and inquired about a plaque, had actually made an application for a plaque, completely independent of the Japanese American groups?

E: We are now aware of this fact, but we didn't find this out until after Manzanar was named a landmark.

B: Mr. Raub at the Eastern California Museum told me that when the Inyo County Landmarks Committee were applying to Sacramento for the plaque, they invited a group of Japanese Americans to Independence, to Manzanar, and that Warren Furutani was one of them. Do you know . . .

E: I knew Warren met with them. I didn't know anybody else had gone with him.

B: Evidently it was quite a group. But was he representing the Manzanar Committee or the JACL at the time? Do you know that?

E: Probably at that point he was just representing JACL, because I don't think the Manzanar Committee had been formed yet. Maybe it was still in the process of forming.

B: This was around 1970.

E: It was around 1970, yes. I think that Warren himself was working on trying to set up a committee, but I don't think that we had actually formed one. He was still working as the National Youth Coordinator of the JACL, so it was through Warren . . . . We were not aware that they had sent a separate application.

B: I see. I think you've answered most of the rest of my questions. But one thing I'd just like to ask you is: Why do you think "concentration camp" on the plaque created such public interest? Why do you think people like Lillian Baker were against this term "concentration camp"?

E: Well, Mrs. Baker's argument is that America never had any concentration camps, that it was Germany that had them, because concentration camps bring up a picture of death chambers, you know, the ovens, and that they really didn't have anything like that in any of the ten camps-- that we had a hospital, three meals a day, and that we were taken care of. We at least had lodging, we could work if we wanted to, and we were paid when we worked. She believes this to be very humane treatment of people, so that it cannot be compared with concentration camps in Germany. The Manzanar Committee has never compared the two. We looked up the term "concentration camp," and it's in Webster's Dictionary; we looked up the term "relocation center," and it's not. We decided that the definition for "concentration camp" according to Webster's Dictionary was a fairly accurate description of Manzanar and the other camps.

Another argument I have heard is that "relocation center" implies that you are able to go in and out freely, of your own free will, and that these centers are set up in cases of emergency, like a flood or an earthquake, and that it's a temporary kind of shelter until you're able to go on to other things. A concentration camp like Manzanar, Tule Lake and the other camps had barbed wire around them. People were not allowed to leave, unless they had permits. There were sentries in the guard towers, and there were searchlights, and the rifles the guards carried had bullets in them. We felt that this in itself connoted "concentration camps."

Someone else said that we should have used the term "internment camp" rather than "concentration camp." I don't know what their argument is. "Internment camp" was used in every one of the episodes in Indian history where they've taken the American Indians and put them on reservations. The orders that came were "internment" orders. One of our Manzanar Committee members, Ron Rundström, who is working on his dissertation, said that there is quite a parallel in the things that the Government did to the Indians. Also, almost all of the administrators who took care of the ten camps, so-called "relocation centers," came from the Bureau of Indian Affairs, because they were the only ones who knew how to run the camps, who knew how to organize people into different work groups and run the administration matters. So most of them came from the Department of the Interior and the Bureau of Indian Affairs.

H: Sue, I want to explore further the response to the plaque itself. You've already alluded to Lillian Baker. Perhaps you could identify this person and tell us a little bit about the nature of her response.

E: Alright. Mrs. Baker is a woman who lives in Gardena--she says of her own choice--among the Japanese Americans there. [Outside of Honolulu, Gardena has the largest population of Japanese Americans among United States cities.] She has been a writer for some years for the Gardena Valley News, which is, I believe, a throwaway paper--I'm not sure. At the time of the Executive Order 9066 exhibit in Pasadena, she wrote a letter of protest and said that if we were going to show photographs of the camps in America, then we should put them right alongside photographs of the Japanese prison camps in the Philippines where her first husband died, and pictures of Buchenwald and Auschwitz in Germany. No one paid much attention to her. The Gardena Valley News printed the letter. They got a lot of replies, and they printed the replies. Then nothing happened until "Months of Waiting," which is an exhibit of drawings and paintings done in camp, came to the Music Center in Los Angeles. Mrs. Baker also protested this exhibit with the same argument as before: that we should put up pictures of the Japanese prison camps in the Philippines for American prisoners of war and the German camps, and give them equal space. Because as far as she was concerned, the camps in America were relocation centers and not concentration camps. This was before she was aware of the fight that we were having with the State; she didn't know that we had applied to the State.

One afternoon when Amy Ishii and Ken Honji and some other people had volunteered to stay at the exhibit and talk to people, answer any questions, Mrs. Baker came to the exhibit. This was evidently her second appearance. She had been invited and attended the preview night that we had, at which time she had made no protest. Eugene Debs of the Los Angeles Board of Supervisors, City Councilman Thomas Bradley's supporters, and a lot of other people who supported the exhibit were there, and Mrs. Baker made no protest. The second time she came she bought a copy of Executive Order 9066 from Amy, wrote out a check to her and started screaming at her, shaking her finger at her, and saying, "You people are causing all this trouble by publicizing this kind of stuff." And she said, "You're to blame for it. We Americans didn't have any concentration camps." Amy didn't really know who she was. Then she looked at the check and said, "Are you the woman 'Elbee' who writes for the Gardena Valley News?" And Mrs. Baker replied, "Yes. I've been opposing all of this for a long time." They got into a loud and spirited argument, and a lot of people gathered around to listen. At which time Ken Honji came up the stairs and heard all the screaming and joined in with Amy. Mrs. Baker was on her way to one of the music halls across the way from the Music Center--she had an afternoon matinee ticket for something--and had stopped at "Months of Waiting" and gotten into this big argument. So anyway, while Amy and Mrs. Baker were

screaming at each other, Ken Honji came up the stairs and joined in
with Amy, and finally was able to escort her down the long flight of
stairs out to the lobby. Mrs. Baker never stopped screaming; she kept
screaming the same things that she'd been saying before, and that was
that America had no concentration camps, they were relocation centers,
humane places where people were treated well, and that we were doing
a disservice to the country by bringing up these unpleasant experiences.

At five o'clock that night Amy called me. I wasn't home, and she said
to my husband, "Sue missed Mrs. Baker." I had just left the Music
Center before Mrs. Baker arrived on the scene. My husband's answer
was: "It's a good thing she did, because I would have had to bail her
out of jail if she had had a run-in with Mrs. Baker." Amy said that
her husband had told her: "It's a good thing you sat there behind that
desk, because if you had gotten up you would have really given her a
big sock and then you would have been in jail." So both of our husbands had the same reaction to that experience.

I have heard that once Mrs. Baker spoke at a JACL meeting at which she requested the time. She completely took over the microphone for an hour
and a half. And all during this time, according to the Governor of
the JACL Pacific Southwest District Council, those nice middle class
Japanese Americans lost their decorum and really gave it to Mrs. Baker.
The next day the Governor called Mrs. Baker to apologize, which I
thought was the wrong thing for him to do, because she immediately used
that in a letter to the editors of all the ethnic papers, saying how
much better she felt, that she had been denied her right to speak at a
public meeting, and that she had been called a "liar" and booed down,
and if the invitation was still open, she would be happy to join the
Gardena Valley Japanese American Citizens League. I've been told that
that invitation has been open for many years, and that she has never
paid her dues. At this point, she says that her publisher will not
allow her to write anything in the Gardena Valley News about any of
the camps.

H: Has she been reacting to the plaque too?

E: Yes, very much so. She has written letters to Governor Reagan and
to all the legislators. She has been on both Ray Briem and Marv
Gray's radio talk shows on KABC. And just before Marv Gray died
she was on his show on KFI, I think, because his contract was not
renewed by KABC. I have not seen her on television yet, but the
Los Angeles Herald Examiner called me one day and said that they had
gone out to interview her--she had made some very strong accusations
against the Manzanar Committee--and the reporter felt that at least
the Manzanar Committee's side should be presented. I talked to the
reporter on the phone, and a couple of days later I asked her to read
what she had written. It sounded pretty good; it sounded like we were
given fairly equal space, but the article that came out was quite
different. The city editor evidently has the final say on what goes
in the paper. I was kind of disturbed, but most people said that they

thought I came out better in my interview than Mrs. Baker did in her's. Her complaint was that of all the pictures they had taken of her in her home, they used the worst one in the _Herald Examiner_. So she, I think, is a kind of complaining person anyway.

H: Is she just the most vocal of those people that have objected to the plaque? Or does she speak for a large segment of the population of Los Angeles?

E: Well, she claims now that she has formed a California Committee for Historical Accuracy, and that she is the Chairperson. How many are in her committee, I don't know, but a young man came to interview me last week, at which time I suggested to him that he ask her how many members she has on her committee, because the Manzanar Committee is willing to let her see the names of the persons on their committee. And I told him we had a core of twelve people. So I said, "Ask her, please, whether she would be willing to give you the information; I don't know."

H: Has KABC interviewed either yourself or Amy Ishii or anyone else from the Manzanar Committee?

E: No. They offered us air time, and we said we did not want time on Ray Briem's show. We want time for a separate response, so they haven't asked us back at all.

H: Are you getting any correspondence from people in the larger community reacting to the plaque?

E: Just what we see in the papers. Yesterday there was a reaction in the _Rafu Shimpo_ [a Little Tokyo-based venacular newspaper], in which a non-Asian, I think his name was Blackwell, wrote a letter supporting the term "concentration camp."

H: But you haven't received any personal correspondence?

E: None at all. Nothing. In fact, all the publicity we've gotten . . . none of us have received any kind of negative reaction, except from Mrs. Baker.

H: Do you receive any informal criticism from radicals, to the effect that the language on the plaque isn't strong enough? Or that by working through the State the Manzanar Committee has in any way compromised its position?

E: Well, the only thing is that a lot of people couldn't understand why we were working through the legislators. We explained to them that we had reached the point where there was no way of getting any kind of agreement on the plaque, so this is why we went to the legislators, why this was the next step that we took. Most people that I've talked to didn't like the word "hysteria" on there. That was the word that the State hung onto and insisted on, because these people said that it was not really "hysteria," but "racism" and "exploitation" that were the true facts. But when you explain how the wording came about, I think people were willing to accept it. The people in San Francisco said that they thought it was as accurate as it could be.

Then Mrs. Baker said that the plaque should have said that you had hospitals, good medical care, humane treatment, and that all of these things should have been included in the wording. Well, you just can't do it. The Manzanar Committee itself has made a decision not to be on the defensive with Mrs. Baker. We refuse to argue with her, we refuse to correspond with her. She has never actually confronted us as a committee. There are notices in the paper saying where our meetings are held, and she has never come to them. She has never talked to me personally, but she has accused us of being radicals and militants. She has accused us of threatening her life, calling her on the telephone. We haven't done that. Nobody in our committee has time for that kind of activity. We decided that rather than put ourselves on the defensive and constantly have to answer her charges, which are false anyway, that we would try to always present a positive kind of picture to the community.

H: Where does the Manzanar Committee go from here? You've gotten the plaque, and you were sort of plaque-oriented for the past year. Do you revert back to your original status as an educational committee, or do you now have a larger range of activities over and beyond education?

E: Well, we'll be doing our educational part; like last night we spoke on Tak Shindo's series on the evacuation for Venice Adult School; you know, brought people up to date as to what happened. Right now there's a feasibility study that the legislature has recommended to the State Parks and Recreation. $150,000 has been allocated to several different studies considering sites to be incorporated into the Parks and Recreation system, one of them being Manzanar. It was given $20,000. So we're in touch with the man who is doing the study, a Mr. Kenneth Collier. Collier is the State landscape architect, who says he was a very young boy in grammar school when the evacuation happened, and he really doesn't know anything about it. I don't think he's done any homework either; he hasn't read any relevant books. He didn't even seem to have the files on the Manzanar application, because he called me the other day and asked me if we had any photographs of any existing conditions at the camp. And I said, "They're in the application form. We have many pages of photographs that the State requested, and you should have them." But he did come down to Los Angeles for a meeting with the Manzanar Committee. He said he wasn't sure what to expect from the Committee, because he had been told that we were radicals. He sat there and listened, and told us what he had done so far. And he called me last week to tell me that he would like to have another meeting

with us. And when he writes us his draft, he would like us to see
it before he turns it in. He has some aerial photographs he took
which he offered to give us. We may possibly have to meet with him
before that, because at this point he says he only has $10,000; he
doesn't know where the other $10,000 is. We asked him about getting
money for consultants, who could help him and give him ideas of what
we could do with the camp, and he said, "The money is not for consultant
fees, but for expenses and salaries." Well, he's already on the State's
payroll. If nobody else is helping him, who is getting the $10,000?
Besides his flying to Manzanar and back, or staying overnight, and
paying for photographs that he's taken or that he's ordered from the
National Archives, where is the money going? So I have put in a call
to Bob Moretti's office to find out how extensive the Assembly resolution was that covered Manzanar. We were even thinking of the possibility of asking that the other $10,000 be frozen until we can get
an agreement on consultants' fees, because the Manzanar Committee has
already spent about six hours with Collier, and we haven't gotten paid
ourselves. We feel that if we're going to provide input into the
State, if we're going to recommend people doing blueprints and giving
ideas to the State, that these people should be paid. And if we're
going to furnish Collier with photographs that we've taken, then we
should be paid for those. We'll probably talk about that at our
meetings, and then decide what to do.

H: I noticed at the 1973 pilgrimage--at the dedication ceremony--that
there were several speakers from Chicago, New York, and San Francisco,
all claiming to represent chapters of the Manzanar Committee. Are
those just paper organizations, or do they have some viability in
terms of membership?

E: Okay. At the time we started having this debate with the State about
the wording, which was sometime in December, I called Edison Uno
and Karl and Elaine Yoneda, and asked them to be the Manzanar Committee
of San Francisco. To which they said, "Okay." Then Warren wrote to
New York and asked a group there, which is quite active, called Asian
Americans for Action, if they would form a Manzanar Committee out of
that group and support us on our wording. Rex Takahashi, who had been
on our original committee, was living in Chicago, and I wrote to him
and asked him if his Asian American Studies group could get some support for the Manzanar Committee, and call themselves the Chicago
Manzanar Committee. So he was able to do that. As the pilgrimage
approached we wrote to them and asked them, if possible, to send a representative to the pilgrimage to represent their chapters. As of now
these chapters are not doing very much, but we keep in touch with
them and we do send them reports as to what is going on. If we have
a fight again, like on this feasibility study, then we will ask them
to help us.

H: A couple of final questions. I know you tried to involve some of the
former Manzanar internees in the ceremonies during the 1973 pilgrimage,
in particular in the placement of the plaque. Could you relate that
incident?

E: Mr. R. F. **Kado** is eighty-two years old, and he contacted the Manzanar Committee **when the copy** of my booklet The Lost Years went on sale in Little Tokyo. He **went to the** Amerasia Bookstore and asked for a copy and said that he **wanted to** make a contribution to the Manzanar Committee. So the young fellow that was there started talking to him and found out that Mr. Kado had built the monument **at the cemetery and had** built the two houses that were at the **entrance of the camp.** So he got his name and address and phone number and said that the man had left a check for $100. I said, "Gee, he's a man we should get hold of, because if we get the plaque, we're going to need someone to put it in and get some kind of advice." I called Mr. Kado and asked him to come to one of our meetings. He came to several meetings, talked with us and told us of his experiences. He was very reluctant to comment on our wording, but it later turned out that he felt **that** even though we had lost all of this property and been interned, that America had been good to him, although he was not a citizen. And that if at all possible, he wanted to avoid a confrontation with the State over the wording. He said, "At least **we got the** landmark; we're going to preserve that. Do we need to **fight the** State? Could we sort of compromise and get the wording so that the plaque will be there?' And we said to him, "That's something that we could work on, but wouldn't it be better if we at least made an effort to try to get what we want on it?" And he said, "Yes, it would be better." He agreed with us, but he said that from his point of view, although he'd lost something like $40,000, a brand new house, at the time of evacuation, that he has been able to rehabilitate a lot of that, and that as a stonemason he was still making good money, and he just didn't want that kind of confrontation.

Mr. Kado was ill at the time that the plaque was approved. I called him to tell him that they were ordering it and sending it to Independence, and asked him if he knew someone who was a stonemason to put the plaque in place, because the State was paying only for transportation and the rest was up to us. And I said, "We would like your advice on where to put it, since you built the stone houses." He said to me, "I have to go to the doctor tomorrow, and I will explain to him what you said, and maybe the doctor will give me permission to do it myself." I said, "Well, I hate to impose on you, because you've been ill." And his answer was, "I would like to finish it. I started it and I would like to finish it."

What happened was that he went to the doctor, and the doctor okayed him to go back to work. He called me and said, "If you will give me the permission, I would like to get hold of the young men who helped me build the stone houses originally, when they were sixteen years old, and have them go up with me to Manzanar, with the blueprint, and figure out a place to put the plaque." And this is what he did. He spent two weekends up there with five or six people who had helped him originally--who are now grown men. They asked to be anonymous because they said they were just finishing a job they started. They didn't want to get any credit for it. They would not let us pay them for gas, or any of their expenses. Mr. Kado put the plaque in after they had collected all **the rocks**. He paid for the cement and everything else, and brought his own **tools**. He was still there at three-thirty that afternoon of the pilgrimage, when I was ready to leave. And I said to him, "It's time for you to go home." And his answer was, "I want to make sure it stays in place."

H: Who were the main speakers at the dedication ceremony?

E: We had Diane Kawano, from the Manzanar Committee of Chicago, who flew in. Her parents **had** been in Manzanar. We had Mary Kochiyama, who is a Nisei, and who is a paid representative of the Asian Americans for Action. She flew out from New York and was one of the speakers. Edison Uno was not able to come from San Francisco, so we asked Pat Sumi to speak in his place. That was sort of a last minute thing. Karl Yoneda was there and did some of the translating in Japanese.

H: What continuing function do you find the plaque playing with respect to community involvement, not only in the Japanese American community but also the larger American community? And what impact has your in-volvement in the Manzanar Committee--and the politics of "plaque creation"--had upon yourself?

E: Okay. The first question. There is still a lot of interest, and, as far as the Japanese community is concerned, Manzanar is now legitimate. When we first started our committee, we had very little support. We got, from one person, who is a **Nisei**: "Why are you bringing up the past? Most of my friends say that they never got to UCLA, but their kids are able to go. They own a house, they have a car, they've made a good living. Why are you bringing up the past?" They don't want to talk about it anymore. This was the reaction we had from most of the Nisei generation. In fact, at the heat of the controversy over the plaque, my mother said to me, "You better stop. You're going to get beaten up like those people got beaten up in camp. They'll come and find you. You know, your name has been in the papers." And I said, "Well, there are a few people who might do something like that, but there's nothing I can do about it." Evidently they'd been translating all of the news reports and Mrs. Baker's letters into the Japanese sections of the <u>Rafu Shimpo</u> and <u>Kashu Mainichi</u>, and my mother had been reading them. She was quite up-set that one time when I saw her.

Does that answer your question?

H: With respect to the Japanese American community. What about the larger community?

E: I think a lot of interest has been generated. For instance, KNX Radio has had several editorials recently. Because of the high winds at the last pilgrimage, a lot of the newsmen were not able to fly into Manzanar

to cover it, so we got very little coverage in April, and KNX Radio
did not know that the plaque was there and had been dedicated. They
got a reply from Mrs. Baker, and they gave her air time. They got
a reply from Mayor Tom Bradley, who gave them a rundown on the history
of what happened; he told them that the plaque is there, that the
Manzanar Committee has an unlimited lease on the land, and that the
City Council had unanimously passed a resolution on the day of the
pilgrimage commending the Manzanar Committee for its work.

I think the fact that we have non-Asians on our committee who have
been working with us from the beginning is an indication of some kind
of interest. I think most of the interest, though, is in the community. Although recently some of the younger kids have said to me that
they thought that all the things that could possibly be said about the
evacuation have already been said, I reply, "Well, I don't think so.
Not until the Nisei start talking. There have been a lot of books
written--sociological studies done and political things written--but I
don't think the whole story has come out." At one point in one of my
speeches I had said that the evacuation had had such a traumatizing
psychological effect on the Nisei that none of this would really come
out, and that the Nisei themselves would never be able to lead a normal
life until they got it out of their system. That the anger, the
bitterness, and the resentment were all inside of them, and that I
thought that it would be healthy for them if they got it out. Some
people have objected to my theory. I wrote that to the Houstons [James D.
and Jeanne Wakatsuki],when they sent me their book, Farewell to Manzanar,
because Jeanne Wakatsuki Houston sent along with it an interview that
they had done, at which time she says that every time she would start
talking about Manzanar she would break out into tears. So her husband
said, "Let's find out what the rest of your family thinks," and they
took the tape recoreder and went over to her sister's house, her
eldest sister, who remembers much more of Manzanar than Jeanne does.
And James said to her, "You know, every time Jeanne starts talking
about Manzanar she bursts into tears and she starts crying." And
her sister said, "What's there to cry about?" They said, "Are you
willing to be taped?" And she answered, "Sure, go ahead." And they
put the tape recorder on and said, "Okay, tell us what it felt like
that first day you got to Manzanar." And she started talking about
the dust storms, started talking about putting the hay into the mattress tick, and she burst into tears. And Jeanne said that after her
sister got over that, she said, "What a relief!" It was such a relief.
And then she was able to talk for hours and hours on the tape about
her experience. Jeanne said it happened to everyone in her family:
her brothers, who are still alive; her sisters; and her sisters-in-law.
She said that the book is a result of her twenty-five year old nephew
coming to her and saying, "I was born in Manzanar and I know nothing
about it. Will you please tell me?" And she said, "Why didn't you
talk to your parents?" And he replied, "They won't talk about it."
And she said, "I looked at him and I opened my mouth and nothing came
out. I decided that it was time." It was kind of a catharsis for
her family. So when she sent me the book, this is what I wrote. I

said to her, "I think for everyone it has to be some kind of catharsis, or the community is not really going to function properly psychologically. They're not active in politics, they're not active in anything, really, of any importance."

I think for the larger community, too, in terms of what's been happening with Watergate and with President Nixon, it was an executive order that sent the people to camp, not a law on the books. And if someone as President wanted to he could just reactivate the order. I understand that executive orders are never cancelled; they stay on the books. They may not be used again, but they're always there. They're not like laws that are adopted and then cancelled out.

I think more and more young people are getting interested in the whole subject of internment, in terms of constitutional law and in light of Vice-President Agnew's constant crusades against the newsmen. I said to one newsreporter, "You know, the next people could be the newsmen." And for awhile there were two cases where two newsmen went to jail because they refused to reveal the sources of their information. So I think when it's connected in that sense, people will see the importance of knowing about this kind of thing so that it doesn't happen again.

H: Sue, you said it's been, or it is increasingly becoming, a form of catharsis for the Nisei generation to talk about their evacuation experiences. Has your involvement in the struggles of the past few years been cathartic for you? If you perhaps disavow the label "radical," has your entire participation since 1969 in the Manzanar Committee and related activities succeeded in "radicalizing" you somewhat?

E: I think so. In the fifties and early sixties I had somehow left the Japanese community to work on my own in other areas. I worked with the credit union movement in the food co-ops, and I was often the only Japanese in these groups. My husband and I became members of the Unitarian Church, and we were members for a couple of years, and most of the people that I met were non-Japanese or non-Asian. Most of the activities were centered around issues like the Pentagon Papers and the Vietnam War, although we were active in precinct work and things like that, and supported some groups. My husband's always been a union man, so I've been aware of things like that. I guess I've come out much more strongly since I've been working with the Manzanar Committee. I've reached the point where I don't even care what anybody calls me, and I feel that it's now become part of my life. I was asked to speak at an anti-war rally as representative of a group that called themselves Asian Americans for Peace. I had never done anything with the group, really, except maybe go to their meetings or fund raisings, and made some donations to them. George Takei [the actor and unsuccesful candidate for a seat on the Los Angeles City Council] insisted that I was the only one that could do it because I had worked on the Manzanar Committee, and he felt that I could articulate myself in terms of relating what was happening in Vietnam with what had happened at

Manzanar. So I spoke for just a few minutes at that rally, which was held in Los Angeles. Then I've been on the Education Commission. It's gotten to the point now where **when** people say "Sue Embrey," they automatically say the "Manzanar Committee." One person said, "Yes, the infamous one!" I guess it has radicalized me more in terms of what I say, although some people say I still say things so that it doesn't come out as strong, because I don't use profanity, I don't use the terminology that the young people use. And sometimes I become very academic when I say something, like at the 1972 pilgrimage. Karl Yoneda and I were the two speakers. My husband read the speech before I took it up to Manzanar and he said, "Well, it's pretty good, but I just wonder if any of the young people will really get it. It's kind of really intellectual." I found out later; Warren Furutani said to me, "Boy, you really blew their minds!" And I said, "With what?" And he answered, "Your speech." What I had said was that whether Manzanar becomes a landmark or not, it was a symbol. It symbolized the ultimate negation of American democracy, and that was the racism that's been in the United States. And that even today, while we were there at the pilgrimage, it was going on in Vietnam, with the strategic hamlets and Asians killing Asians, because there were Asian Americans being drafted into the service to fight in Vietnam. And that the people who spend the day there at Manzanar should keep it in their minds that it could happen to someone else, and that I hoped that they would be in the very forefront of defending people so that it doesn't happen to them. Karl Yoneda spoke about Hiroshima, the Indian reservations, the ghettos, and how man's inhumanity to man is still going on. Then he spoke a few words in Japanese to the Issei there. Warren said that the young people really related to those two speeches more than they had to anything else.

In terms of my personal life, I can tell you that my family is fed up with Manzanar! We're eating dinner, the phone rings, and I'm on. We're asleep and the phone rings late at night. And they're coming, like calls from all over. Now I'm getting a lot of calls from Sacramento, because I've written to them already about the feasibility study, and all these different people keep calling me about one thing or another. For my family, I guess, the pilgrimages haven't been that exciting, because I'm working all the time I'm up there, and they're trying to find something to do to keep themselves occupied. At the December 1969 pilgrimage my husband helped paint the monument and cleaned up the cemetery area. He thought that it was a very good way of at least letting the young people know what happened.

I remember at one point I thought it had all been a cathartic experience and I was over many of the remnants of the evacuation. But during the trial of the soldiers who were involved in My Lai, in the massacre, I think it was like the fourth or fifth day of the trial, one fellow said, "Well, I was just following orders." One of the questions was, "Didn't you realize these people were human beings? And that you were shooting helpless people in the village?" And he said that he was just following orders. Then there was a letter to the editor from a woman in Iowa, I think, saying, "Oh well, that area is overpopulated anyway, so what's a few more people, a few hundred bodies?" I just blew up; it just came out without any thinking on my part. I said to my husband, "Damn it! We were lucky we got out of Manzanar!" Just like that; then it was all over. And he said, "Gee, I didn't really think you felt that deeply about it." And I said, "Well, I hadn't really thought about it." Just because of what they were saying on the radio and in reporting what was happening at the trial . . . and it just made the connection to me, and I just said what I thought. I know when I was telling Warren Furutani about it, he said, "That must have really been something for you to say that after all these years, because to me you're the one person who had sort of made your peace with the past. You're able to talk about it more in a historical way than in a personal way."

H: Sue, you mentioned the book by the Houstons called <u>Farewell to Manzanar</u>. You've no doubt done some thinking on this, but what exactly does it mean to say, "farewell to Manzanar?"

E: I'm not sure, really, except that you can talk about what happened to yourself and talk about what happened to people as Asian immigrants. After the 1969 pilgrimage, I sort of retreated into the past, because the pilgrimage had such a traumatic effect on me. I didn't realize it. I was going up there for a day, and I thought it would be adventurous--I hadn't been back to Manzanar since I left. But for about a month I would wake up in the middle of the night with nightmares. I would say to my husband, "I couldn't sleep last night." And he would reply, "You were thinking about Manzanar." And I would then say, "I guess it must be that, because I can't think of anything else that would bother me." So I started to read history, Asian American history, Japanese history, and I began to see that the internment was not just an isolated case. We blow it up so that it seems that it's the only thing that has happened to the Japanese in America. As I read over what had happened to Asians before the evacuation, I began to realize that laws had been enacted against the Chinese, and that laws had been enacted against the Japanese keeping them from doing business in certain areas, like fishing and buying land. And I realized that the evacuation was only part of what had been happening to the Asian immigrant. So I could put it in better perspective, not blow it out of shape, see it as part of a continuum. I think that the most important thing about saying "farewell to Manzanar" is facing the fact that there is racism in America, which is the word--"racism"--more than any other, really, that most of the Nisei didn't want to put on the plaque. I think once the Nisei realize that there are these things that are done to people, and that it's all due to racism, then I think they can go on from there. A lot of people will say, "Oh, I've never faced that kind of prejudice. I've never been refused service. I've never been refused an apartment." But there are cases where that has happened, and then people say, "Oh well, they're just exceptions." They don't want to face the fact of racism. I think once you face it, know it's there, possibly find ways and tools of coping with it, I think then you can let go of the past and say "farewell."

PART THREE: BIBLIOGRAPHY

CSUF JAPANESE AMERICAN ORAL HISTORY COLLECTION, 1974

Compiled by
Betty E. Mitson
Arthur A. Hansen

INTRODUCTION

At the time of this volume's publication, the listed interviews are at varying stages of completion. The ultimate goal is to bind each into a permanent volume, while the tape is preserved as well. In those instances where only the minutes or the hours are indicated, the interview has not been transcribed. Where numbers of pages are shown, the interview has been transcribed and may or may not already be in final form. If it is not in final form, the number of pages may vary slightly in future editions of this bibliography. While the interviews are herein listed alphabetically, they are filed according to the designated O.H. numbers. Several interviews were taped with residents of the town of Tulelake, which is not to be confused with the spelling of the former nearby Tule Lake camp.

GENERATIONAL DESIGNATIONS:

    Issei   - Immigrant generation
    Nisei   - Second generation
    Kibei   - Nisei; raised and educated in Japan
    Sansei - Third generation
    Yonsei - Fourth generation

RELOCATION CENTERS:

    Central Utah, Topaz, Utah
    Colorado River, Poston, Arizona
    Gila River, Rivers, Arizona
    Granada, Amache, Colorado
    Heart Mountain, Heart Mountain, Wyoming
    Jerome, Denson, Arkansas
    Manzanar, Manzanar, California
    Minidoka, Hunt, Idaho
    Rohwer, McGehee, Arkansas
    Tule Lake, Newell, California (later a segregation center)

AGER, Earl F.   O.H. 1348
     A Tulelake, California businessman recounts his dealings with
     and attitude toward the nearby segregation center.
        Interviewer: Sherry Turner
        Date: August 27, 1973   10 pp.

AIGNER, Albert E.   O.H. 1397
     Lone Pine native and longtime employee of a trucking company,
     which serviced Manzanar, recollects wartime impressions of
     camp, personal and community reaction, local economic impact,
     attitudes toward Director Ralph P. Merritt, necessity of evacua-
     tion, and town's treatment of Native Americans.
        Interviewer: David J. Bertagnoli; Arthur A. Hansen
        Date: December 20, 1973   20 min.

ANONYMOUS   Nisei   O.H. 11
     With father detained by FBI, one brother in Army, and other
     brothers relocated inland during voluntary evacuation period,
     interviewee was caught in the mass evacuation. Describes Poston,
     resettlement out of camp, and hostility toward former internees
     upon return to California.
        Interviewer: Richard D. Curtiss
        Date: March 4, 1966   24 pp.

ANONYMOUS   Nisei   O.H. 1331
     Childhood in Fresno, California area, schoolboy impressions of
     Fresno Assembly Center and Jerome and Gila camps, and current
     feelings about evacuation.
        Interviewer: John Wiedmann
        Date: December 17, 1973   27 pp.

ANONYMOUS   O.H. 1344
     Matron whose husband worked on internal security force at both
     Manzanar and Tule Lake recalls experiences. On Manzanar: Inyo
     County treatment of Native Americans; economic impact of camp
     and treatment of internees. On Tule Lake: pro-Japan activities;
     internee killing; riot and aftermath: social, cultural, and
     economic life of camp; and reaction of nearby community
        Interviewer: David J. Bertagnoli
        Date: July 14, 1973   10 pp.

ANONYMOUS   O.H. 1396
     Longtime Lone Pine resident and manager of trucking company
     focuses on firm's employment of six internees to unload train
     shipments of materials for Manzanar, camp's establishment and
     administration, effect on local economy and opinion, Manzanar
     Riot, internee-town relationship, and propriety of evacuation.
        Interviewer: David J. Bertagnoli; Arthur A. Hansen
        Date: December 20, 1973   20 min.

BELL, Rollin O.   O.H. 1346
    Inyo County highway patrolman recalls prewar Japanese Americans
    in Owens Valley, public response to Manzanar, camp conditions,
    internee-administration relations, camp internal security, evacua-
    tion policy, and personal attitude toward commemorative plaque
    at Manzanar site.
        Interviewer: David J. Bertagnoli
        Date: July 15, 1973   11 pp.

BRANSON, Donald H.   O.H. 1402
    Owens Valley resident since 1919 relates experiences as foreman
    of plumbing gang at Manzanar. Commentary on economic impact of
    camp, attitude of local citizens, conditions of Manzanar, treat-
    ment of internees, and evacuation decision.
        Interviewer: Arthur A. Hansen
        Date: December 20, 1973   14 pp.

BRIERLY, A. A.   O.H. 1378
    Lifetime resident and civic leader in Owens Valley discusses
    socio-political composition of area and response to Manzanar
    center: economic impact on Valley, views about internment policy,
    rumors about the camp director, and opinion concerning Manzanar
    plaque.
        Interviewer: David J. Bertagnoli; Arthur A. Hansen
        Date: December 6, 1973   12 pp.

BROWN, Robert L.   O.H. 1375
    Former Reports Officer and Assistant Project Director of Manzanar
    center discusses experiences as Inyo County teacher in the 1930s;
    prewar job as Executive Secretary for Inyo-Mono Association;
    social, political, and economic makeup of prewar Owens Valley
    communities; and formation and development of Manzanar. Special
    attention to public relations work for camp, biographies of
    prominent administrative and internee personalities, origination
    and growth of Manzanar Free Press, and causes and consequences of
    Manzanar Riot.
        Interviewer: Arthur A. Hansen   103 pp.
        Date: December 13, 1973; February 20, 1974

CAMPBELL, Arline   O.H. 1349
    Postmistress of Tule Lake camp discusses experiences there.
        Interviewer: Sherry Turner
        Date: August 26, 1973   16 pp.

CAMPBELL, Ned   O.H. 1329
    Experiences as Assistant Project Director at Manzanar, with
    particular reference to Manzanar Riot. Prewar background; recruit-
    ment by War Relocation Authority; profiles of administrators, staff,
    and evacuee leaders; resignation from WRA; and evacuation policy.
        Interviewer: Arthur A. Hansen
        Date: August 15, 1974   2 hrs. 30 min.

CHARNESS, Lee, Jr.   O.H. 78
    Describes participation of father as coordinator of Civil Defense
    in Huntington Beach, California, in assisting FBI roundup of
    "potentially dangerous enemy aliens." Discussion of family's
    produce market and expertise of Japanese-American truck farmers.
        Interviewer: John Sprout
        Date: November 25, 1968   29 pp.

CRAGEN, Dorothy C.   O.H. 1347
    Former superintendent of Inyo County schools discusses refusal
    of county Board of Education to administer Manzanar's schools;
    teaching and administration of camp schools; evacuation; local
    attitudes, particularly the incident of a Japanese-American
    soldier in Lone Pine; and Manzanar plaque wording.
        Interviewer: David J. Bertagnoli
        Date: July 14, 1973   11 pp.

CUSHMAN, Joyce   O.H. 1350
    Impressions as young woman living in town near Tule Lake camp
    while fiance served overseas with Army.
        Interviewer: Sherry Turner
        Date: August 27, 1973   8 pp.

DREW, Elodie M.   O.H. 1389
    Eastern California Museum employee from pioneer Owens Valley
    family relates experiences relative to Manzanar center, personal
    and community reaction to internment policy and camp, effect on
    postwar attitudes in area toward minority groups, and meetings
    with former internees visiting museum.
        Interviewer: David J. Bertagnoli
        Date: December 6, 1973   9 pp.

EMBREY, Sue Kunitomi   Nisei   O.H. 1366a
    Co-chairperson of Manzanar Committee and former editor of
    Manzanar Free Press discusses parental background in Okayama,
    family business activities in Los Angeles, prewar Los Angeles'
    Japanese-American community, Pearl Harbor and evacuation, and
    Manzanar camp. Commentary on internee subculture, factions,
    personalities, administrator profiles, role of camp newspaper,
    and Manzanar Riot.
        Interviewer: Arthur A. Hansen; David A. Hacker
        Date: August 24, 1973   61 pp.

EMBREY, Sue Kunitomi   Nisei   O.H. 1366b
    Wartime resettlement to Madison, Wisconsin, and Chicago; postwar
    experiences as Los Angeles city employee; problems of mixed
    marriage; and in-depth history of Manzanar Committee and its
    successful struggle to place a controversial commemorative plaque
    on Manzanar site.
        Interviewer: Arthur A. Hansen; David J. Bertagnoli
        Date: November 15, 1973   61 pp.

FUJIYAMA, Margie M.   Sansei/Nisei   O.H. 1383

  Cal State Fullerton secretary recollects farm life in prewar
Sacramento area, camp life at Pinedale Assembly Center and Poston,
educational and employment conditions in camp, resettlement in
St. Louis, and personal and community consequences of internment.

   Interviewer: Susan Fowler
   Date: January 11 and 12, 1973   21 pp.

FUKASAWA, George T.   Nisei   O.H. 1336

  Communications professor at Cal State Fullerton examines prewar
Ventura County Japanese-American community, intelligence activities
in post-Pearl Harbor roundup of Issei leaders in Los Angeles, evacuation role of JACL, personal role as evacuee policeman relative
to Manzanar Riot, Manzanar factions and personalities, and internment policy.

   Interviewer: Arthur A. Hansen
   Date: August 12, 1974   3 hours

GILLESPIE, Mary   O.H. 1345

  Longtime resident of Independence recounts impressions of Manzanar:
description, treatment of internees, local employees in camp,
impact on local economy, personal attitude toward internees,
Manzanar Riot, and postwar usage of Manzanar facilities.

   Interviewer: David J. Bertagnoli
   Date: July 14, 1973   10 pp.

GRIFFITH, Duff   O.H. 1365

  Girlhood memories of Japanese house servants in home of U.S. Territory of Hawaii governmental officer during pre-World War II period.
Details respecting martial law on Hawaiian Islands; personal
reactions to Japanese-American evacuation; and Japanese community
in Brazil.

   Interviewer: Betty E. Mitson
   Date: September 21, 1973   40 pp.

HARRY, Frank   O.H. 1395

  An Inyo County lifetime resident's impressions of Manzanar center;
automobile caravan of voluntary evacuees; internees fishing back
of camp; brother-in-law's employment as military police guard at
Manzanar; and Nisei soldiers in postwar Army.

   Interviewer: Arthur A. Hansen; David J. Bertagnoli
   Date: December 20, 1973   10 min.

HOPKINS, Jack B.   O.H. 1394

  Longtime Inyo County business and civic leader recounts impressions
of Manzanar: economic impact of camp on Lone Pine, local attitudes
toward camp, administrative staff, and internment policy.

   Interviewer: Arthur A. Hansen
   Date: December 20, 1973   23 pp.

HORI, Soichiro   Kibei   O.H. 1337
  Born in the United States but raised in Japan, interviewee was
  seventeen when he first learned English language. Interned with
  family at Manzanar, he later worked as a civilian Japanese
  language teacher for U.S. Navy.
   Interviewer: Paula Erickson
   Date: July 16, 1973   21 pp.

IHARA, Craig Kei   Sansei   O.H. 1230
  Cal State Fullerton philosophy professor, born at Rohwer camp,
  discusses family history, focusing on religion, education,
  aspirations, and cultural heritage. Relates recent overnight
  stay at old camp site.
   Interviewer: Betty E. Mitson
   Date: December 18, 1972   34 pp.

ISHIDA, Frank Kiyoshi   Sansei   O.H. 1338
  Insurance agent discusses family history: immigration from
  Hiroshima Ken, arranged marriage, produce business, internment
  at Manzanar, and father's service as interpreter with U.S. Army
  in Philippines.
   Interviewer: Robert M. Kasper
   Date: July 18, 1973   23 pp.

ISHIDA, Seiko   Kibei   O.H. 1339
  Retired teacher recounts samurai parents' background, their
  emigration to Seattle, socio-economic composition of Seattle
  Japanese community, and her teacher training. Prewar stays in
  Japan as child and later as tutor in missionary family. Unable
  to find work as a teacher in Los Angeles during late 1930s, she
  taught at Manzanar. Resettlement in New York and postwar return
  to Los Angeles.
   Interviewer: Arthur A. Hansen
   Date: August 6, 1974   2 hours

ISHII, Amy Uno   Nisei   O.H. 1342a
  President of the Hollywood Japanese American Citizens League
  relates family history prior to World War II. Mother and father
  attended missionary schools in Japan and immigrated early in
  twentieth century. An uncle, Domoto Takanoshin, was first
  Japanese to obtain a U.S. patent, owned North American Mercan-
  tile Company (NAMCO), and was instrumental in several family
  immigrations.
   Interviewer: Betty E. Mitson
   Date: July 9, 1973   26 pp.

ISHII, Amy Uno   Nisei   O.H. 1342b
  Prewar employment as "schoolgirl" domestic; Pearl Harbor and
  evacuation; father's work as Department of Agriculture entomol-
  ogist and subsequent detention in five "enemy alien" camps;
  life in Santa Anita Assembly Center and Heart Mountain camp;
  resettlement to Chicago; and return to Los Angeles in 1946.
   Interviewer: Kristen Mitchell
   Date: July 18, 1973   54 pp.

JONES, Robert L.   O.H. 1351
   Present city clerk of Tulelake, California recalls wartime
   experiences as a farmer living near a segregation center.
     Interviewer: Sherry Turner
     Date: August 25, 1973   11 pp.

JOSEPH, Ethelyne   O.H. 1385
   Wife of a prominent Inyo County grocer discusses economic impact
   of nearby center on Lone Pine, attitude of area citizens toward
   evacuation, internees at Manzanar, and historical marker at camp
   site.
     Interviewer: David J. Bertagnoli
     Date: October 4, 1973   7 pp.

KAIHARA, Rodney   Sansei   O.H. 1277
   Landscape architect analyzes life since a child at Poston:
   prejudice in a Mexican-American community, Japanese culture,
   mixed-dating, effects of broken home, attitude toward dominant
   culture, cultural stereotyping, and effects of evacuation.
     Interviewer: Patricia Morgan
     Date: March 25, 1973   1 hr. 20 min.

KANEGAE, Henry   Nisei   O.H. 4
   Former block manager at Poston refers to role of Bureau of
   Indian Affairs in camp administration, a riot, and camp agricultural program. In connection with his produce business, he made
   a recent trip to area and revisited old camp site.
     Interviewer: Richard Curtiss
     Date: February 12, 1966   33 pp.

KANNO, George   Nisei   O.H. 10
   Description of father's arrest by FBI, status of property during
   internment at Poston, and temporary release to Colorado where
   family was treated sympathetically by local farmers who were
   German immigrants.
     Interviewer: Richard Curtiss
     Date: February 25, 1966   16 pp.

KANNO, James   Nisei   O.H. 1069
   First mayor of Japanese ancestry in United States (Fountain
   Valley) describes Poston camp and temporary release to Colorado,
   orderly work at University of Michigan Hospital, and student
   entrance to Marquette University. Became local president of
   JACL and entered politics when area was incorporated.
     Interviewer: John McFarlane
     Date: April 26, 1971   1 hr. 30 min.

KELLEY, Anna T.   O.H. 1401
    Former Inyo County Welfare Director recollects experiences as
    first-aid operator for firm insuring the five construction
    companies that built Manzanar, social and economic effects of
    camp on local area, and early conditions of camp. Evaluates
    Manzanar historical marker's wording.
        Interviewer: Arthur A. Hansen; David J. Bertagnoli
        Date: December 6, 1973   28 pp.

KELLY, Bette   O.H. 1352
    Former postal clerk at Tule Lake camp relates impressions of
    life there and status of land and buildings after closure.
        Interviewer: Sherry Turner
        Date: August 26, 1973   12 pp.

KIKUCHI, Yoriyuki   Issei   O.H. 1340
    Practicing dentist recollects boyhood in samurai family, immigra-
    tion to America, early employment and education in Southern
    California, and prewar dental practice. Head of dental services
    at Manzanar, he discusses camp problems and personalities. Post-
    war experiences in Boyle Heights, Los Angeles.
        Interviewer: Arthur A. Hansen
        Date: July 29, 1974   1 hr. 30 min.

KING, Ruth E.   O.H. 1353
    Correspondent for Herald and News of Klamath Falls, Oregon dis-
    cusses problems relating to Tule Lake camp.
        Interviewer: Sherry Turner
        Date: August 28, 1973   15 pp.

KISHIYAMA, J. S.   Issei   O.H. 1272
KISHIYAMA, K.   Kibei
    Reflections of elderly couple on experiences in America. Husband
    recounts early years as youthful immigrant; wife discusses her
    family's background and generational makeup of Japanese-American
    community. Picture bride system, first impressions of America,
    and Japanese-American rural living.
        Interviewer: Patricia Morgan
        Date: April 6, 1973   1 hour

KOBAYASHI, Irene M.   Sansei/Nisei   O.H. 1077
    Japanese family in Hawaii during World War II, harassment by FBI,
    problems of dual citizenship, overt racism, cultural suppression,
    integration, child rearing, and political activism.
        Interviewer: Betty E. Mitson
        Date: April 11, 1972   33 pp.

KRATER, Katherine   O.H. 1343
    Wife of Independence grocer details Manzanar: personal and
    community reaction, camp visits, Manzanar Riot, Director Ralph
    Merritt, evacuation policy, and historical marker at camp site.
        Interviewer: David J. Bertagnoli
        Date: July 14, 1973   17 pp.

KUNITSUGU, Kango   Nisei   O.H. 1334a
    Civil engineer reflects on internment at Rohwer. Details concerning loyalty questionnaire and current involvement with Los Angeles' Little Tokyo redevelopment.
      Interviewer: Sherry Turner
      Date: August 4, 1973   68 pp.

KUNITSUGU, Kango   Nisei   O.H. 1334b
    Manager of Little Tokyo Redevelopment Project discusses wartime conversion of the area into a black community--Bronzeville-- and postwar reconversion into Japanese American cultural, commercial, and spiritual center. Anti-Japanese legislation, and pre- and post-war symbolic meaning of Little Tokyo.
      Interviewer: David Biniasz
      Date: November 28, 1973   30 min.

KUNITSUGU, Katsumi   Nisei   O.H. 1333
    English section editor of Kashu Mainichi describes her brief childhood years in Japan, internment at Heart Mountain, and resettlement to attend college.
      Interviewer: Sherry Turner
      Date: July 15, 1973   52 pp.

KURATOMI, Iwami   Issei   O.H. 1236a
    Born into samurai family in 1884 and came to America in 1901, interviewee outlines life and wartime internment at Santa Fe, New Mexico (a Department of Justice camp) and later at Jerome and Rohwer camps.
      Interviewer: Joyce Eakens
      Date: May 3, 1973   2 hrs. 15 min.

KURATOMI, Iwami   Issei   O.H. 1236b
    Ninety year old describes life in landed family in Japan: family armor, school, childhood play and discipline, mother's duties, loss of family estate. Recruitment into labor gang, school in San Francisco, earthquake of 1906, ventures into laundry and rice-growing businesses, trip to Cuba, comments on Pres. Theodore Roosevelt and William Randolph Hearst, details on Japan's navy, arrest and detention at Santa Fe, New Mexico, detailed description of life there, work as agricultural director at Jerome and Rohwer Relocation Centers. and postwar work as "French" chef for violinist Mischa Elman. Considerable information on diet to which he ascribes his longevity.
      Interviewer: Betty E. Mitson
      Date: May 10, 1973; March 16, 1974   310 pp.

MILLER, Hubert E.   O.H. 1384
     Lone Pine automobile dealer discusses conditions at Manzanar
     center, arrival of caravan from Los Angeles, sale of internee
     automobiles, economic impact of camp on neighboring communities,
     personal and area reaction to evacuation.
          Interviewer: David J. Bertagnoli
          Date: October 4, 1973   25 min.

MILLER, Pauline   O.H. 1393
     Wife of auto dealer assesses economic impact of Manzanar camp
     on Lone Pine and internee-townspeople interaction respecting
     both wartime and present. Reflects on controversial wording on
     Manzanar historical marker.
          Interviewer: Arthur A. Hansen; David J. Bertagnoli
          Date: December 20, 1973   15 pp.

MORI, John Yukio   Sansei/Nisei   O.H. 1231
     Young conscientious objector to Vietnam War discusses alternate
     service as partner in Amerasia Bookstore, a nonprofit organiza-
     tion serving Los Angeles' Little Tokyo, store's educational
     projects serving community, activities in Young Buddhist Associa-
     tion to renew cultural roots, parents' reaction to his current
     life-style, and long-term effect of wartime evacuation.
          Interviewer: Betty E. Mitson
          Date: December 21, 1972   44 pp.

MUKAEDA, Katsume   Issei   O.H. 1341
     Chairman of Japanese American Cultural Center and former
     President of Japanese Chamber of Commerce recounts conditions
     of prewar Los Angeles' Little Tokyo, its wartime conversion into
     a black community, and postwar reestablishment as Japanese
     American cultural and commercial center. Prewar discriminatory
     legislation, prewar Japan-America relations, camp conditions,
     wartime repatriation procedure, consequences of internment, and
     contemporary civil rights movement.
          Interviewer: David Biniasz
          Date: November 28, 1973   45 min.

NAKAMURA, Harry   Nisei   O.H. 649
     Recollections of farm boy evacuated from San Luis Obispo area to
     Poston camp. Comments on military service of brothers, himself,
     and all-Nisei 442nd Regiment.
          Interviewer: John McFarlane
          Date: May 2, 1971   13 pp.

NAKASHIMA, Meri Hanako   Nisei   O.H. 1368
     Memories of athletic girlhood, evacuation to Santa Anita
     Assembly Center where witnessed a riot, and eventual move to
     Rohwer and marriage in an out-of-camp ceremony.
          Interviewer: Janis Gennawey
          Date: July 17, 1973   37 pp.

NICHOLSON, Herbert V.   O.H. 1235
    Quaker missionary who lived in Japan from 1915 to 1961, except
for World War II years in U.S., recounts 58 years of association
he and wife have had with people of Japanese ancestry. Biographical account of childhood; work in missionary field before and
after war and after retirement in U.S. Particularly detailed
are experiences connected with Japanese-American evacuation:
appeals to FBI, experiences at Department of Justice detention
camps as interpreter and witness, repeated trips to most camps
to deliver personal goods and Christmas gifts, evangelical
efforts among internees and administrative personnel, visits to
442nd Regiment training camp and to Washington, D.C. which
prompted a letter writing campaign to open camps. Postwar
project which brought 5,000 goats to wartorn Japan.
    Interviewer: Betty E. Mitson   355 pp.
    Date: April 19, 24, July 19, and November 20, 1973

NISHIZU, Clarence I.   Nisei   O.H. 5
    Former block manager at Heart Mountain center details evacuation
from Buena Park, California, life within camp, and resettlement
to North Dakota, Idaho, and Colorado, and escheatment court case
over family property.
    Interviewer: Richard Curtiss
    Date: January 1, 1966   24 pp.

NITTA, Hitoshi   Nisei   O.H. 3
    Orange County rancher discusses management of truck farming
business from Poston camp through a bank trust and Mexican-
American foreman. Married in camp and family was first to
return to Orange County when ban was lifted. Description of
Poston and personal reaction to evacuation.
    Interviewer: Richard Curtiss
    Date: February 7, 1966   25 pp.

NITTA, Mary   Nisei   O.H. 1127
    Among last evacuated from California, interviewee served as a
nurse at Poston hospital where she met Hitoshi Nitta when he
came in for treatment. They married and had a son born in
camp. Camp life and views on evacuation.
    Interviewer: Ruth Wilkerson
    Date: March 27, 1972   28 pp.

NITTA, Minoru   Nisei   O.H. 114
    Poultry rancher who married to be evacuated with bride to
Poston details camp life, resettlement to Cleveland, and return
to California. While family was interned, State of California
initiated escheatment action against their land holdings purchased after 1913. However, the Supreme Court struck that down,
thereby establishing a precedent.
    Interviewer: John McFarlane
    Date: March 21, 1972   29 pp.

ODANAKA, Woodrow   Nisei   O.H. 1382
  High school student whose family ran retail produce business was
  evacuated to Santa Anita Assembly Center, where he witnessed a
  riot. Later graduated in Granada camp and relocated to college
  in Minnesota. Drafted with camp group and served with Army
  millitary intelligence in Philippines and in occupation of Japan.
    Interviewer: Patrick H. West
    Date: July 16, 1973   30 pp.

OKIMOTO, Elaine S.   Nisei   O.H. 1080
  Farm girl evacuated from Dinuba, California to Poston who recounts
  life in camp, resettlement to college in Ohio, eventual attendance
  at UC Berkeley, translation work with occupation forces in Japan
  where met and married a Kibei. Effect of Illegal entry and
  cultural factors on behavior.
    Interviewer: Betty E. Mitson
    Date: April 4, 1972   23 pp.

PARKER, C. R.   O.H. 1354
  Retired fire chief for Tule Lake Center briefly recounts impressions of camp life.
    Interviewer: Sherry Turner
    Date: August 26, 1973   8 pp.

PEDERSEN, O. E.   O.H. 1364
  Wife of former Tulelake, California police chief relates her
  experiences at Tule Lake center during husband's employment
  with internal security force. War Relocation Authority
  personnel, camp life, reaction of surrounding communities to
  camp, and attitudes of internees.
    Interviewer: Sherry Turner
    Date: August 27, 1973   12 pp.

PEDNEAU, Bessie K.   O.H. 1400
  Third generation American of Chinese ancestry living in Owens
  Valley remembers Manzanar and comments on State historical
  marker; had a baby delivered by Army doctor from camp.
    Interviewer: David J. Bertagnoli
    Date: October 4, 1973   5 pp.

PEDNEAU, Frank L.   O.H. 1399
  Local resident reflects on Japanese-American evacuation and
  historical marker placed at Manzanar.
    Interviewer: David J. Bertagnoli
    Date: October 4, 1973   4 pp.

RAUB, Henry   O.H. 1398
  Director of Eastern California Museum traces historical origins
  and political circumstances of Manzanar historical plaque.
  Impressions of wartime internment shown by recent Japanese-
  American visitors to museum in Independence.
    Interviewer: David J. Bertagnoli
    Date: October 12, 1973   7 pp.

RUNCORN, Ed. H.   O.H. 1332
    Former War Relocation Authority Cooperative Enterprises assoc-
iate superintendent discusses how internees, largely Issei,
invested in "canteens;" how profits were shared; and religious
influence, morale, and unrest at Amache and Tule Lake camps.
    Interviewer: Janis Gennawey
    Date: July 8, 1973   19 pp.

RYCHMAN, Fannie   O.H. 1355
    Wife of retired farmer expresses attitude toward nearby Tule
Lake camp.
    Interviewer: Sherry Turner
    Date: August 27, 1973   8 pp.

SCHINDLER, Wesley   O.H. 1356
    Commentary by a farmer living in the area of Tule Lake camp.
    Interviewer: Sherry Turner
    Date: August 26, 1973   6 pp.

SCHINDLER, William E.   O.H. 1357
    Views of Tule Lake as seen by a farmer in the area.
    Interviewer: Sherry Turner
    Date: August 27, 1973   5 pp.

TAKETA, Roy Y.   Nisei   O.H. 1330
    Assistant principal of an Anaheim high school recollects prewar
experiences as son of a Japanese language schoolteacher in
Los Angeles, family's voluntary relocation to Colorado and
eventual return to California. Events surrounding Pearl Harbor,
reaction to internment policy, wartime experience of wife's
family in Hawaii, and postwar housing and employment discrimination in Orange County.
    Interviewer: Mary M. McCarthy
    Date: July 13, 1973   28 pp.

TANAKA, Togo W.   Nisei   O.H. 1271a
    Graduate of UCLA and English language editor of Rafu Shimpo,
leading newspaper of Little Tokyo in Los Angeles, discusses
prewar history of family of samurai ancestry. Information about
a riot at Manzanar camp at which time he was evacuated with
others to Death Valley for protection.
    Interviewer: Betty E. Mitson; David A. Hacker
    Date: May 19, 1973   62 pp.

TANAKA, Togo W.   Nisei   O.H. 1271b
    In-depth analysis of discontent erupting into "Manzanar Riot" of
December 6, 1942. Having been one who was subjected to harassment, he discusses camp factions and personalities in relation
to some contemporaneous writing on the subject done by him in
capacity of War Relocation Authority documentary historian.
    Interviewer: Arthur A. Hansen
    Date: August 30, 1973   42 pp.

TASHIMA, Masaka Yagi   Kibei   O.H. 1359
    Born in San Francisco in 1896 where parents owned hotel business,
interviewee spent years from 2 months of age to 16 years in Japan.
Family established hotel business in Los Angeles in 1912. Discusses marriage to an Issei entailing relinquishment of citizenship
and prewar family life in Orange County. Evacuation to Poston, son
Masayuki Tashima's military involvement, and current occupations
of other children.
    Interviewer: Pat Tashima (granddaughter)
    Date: June 1, 1974   1 hour

TASHIMA, Mary Yoshie   Issei (Nisei)   O.H. 1360
    Born to Issei parents visiting in Japan, interviewee's experience
is that of a Nisei excepting for naturalization of citizenship.
Prewar Los Angeles, evacuation to Santa Anita Assembly Center;
and later schooling, jobs, and outside community contacts at Amache.
Postwar return to Los Angeles, affect on family life, and attitudes
respecting allegiance.
    Interviewer: Pat Tashima (daughter)
    Date: February 20, 1974   1 hr. 30 min.

TASHIMA, Masayuki (Masy)   Sansei/Nisei   O.H. 1361
    Graduate of Army officer's school looks at postwar Italy; rise to
officer's status; problems with troop morale, conduct, discipline;
Japanese Americans today; and involvement in JACL.
    Interviewer: Pat Tashima (niece)
    Date: July 15, 1974   1 hr. 30 min.

TASHIMA, Yoshiyuki (Yas)   Sansei/Nisei   O.H. 1362
    Supermarket produce manager discusses prewar Wintersburg and
Garden Grove in Orange County; father's detention as "enemy alien;"
interviewee's graduation from Huntington Beach High School after
relocation to Poston camp and subsequent Army experiences.
    Interviewer: Pat Tashima (daughter)
    Date: February 15, 1974   30 min.

THALER, Victoria   O.H. 1358
    Judge residing in Tulelake recalls her life in nearby camp as
wife of a man working there, reactions of townspeople upon her
decision to reside in town after the camp's closure.
    Interviewer: Sherry Turner
    Date: August 27, 1973   13 pp.

UNO, Roy   Nisei   O.H. 1070
    Advertising man who serves on Human Relations Council in Santa
Ana, California, reflects on issues involved in evacuation. As
a college student, he went to Santa Anita Assembly Center and
later to Rohwer camp, resettled to Chicago, and served in Allied
Translator Interpreter Service in the Philippines.
    Interviewer: John McFarlane
    Date: April 25, 1971   32 pp.

UYESUGI, Mas   Nisei   O.H. 1071
     First Japanese-American jeweler in Orange County, California reflects on life in Granada camp. Completed high school there, resettled to college and later served as interpreter for war crimes trials in Philippines. Considerable discussion of attitudes, philosophy, and need for community involvement.
       Interviewer: John McFarlane
       Date: April 16, 1971   32 pp.

WATANABE, Dorothy   Nisei   O.H. 1363
     District manager of an educational corporation discusses samurai ancestry, childhood on Bainbridge Island, Washington, and makeup of Bainbridge Japanese community. Interned at Manzanar, she relates circumstances and why Bainbridge Islanders were transferred to Minidoka. Resettlement to Chicago and postwar years in California with attention to discriminatory housing policies.
       Interviewer: Arthur A. Hansen
       Date: July 24, 1974   3 hours

YAMADA, Takeo   Nisei   O.H. 1279
     Orange County produce clerk comments on prewar agriculture and marketing in Southern California, pre-evacuation period in Irvine, life at Poston, and controversy about military classification. Parents' earlier immigration via Mexico, Buddhism, postwar response by dominant culture, Japanese language schools, generational differences, comparison of contemporary Japan and America, and effects of evacuation.
       Interviewer: Patricia Morgan
       Date: March 26, 1973   90 min.

YAMAKI, Emi   Nisei   O.H. 1335
     Experiences of a family who voluntarily relocated to Utah. Presently serving on a State of California committee to develop curriculum to teach Asian-American history in public schools.
       Interviewer: Sherry Turner
       Date: August 17, 1973   53 pp.

YAMAMOTO, Harry K.   Sansei   O.H. 1072
     A Santa Ana, California city councilman describes Heart Mountain camp, resettlement to Utah and Chicago, conscription into Army military intelligence, return to a black community in California, and eventual move to Orange County.
       Interviewer: John McFarlane
       Date: April 21, 1971   13 pp.

YONEDA, Elaine Black   O.H. 1377a
     Born in New York City to parents who were immigrants from Russia, interviewee became West Coast vice-president of International Labor Defense in which capacity she met and married labor activist Karl G. Yoneda. She acted in her own defense in a precedent setting "red baiting" case in 1930s.
       Interviewer: Betty E. Mitson
       Date: March 2, 1974   2 hours

YONEDA, Elaine Black   O.H. 1377b
    Former internee of Manzanar, by choice, treats impact of Pearl
    Harbor on San Francisco Japanese-American community, response of
    Japanese-American Left to evacuation, husband's illegal arrest by
    FBI and his voluntary evacuation, conditions in camp, work in camp
    library and camouflage net factory, factions and personalities,
    Manzanar Riot, and removal to Death Valley with "pro-American"
    group.
        Interviewer: Arthur A. Hansen
        Date: March 3, 1974   7 hours

YONEDA, Karl G.   Kibei   O.H. 1376a
    Born in Glendale, California, but raised in Hiroshima prefecture,
    Japan, he fled to his native land when drafted into Japanese
    army in 1926. Already politically active in both Japan and
    China, he entered labor movement in United States in behalf of
    farm workers and was first of Asian ancestry to run for California
    Assembly, on Communist ticket. Met future wife when she, as a
    union officer, bailed him out of jail after Hunger March of 1931.
    She later accompanied him and their son to Manzanar camp.
        Interviewer: Betty E. Mitson
        Date: March 2, 1974   2 hrs. 30 min.

YONEDA, Karl G.   Kibei   O.H. 1376b
    Prewar Japanese-American leftist organizations, leadership, and
    strategies, personal involvement as labor activist, editor of
    Rodo Shimbum (Labor News) and San Francisco agent for Doho
    (Brother), unconstitutional arrest and imprisonment following
    Pearl Harbor, voluntary evacuation to Manzanar center, conditions
    and controversies culminating in "Manzanar Riot."
        Interviewer: Ronald C. Larson; Arthur A. Hansen
        Date: March 3, 1974   2 hrs. 30 min.

LECTURES

TAPE RECORDED LECTURES FROM A SERIES: ARTHUR A. HANSEN, COORDINATOR, JAPANESE AMERICAN INTERNMENT DURING WORLD WAR II: A SOCIO-HISTORICAL INQUIRY (Univ. of Calif. Extension, Irvine, March 20-June 12, 1973).

EMBREY, Sue Kunitomi
Co-chairperson of Manzanar Committee and former editor of Manzanar Free Press analyzes SYMBOLIC MEANING OF THE CONCENTRATION CAMP EXPERIENCE TO THE CONTEMPORARY ASIAN AMERICAN CONSCIOUSNESS MOVEMENT. Brief history of anti-Oriental agitation in California leading to evacuation, discussion of "Yellow Power" activists and emphasis on internment experience to develop identity and unity, and commentary about the film "Manzanar" produced by Bob Nakamura, an activist interned as a child in Manzanar. Supplementary information respecting objectives, issues, and strategies of Asian American radicals provided by Charles Igawa, Acting Assistant Professor in Department of Comparative Cultures, University of California, Irvine. Embrey is joined by Igawa and Amy Uno Ishii, president of the Hollywood Chapter of the Japanese American Citizens League, for a question and answer session.
Date: June 5, 1973   3 hours

HATA, Donald Teruo, Jr.
Associate Professor of History and Director of Asian American Research Project at California State College, Dominguez Hills traces THE ROAD BACK, 1945-1960. Discussion of major problems and patterns encountered by Japanese Americans after release from concentration camps and readjustment to postwar American life, with examples drawn from personal experiences. Question and answer period highlights wide range of subtopics from socioeconomic to political and philosophical concerns.
Date: May 29, 1973   3 hours.

ISHII, Amy Uno and Ken Honji
Woman president of Hollywood Chapter of Japanese American Citizens League and youth worker affiliated with Services for Asian American Youth, Los Angeles offer multimedia presentation on THE JAPANESE AMERICAN EXPERIENCE. Aftermath of Pearl Harbor and newspaper campaign for Japanese-American evacuation, roundup and removal to concentration camps, and personal recollections of camp life. Includes discussion by panel consisting of Ishii and Honji, plus Estelle Ishigo, a Caucasian artist interned at Heart Mountain and author of Lone Heart Mountain, and Hana Uno Shepard, Mrs. Ishii's sister and a former internee at the Granada camp.
Date: April 17, 1973   3 hours.

KAGIWADA, George

Assistant Professor of Applied Behavioral Sciences and Coordinator of Asian American Studies at University of California, Davis evaluates THE IMPACT OF THE INTERNMENT ON THE JAPANESE AMERICAN COMMUNITY. Discussion of consequences of internment experience on Japanese Americans, with emphasis upon peculiar character of American racism and emasculating effect of "assimilation" for ethnic minorities. Includes question and answer commentary.

Date: May 15, 1973   3 hours

KUNITSUGU, Katsumi

English section editor of Kashu Mainichi (California Daily News) former internee at Heart Mountain speaks on LIFE IN AN AMERICAN "CONCENTRATION CAMP" AND HOW EDUCATION GOT ME OUT. Details experiences at Heart Mountain center based upon diary entries, emphasizing schooling in camp and student relocation program. Question and answer supplement includes commentary by her husband Kango Kunitsugu who was interned at Rohwer camp.

Date: April 24, 1973   3 hours

MITSON, Betty E.

American Studies and History major specializing in Oral History at California State University, Fullerton considers the topic, ORAL HISTORY AND THE JAPANESE AMERICAN EXPERIENCE. Discussion of the development of oral history and rationale for its use, particularly among Japanese Americans interned during World War II. Brief tape-recorded excerpts illustrating experiences and attitudes. Supplementary talks by two interviewees: John Yukio Mori, partner in Little Tokyo's Amerasia Bookstore details participation in that enterprise and concerns as a Sansei; and Herbert V. Nicholson relates experiences assisting interned people.

Date: May 22, 1973   3 hours

MORIYAMA, Alan Takeo

Curriculum Coordinator for Asian American Studies Center at University of California, Los Angeles focuses on JAPANESE IMMIGRATION TO THE UNITED STATES. Conditions in Japan and the United States related to immigration, reactions of American society to Japanese, and ways in which seeds of evacuation were laid early in twentieth century. Questions and answers pertinent to topics.

Date: March 27, 1973   3 hours

ODO, Franklin S.

Lecturer in Asian American Studies program at California State University, Long Beach addresses topic of JAPANESE AMERICAN HISTORY AND THE CAMPS: ASPECTS OF SUBCULTURAL CONTINUITY AND DISCONTINUITY. Historical experience of Japanese Americans before World War II, evacuation to inland camps, how attitudes and behavior patterns within camps were shaped by long history of racism and resistance, and political and ideological disputes within Japanese American community at time of evacuation.

Date: May 1, 1974   3 hours

OKIMOTO, Joe Y.
Hughes Aircraft Marketing Manager who was living in Japan during World War II discusses KIBEI AND NISEI, detailing how social and cultural experiences of Kibei differ from those of other Japanese Americans. Lecture emphasis is academic, however, some biographical material in subsequent discussion.
Date: May 8, 1973   2 hours

TANAKA, Togo W.
Publisher and Editor in chief, School Industrial Press, Los Angeles, and former English language editor of Rafu Shimpo (Los Angeles Daily Japanese News) from 1936 to 1942 speaks on HOW TO SURVIVE RACISM IN AMERICA'S FREE SOCIETY. Capsule review from perspective of Japanese Americans of what happened on West Coast during decade before Pearl Harbor, how Japanese Americans coped with racist pressures, and resources developed in prewar period to survive punishment without crime during wartime. Topics considered in light of speaker's personal experiences. Question and answer session included.
Date: April 3, 1973   26 pp.

MISCELLANEOUS ORAL DOCUMENTS

HANSEN, Arthur A.
    Associate Professor of History and Project Director of
California State University, Fullerton, Japanese American
Oral History Project explores topic of ORAL HISTORY AND
ASIAN AMERICAN STUDIES in an interview-lecture delivered
before a graduate seminar in research methodology at the
University of California, Los Angeles, Asian American Studies
Center. Discussion of oral history's growth and development,
applicability as a research tool, interview techniques, uses
and misuses of oral documentation, collections relevant to
Asian American studies, and utility of oral history in under-
standing Japanese-American wartime evacuation.
    Interviewer: Betty E. Mitson
    Date: April 26, 1974   1 hour

NICHOLSON, Herbert V.
    Details personal knowledge of JAPANESE-AMERICAN RELATIONS FROM
1915 TO 1961. As secretary to Gilbert Bowles, a Quaker missionary who was an executive of the Japan Peace Society, and as
Secretary of the Fellowship of Reconciliation, Nicholson had a
unique opportunity, beginning in 1915, to meet many Japanese
governmental officials and to observe rise of militarism and
influence of Hitler in Japan's affairs. Due to international
tensions, he returned in 1940 to U.S. and served a West Los
Angeles Japanese Methodist Church until congregation was evacuated. When Fair Play Committee refused to start a letter writing campaign to prevent evacuation, he helped form Friends of
the American Way, a Pasadena-based group, too small and too late
to stop it. Particularly detailed are his contacts in "alien
enemy" camps, where he served as interpreter and witness in
hearings, and a letter writing campaign he instigated on March
20, 1944, which he indicates triggered official opening of camps
on Jan. 2, 1945, and not a Supreme Court decision. Returned to
Japan in 1947 with 5,000 goats and stayed in missionary work
there until official retirement in 1961; however, work amongst
people of Japanese ancestry continues to date. Observations
about positive and negative aspects of U.S. occupation policies
in Japan are included.
    Recorded by: Herbert V. Nicholson
    Date: April 10, 1974   3 hours

OAKI, Rocky

Thirty-three year old owner of Benihana of Tokyo, a distinctive restaurant chain, is interviewed by Michael Jackson on KABC-Talk Radio. Aoki came to America thirteen years ago with the Japanese Olympic wrestling team and decided to stay. Beginning in Harlem by selling ice cream from a truck, he now has eighteen establishments in such places as New York City, Chicago, San Francisco, Las Vegas, and several in Southern California. As a budding entrepreneur, he is expanding into the production of Broadway shows, establishment of sports clubs, and publishing a magazine, "Genesis." Jackson dubbed him "The Japanese Horatio Alger."

Recorded by: Brian L. Mitson

Date: July 9, 1973   45 min.

INDEX BY CAMPS